WOMEN'S WORK

STUDIES IN DANCE HISTORY

A Publication of the Society of Dance History Scholars

TITLES IN PRINT

The Origins of the Bolero School, edited by Javier Suárez-Pajares and Xoán M. Carreira

Carlo Blasis in Russia by Elizabeth Souritz, with preface by Selma Jeanne Cohen

Of, By, and For the People: Dancing on the Left in the 1930s, edited by Lynn Garafola

Dancing in Montreal: Seeds of a Choreographic History by Iro Tembeck

The Making of a Choreographer: Ninette de Valois and "Bar aux Folies-Bergère" by Beth Genné

Ned Wayburn and the Dance Routine: From Vaudeville to the "Ziegfeld Follies" by Barbara Stratyner

Rethinking the Sylph: New Perspectives on the Romantic Ballet, edited by Lynn Garafola (available from the University Press of New England)

Dance for Export: Cultural Diplomacy and the Cold War by Naima Prevots, with introduction by Eric Foner (available from the University Press of New England)

José Limón: An Unfinished Memoir, edited by Lynn Garafola, with introduction by Deborah Jowitt, foreword by Carla Maxwell, and afterword by Norton Owen (available from the University Press of New England)

Dancing Desires: Choreographing Sexualities on and off the Stage, edited by Jane C. Desmond

Dancing Many Drums: Excavations in African American Dance, edited by Thomas F. DeFrantz

Writings on Ballet and Music, by Fedor Lopukhov, edited and with an introduction by Stephanie Jordan, translations by Dorinda Offord

Liebe Hanya: Mary Wigman's Letters to Hanya Holm, compiled and edited by Claudia Gitelman, introduction by Hedwig Müller

The Grotesque Dancer on the Eighteenth-Century Stage: Gennaro Magri and His World, edited by Rebecca Harris-Warrick and Bruce Alan Brown

Kaiso!: Writings by and about Katherine Dunham, edited by VèVè A. Clark and Sara E. Johnson

Dancing from Past to Present: Nation, Culture, Identities, edited by Theresa Jill Buckland

Women's Work: Making Dance in Europe before 1800, edited by Lynn Matluck Brooks

Women's Work

Making Dance in Europe before 1800

Edited by

LYNN MATLUCK BROOKS

THE UNIVERSITY OF WISCONSIN PRESS

The University of Wisconsin Press
1930 Monroe Street, 3rd Floor
Madison, Wisconsin 53711-2059

www.wisc.edu/wisconsinpress/

3 Henrietta Street
London WC2E 8LU, England

1   3   5   4   2

Printed in the United States of America

Library of Congress Cataloging-in-Publication Data
Women's work : making dance in Europe before 1800 /
edited by Lynn Matluck Brooks.
     p.   cm.—(Studies in dance history)
Includes index.
ISBN 0-299-22530-5 (cloth: alk. paper)
ISBN 0-299-22534-8 (pbk.: alk. paper)
1. Women dancers—Europe—History.   2. Dance—Europe—History.
I. Brooks, Lynn Matluck.   II. Series: Studies in dance history (Unnumbered)
GV1799.4.W65   2007
792.8094—dc22   2007011730

This volume is dedicated
with gratitude and affection to

GENEVIEVE OSWALD

Curator Emerita of the Jerome Robbins Dance Division
of the New York Public Library for the Performing Arts.

Contents

Acknowledgments   ix

Introduction: Women in Dance History,
    the Doubly Invisible   3
    LYNN MATLUCK BROOKS

PATRONAGE AND POWER

1   Isabella and the Dancing Este Brides, 1473–1514   19
    BARBARA SPARTI
2   Fabritio Caroso's Patronesses   49
    ANGENE FEVES
3   At the Queen's Command: Henrietta Maria and
    the Development of the English Masque   71
    ANNE DAYE

PROFESSIONAL PERFORMANCE

4   The Female Ballet Troupe of the Paris Opera
    from 1700 to 1725   99
    NATHALIE LECOMTE
5   Françoise Prévost: The Unauthorized Biography   123
    RÉGINE ASTIER
6   Marie Sallé, a Wise Professional Woman
    of Influence   160
    SARAH MCCLEAVE
7   In Pursuit of the Dancer-Actress   183
    MOIRA GOFF

WORLDVIEWS

8   Elisabeth of Spalbeek: Dancing the Passion   207
     KAREN SILEN
9   *Galanterie* and *Gloire:* Women's Will and
     the Eighteenth-Century Worldview
     in *Les Indes galantes*   228
     JOELLEN A. MEGLIN

     Contributors   257
     Index   261

Acknowledgments

This volume began at the urging of Barbara Sparti, who suggested this theme to me in June 2001 at a conference of the Society of Dance History Scholars (SDHS). I then pursued work on this collection of essays with the support of Sandra Noll Hammond, then on the editorial board of SDHS; Sandra's wisdom, warmth, and knowledge were and have remained indispensable as I progressed with this project. I am also grateful to Lynn Garafola, then chair of the SDHS editorial board, who guided this volume through its early stages of conception and development. More recently, Ann Cooper Albright has taken over the chair and has become a valued and generous advisor. Editors Raphael Kadushin and Sheila Moermond of the University of Wisconsin Press have been prompt and thorough in responding to my numerous queries, and I thank them for their patience.

All the authors who contributed to this volume were wonderful collaborators, sharing their knowledge, revising their essays, and providing information and suggestions whenever queried. I feel honored to have shepherded their articles to publication. My own dedication to dance history has been stimulated and shaped by many fine teachers, without whom I would not have kept going: Fran Bowden and Edrie Ferdun of Temple University, Ingrid Brainard, and my great mentor, Genevieve Oswald. Like the remarkable ladies who are the theme of this volume, these wonderful teachers have served the field of dance unstintingly, and for me, they have *made* dance history.

WOMEN'S WORK

Introduction

Women in Dance History, the Doubly Invisible

Lynn Matluck Brooks

Women have been difficult to capture as historical realities. They appear far less often than men as players in the documented historical record. Somewhat surprisingly, this is true also in the historical record of dance, a field currently closely associated with women. Like the history of women, dance has been difficult to capture as a historical subject. Bringing together these two elusive subjects—women and early dance—is the objective of this volume.

In his introduction to *Retrieving Women's History,* editor S. Jay Kleinberg notes "women's invisibility" in historical accounts, which have "systematically omitted" them from the record.[1] One objective, then, of recent research into women's history is to provide women with a place in the sweep of human history, a place that is recorded, and thus remembered, evaluated, and in many cases, newly appreciated. As women have begun to emerge from "the shadows of history,"[2] Natalie Zemon Davis and Arlette Farge have remarked, it becomes ever clearer that "wherever one turns, they were present, infinitely present: from the sixteenth through the eighteenth centuries, at home, in the economy, in the intellectual arena, in the public sphere, in social conflict, at play, women were there."[3] And during this same time period, women were there on the dance floor as well—on public stages, in the king's court, and under the roofs of religious institutions. As an investigation of women's work in the field of dance, this volume encompasses the period Davis and Farge identified in the quote above—the sixteenth through the eighteenth centuries—but embraces it in a wider stretch; one article (Barbara Sparti's "Isabella and the Dancing Este Brides, 1473–1514") reaches back to the fifteenth century, and another (Karen Silen's "Elisabeth of Spalbeek: Dancing the Passion") even further.

Dance from the eighteenth century and earlier is often lumped into a category of "early dance," partly because it preceded the establishment of ballet technique as we know it today, but also because documentation from periods preceding the nineteenth century is considerably sparser than from later periods, and the nature of the documentation often makes it difficult to interpret. This volume demonstrates some common themes that connect women and dance through this long stretch of time: women exercised patronage and power over dancing, women danced in professional performance contexts, and women explored and expressed their worldviews through dance.

We open this volume with an exploration of the ways that patronage and power allowed women to move into and through the world of dance before and during the early modern period. While men were the visibly active architects of the political and social order in this period, women were able, through patronage of the arts, directly to stage performances that had social and political impact. Women as art patrons were not a new phenomenon, and documentation specific to this role in dance has yet to be fully explored.[4] Articles in the current volume demonstrate that ladies, like the Este brides and Queen Henrietta Maria, not only patronized dance and dancing masters, but they performed dances in highly public settings—and did so with skill and finesse, as well as with astute social and political judgment. The women of the powerful Este family of Ferrara, for example, displayed their magnificence, power, and prestige through the danced entertainments they supported and, in some cases, performed in. As revealed by Barbara Sparti, these women studied dance, commissioned dances, appeared as dancers on important public occasions, and judged one another by their appearance, taste, and performance in such events. Yet in tracing ways that "dance was used by the various Este women to display magnificence and power," Sparti concludes that even these established patronesses are difficult to document fully. One reason for this difficulty is the fact that, for the dances that were "the most popular at the time of the Este sisters, we have the least information." As Sparti points out, here again "is a great gap in written dance history—one that is pregnant with rich and varied kinds of narrative dancing and virtuosic leaps and capers." This is but one example of glimpses this volume repeatedly allows us into historical treasures awaiting further research.

The Este sisters were certainly not alone in wielding their influence through patronage of danced entertainments. A similar set of powerful, interconnected women is brought to light in Angene Feves's "Fabritio Caroso's Patronesses." The critical role that these powerful women played in Caroso's success as a teacher, author, and choreographer in the late sixteenth century is evident from his grateful dedications to them, repaying in his dance titles his obligations for their patronage and support. Through tracing their connections and lives, Feves sheds light on the elusive biography of one of Italy's important early dancing masters as well as on the lives of these powerful and highly placed women. Further, she clarifies the importance of women—powerful women—in the world of Italian late-Renaissance dance. Concluding her article, Feves, like Sparti, identifies a list of questions about Caroso's life and work and his connections to the women discussed in her article. These questions suggest directions for future research in this important period of European dance history.

Women beyond Italy served as patrons of dance in the period covered by this volume, as Anne Daye's article, "At the Queen's Command: Henrietta Maria and the Development of the English Masque," illustrates. The display of skill in dancing, taste in commissioning, and diplomacy in accommodating different national styles to one another were key to the acceptance of Queen Henrietta Maria at the English court into which she married in the early seventeenth century. Having performed since childhood in the impressive danced entertainments of the French court, dance was an obvious medium for Henrietta Maria to use as a means of both integrating into her new environment and asserting herself as a woman of taste and power. Even as a young bride, "Henrietta Maria succeeded in a major innovation within months of arrival in England" through her collaboration with renowned designer Inigo Jones on the pastoral play *Artenice*. As her years at the English court unfolded, her dance patronage and contributions to the court masque revealed "a high degree of innovation and a synthesis of French, Italian, and English elements in the exploration of a dance genre that yet remained essentially English." This French-born queen left her mark on the English dance world.

These three articles on women and dance patronage, covering a span of about 170 years and touching on Italy, France, and England, make clear that women were far from powerless and invisible in their own spheres of action. Indeed, as Carole Levin and Patricia A. Sullivan have commented, "By the sixteenth century, in part through the accident of female birth and early male death, women were to achieve power in startling new ways."[5] These changes affected women's behaviors and expressivity, as well as "how the larger society perceived women's roles and nature." It was in this period that a woman, Lucrezia Marinella, could pen a book like *The Nobility and Excellence of Women, and the Defects and Vices of Men* (published in 1600), a theme about which several other Italian women of the period also chose to publish.[6] Among these were such interesting figures as the Benedictine Arcangela Tarabotti, whose three-part parody of Dante's *Inferno, Purgatorio,* and *Paradiso* articulated women's points of view from the perspectives of abusive marriages and the convent;[7] Sara Copio Sullam, a Jewish scholar living in the ghetto of Venice;[8] and Moderata Fonte, author of the two-hundred-page *Il merito delle donne,* highlighting ways that women were excluded from the privileges of the Venetian Republic.[9] A map of the political structures that allowed women power and expression in some states but kept them hidden in others could be a fruitful product of further research into the activity of women in early dance.[10]

The articles in this volume demonstrate that, during the period covered, shifts occurred in the roles women played in the dance world. For example, women came increasingly into view and finally gained primacy in the realm of professional performance, as revealed in Nathalie Lecomte's article, "The Female Ballet Troupe of the Paris Opera from 1700 to 1725." Eventually, female stars were lionized, adored, and extended considerable power within the professional dance world. Lecomte's research focuses on a period when women were relative newcomers to the Paris Opera, the institutional center of French—indeed, of European—culture. But Lecomte points out that "if male dancing was still predominant at the beginning of the eighteenth century, female professional dancing was nonetheless of high quality." The numbers of women dancing professionally as well as their status and their pay typically were lower than were men's, yet these dancers were already laying the groundwork for the ascendance of women to the pinnacle of terpsichorean achievement, a height later female dancers reached with the Romantic ballet. With Lecomte's investigations, "a sizeable slice of dance theater history, which women have so enlivened, has come to light," yet she still notes that "personalities such as Elisabeth Du Fort, Michelle Dangeville, Marie-Catherine Guyot, Madeleine Menés, and so many of their colleagues, who so brilliantly marked their epoch with their talent, are now forgotten." Again, as this volume repeatedly highlights, a wealth of material about women's participation in "early dance" remains to be explored. At the same time, Lecomte's research brings forward important data—names, dates, works, partnerships, salaries, and more—that form the critical factual foundation for such further investigations.

Lecomte points out that the women of the theater often suffered suspicion and slurred characters. In fact, some earned such reputations quite knowingly, since they considered their sexual allure and liaisons to be as much a part of their careers as were their stage appearances. As Eric A. Nicholson has written: "All the world's a stage, and all the stage is a brothel: to early modern European men and women, the latter metaphor was as appropriate as the former. It was also equally complex. On the one hand, the identification of playhouse with bawdyhouse conveyed a negative moral judgment; on the other, it embodied the sexually enticing as well as threatening aspects of defining human relations and identities along theatrical lines. Moreover, whether condemned as a site of debauchery or patronized as both a comprehensive and erotically charged 'mirror of nature,' the early modern theater highlighted woman in all her negative, positive, and, as often as not, ambivalent guises."[11]

Such themes are inescapable in reading about one of history's greatest professional performers, as illuminated in this volume by Régine Astier's "Françoise Prévost: The Unauthorized Biography." An enchanting virtuoso dancer, a choreographer of note, and a teacher of stars, Prévost rose from poverty and obscurity to become the reigning female presence at the Paris Opera in the early eighteenth century and to influence all European art dance. Astier writes: "That such an eminent, multifarious, and accomplished talent appeared so early in the history of professional female dancing is quite startling but that it left historians of the performing arts mostly indifferent is beyond comprehension."

As Astier's article, as well as Lecomte's, makes clear, Prévost was a remarkable artist; she was equally virtuosic at shaping her personal life—
juggling lovers, her daughter's paternity, and her own financial situation
with remarkable wit and daring. The fascinating documentation here
presented reads like a novel, yet it records a real and exceptional life.
Prévost took full advantage of the position to which she rose to wield
artistic and personal control in an environment often hostile to female
power. As Astier concludes, Prévost "steered her course in this unfavorable context with intelligence, energy, and conviction and we sense that
she enjoyed the journey." And with Astier's biography, we enjoy and
learn from it too.

The same drive to shape her own image and career, but differently
realized, was the concern of one of Prévost's students, as discussed in
Sarah McCleave's article, "Marie Sallé, a Wise Professional Woman of
Influence." Like her teacher, Sallé was a star of the professional stage,
both Paris and London, in her case. Yet unlike Prévost, Sallé refused to
work her sexual allures on men to gain position or wealth. Her control
of her private life, and her equally strong insistence on shaping her
dance career, aroused suspicions that caused her image to shift from the
virtuously virginal to the sexually unspeakable. Indeed, dance is here
readily recognizable as "a privileged arena for the bodily enactment of
sexuality's semiotics," as Jane Desmond has noted.[12] Sallé steadfastly retained her focus on her artistry, skillfully crafted groundbreaking dances,
worked with collaborators of the highest caliber, and left the imprint of
her genius on students, staging, and musical scores. Like other authors
in this volume, McCleave poses questions: "How much do we actually
know about [Sallé's] influence on others as a performer? And how can
we measure her impact as a choreographer when no detailed information about any of her works is known to survive?" Despite these gaps in
the available documentation, McCleave provides a provocative analysis
of Sallé as an influential dancer, choreographer, and teacher, whose
"professionalism facilitated the unprecedented creative opportunities
which she, as a woman, enjoyed in the 1730s and 1740s."

Women like Prévost and Sallé were the forerunners of the great ballerinas who came to dominate western Europe's stages in the early to
mid-nineteenth century, women whose descendants are still captivating
audiences with their power, virtuosity, and allure. Beyond France, too,
the female professional dancer made her mark. As Moira Goff explains
in her article "In Pursuit of the Dancer-Actress," women were critical to

the realization of the eighteenth-century reforms undertaken by such dance visionaries as John Weaver, whose choreographies, presaging the *ballet d'action*, required performers of extraordinary skill in both dramatic interpretation and dance performance. These women were professionals, dancers with virtuosic techniques and authoritative presentation. Several of the women performing on London's stages at this time managed to make their ways in the theater world as *both* dancers and actresses, playing featured roles in interludes, ballets, and plays. Goff stresses that the performers who are the subject of her article "were not dancers who occasionally took minor acting roles, nor were they actresses who sometimes danced when required. These women not only danced regularly in the entr'actes and took leading roles in danced afterpieces but they also had their own acting roles, often leading ones, in which they appeared season after season." These were, then, remarkably skilled and disciplined artists who had mastered and managed the complexities of *two* art forms. Their influence on the famous choreographers and directors of their day can now be reconsidered, as Goff suggests. "It is natural to conclude that they were collaborators with, rather than merely interpreters for, John Weaver, John Rich, and others. Indeed, it is possible to claim that expressive dancing developed on the London stage as quickly as it did because of the accomplished performances of the dancer-actresses Margaret Bicknell, Elizabeth Younger, and Hester Santlow." Artists with so broad a theatrical reach are rare today, even in contemporary "dance theater." Drawing connections between the theatricality of contemporary dance and that of the *ballet d'action*, of which Weaver's work was a forerunner, would be another fascinating direction for further investigation.

Further surprising perspectives appear in the worldviews treated in this volume. Two compelling yet utterly different female views of the world conclude this volume, bracketing this collection's reach in time as well as in the philosophies explored. Well over seven hundred years ago, Karen Silen's article documents, a woman was renowned and revered for her religious visions expressed through dance. The remarkable combination of femaleness, religious orthodoxy, and embodied enactment is further astonishing to the contemporary reader when one realizes that this woman, Elisabeth of Spalbeek, was young, was creating as well as performing her movement interpretations, and was understood to be depicting the story of Christ's Passion through her own body. Such surprises allow us "to explode the standard myth that women were always dominated and men always oppressors. The reality was much more complex. There was inequality, to be sure, but there was also a shifting zone in which women found and used a multitude of strategies outside the roles of inevitable victims or exceptional heroines to make themselves active agents in history."[13] That Elisabeth found such an opportunity for expression, communication, and recognition in a sphere where, at other times, women's movement and physicality were suspect and repressed, is evident from the information provided in Silen's article. In fact, as Silen states, "Elisabeth's supporters understood her dances as a divine revelation received directly from God for the purposes of inspiring her audiences and renewing their faith." Elisabeth was one of the fortunate visionaries of her day. Silen points out that, viewed through "the hagiographic lens, women appear only as signs to be read and used for ideological purposes." Was Elisabeth "simply a vessel to be filled with God's . . . purposes? Was she a fraud, who manipulated well-known signs to create a new dance form?" As reported and interpreted by her biographer, Abbot Philip of Clairvaux, Elisabeth's trances were authentic and holy and are accessible centuries later through his documentation of her dancing—documentation in some ways remarkably detailed and in others frustratingly inadequate. The elusive nature of dance as a historical theme is immediately apparent in the attempt to recapture Elisabeth's experience through Philip's record of it. Yet that record, as Silen's analysis brings out, extends our knowledge of women's roles in the Church, in European history, and in dance.

Somewhat midway between Elisabeth's time and our own, women were again shaping the dominant themes of their age—no longer religious in nature, but now themes of exploration, of exoticism, of colonial expansion. Joellen Meglin analyzes the nature of salon culture in eighteenth-century France, a world in which women shaped the tastes, the presentations, the very ethos of the age, while men responded to their visions through action on the world's theatrical and political stages. The theme of intellectual exchange between men and women constitutes the subject of Joellen Meglin's "*Galanterie* and *Gloire:* Women's Will and the Eighteenth-Century Worldview in *Les Indes galantes.*" According to Davis and Farge, "taking women seriously involves reconstructing their actions within the context of the relations that men and women instituted between themselves. It involves viewing relations between the sexes as a social construct whose history can and should be an object of study. . . . There was lively debate between men and women in the early modern period. It was a debate that developed against a background of social and political instability and disorientation, as the established church fragmented in the violence and controversy of Reformation and Counter-Reformation and as states turned to mercantilist economic policies."[14] These forces had affected French theater prior to *Les Indes galantes,* an *opéra-ballet* produced in 1735, but they came to the fore in the salon culture that informed contemporary understandings of *galanterie* and war, of exoticism and sexuality. As Meglin astutely observes, in the *opéra-ballet* "the stuff of gender relations was used to narrate encounters between diverse peoples and the stuff of national character was used to narrate gender relations." In *Les Indes galantes,* "women acted as the regulators of social grace, bespeaking a salon-centered agenda as opposed to an absolutist one," thus creating "a space for alternative views and imagined otherness."

That dancing was part of the armory available to women in expressing their achievement and power in the period covered by this volume is not surprising. As Jean-Paul Desaive writes with reference to English and French literature of the fifteenth through seventeenth centuries, "Sick bodies and remedies and effects are abundantly present in memoirs and letters, but healthy bodies are just as noticeably absent. When the healthy body appeared in works of fiction, it was often in terms so conventional as to be all but meaningless: the most beautiful figure in the world, the most beautiful bosom in the world, and so on. But novels and 'true' reportage did abandon their reticence and move beyond stereotypical description in one area, that of dance. . . . Along with riding, a sport reserved for the nobility, dance was the only form of body language that allowed a woman to express herself as an equal of, and in perfect symmetry with, a man." In most sports of the leisured classes, like tennis and jousting, "men performed while women sat and watched. A ball was thus a unique occasion for women to demonstrate that they too could move gracefully, vigorously, briskly, or with abandon." In the duets that constituted most of these social dances, the ways that male and female performers balanced their partnership and importance must have appealed to women of imagination and energy. The example of a dancing couple could serve as a model for women's roles in other contexts. Interestingly, Desaive comments that "novels and religion were the only avenues open to them [women] for freeing their minds, and dance was the only avenue open to them for freeing their bodies."[15] This avenue to freedom is further explored in the current volume not only in Meglin's analysis but also in the articles preceding it.

The confluence of the three themes listed by Desaive—literature, religion, and dance—is likely to yield much further information about women's participation as dancers, dance supporters, and dance makers. For example, my own research in Spanish Golden Age dance combined investigation of these themes, resulting in a rich yield of information. The glorious dramatic literature from this period was filled with dance references, descriptions, and embodiments, while the dances created for performance during Spain's major religious celebrations were frequently under the direction of female choreographers.[16] In the current volume, Silen's article is evidence of the riches that the study of women's religiosity reveals, while Meglin's mines the literary field for provocative insights. Dance, the third item in Desaive's list, is the constant that runs through the lives and work of the women studied for this volume.

Underlying the research presented in all the articles in this collection is the difficulty of treating dance as a historical subject. An art as ephemeral as dance—lacking a trustworthy, widely used notation form for most of its history, and only recently much recorded—is difficult to capture in the retreating past that constitutes history. In part, this may be due to the fact that dance is difficult to describe in words. Those of us who teach it, who write about it, who seek to explain it to lay people, are acutely aware of this fact; we hone our language skills carefully to become articulate speakers about dance. In her article in this volume, Silen discusses the problems she encountered in using the documentation left by Philip of Clairvaux, who had to tackle the problems of dance description: what movements to describe, what information to leave out, how to create an appropriate context in which to place Elisabeth of Spalbeek's dancing. Such concerns confront every dance historian. Yet another reason for the fleeting references to dance in the historical record might be that the dancing, on the occasions noted, was simply less important to the document's writer than were other factors, such as the sumptuous costumes, the physical charms of the performers, or the particular guests present at an event. Barbara Sparti, for example, in her article about the dancing ladies of the Este family, makes this point in the context of her research. In one form or another, this issue runs through every subject tackled in this volume.

Earlier in this essay, the issue of women's "invisibility" in written histories was raised. Was this also the case in dance history? After all, dance is currently associated in mainstream Western cultures with female presence and influence: more women than men enroll in dance classes, perform on dance stages, and engage in dance education and research. Recent dance history is full of vibrant, powerful women who danced, created dances, promoted the dance field, taught and theorized about dancing—women like Isadora Duncan, Ruth St. Denis, Anna Pavlova, Bronislava Nijinska, Ninette de Valois, Marie Rambert, Mary Wigman, Martha Graham, Doris Humphrey, Hanya Holm, Helen Tamiris, Margaret H'Doubler, Anna Halprin, and so many others. And yet dance scholars Sharon Friedler and Susan Glazer have also noted that "despite a rich history and rampant assumptions that women dominate in dance, when we began our research in 1989 we could find little scholarly work linking women to one another, to their heritage and to their professional environments. . . . As educators and dancers we felt the need for literature focused on women in dance, lore that could provoke discussion within and beyond the field and promote further scholarship."[17] The focus of the book from which this quote was taken—*Dancing Female: Lives and Issues of Women in Contemporary Dance*—is twentieth-century dance. As one reaches further back in history, the absence of an integrative history of women in dance becomes increasingly noticeable, as does the sheer lack of information, data, and any kind of substantial knowledge of women's participation in the world of Western dance. Names arise, some mentioned in the current volume as well, in any survey text covering the history of Western theater dance—fewer and fewer names as we reach into the receding past: Fanny Elssler, Marie Taglioni, Marie Sallé, Marie-Anne Camargo, Françoise Prévost, Hester Santlow, Catherine de Medici, Queen Elizabeth I. But knowledge of these ladies' dancing lives is far from complete, and there are many more women's names, as the authors of articles included in this volume have identified, that deserve to be highlighted and appreciated in the context of dance history.

This volume can be viewed as part of a larger pattern of research in women's history, research that has moved in several directions.[18] One avenue of study is the search to place the missing names and faces of women in the established disciplinary canon appropriate to a specific field, in other words, to fill in the gaps. Another direction investigates the circumstances that excluded women from greater participation in the canon. Yet a third direction questions the very concept of a canon, relegating that notion to the status of an elitist social construct designed in part to close women out of the circle. The articles included in the current volume give evidence of women inside the mainstream of dance (Prévost) yet sometimes pursuing that status with considerable risk or discomfort (Sallé); women influencing the canon (as in *Les Indes galantes* and the projects of Queen Henrietta Maria); and women earning reverence for their dancing in noncanonic contexts (Elisabeth of Spalbeek). In the period under study, women's culture, in some senses quite distinct from that of men, embraced the world of the dance, one of the few arenas in which women could exercise their creativity as well as their bodies. Through their dancing, women were able to pursue varied paths, including the roles of patrons, performers, and arbiters of behavior.[19]

The aim of this volume is to bring to light some of the ways that some women in this hard-to-capture past supported dance, made dances, performed dances, and influenced the dance world. No doubt, further research—and there is an iceberg submerged beneath the superficial tip of our dance history knowledge—will find women in more and surprising roles, for this is truly a field across which women have moved with finesse, expressivity, and power for long centuries past.

NOTES

1. S. Jay Kleinberg, "Introduction," in *Retrieving Women's History*, ed. S. Jay Kleinberg (Oxford: Berg Publishers Ltd., 1988), ix.

2. Georges Duby and Michelle Perrot, "Writing the History of Women," in *A History of Women in the West*, vol. 3, *Renaissance and Enlightenment Paradoxes* (hereafter cited as *A History of Women*), ed. Natalie Zemon Davis and Arlette Farge (Cambridge, MA: Belknap Press of Harvard University Press, 1993), ix.

3. Natalie Zemon Davis and Arlette Farge, "Women as Historical Actors," in *A History of Women*, 1.

4. See, for example, Elizabeth McKenna, "The Gift of a Lady: Women as Patrons in Medieval Ireland," in *Women in Renaissance and Early Modern Europe*, ed. Christine Meek (Dublin: Four Courts Press Ltd., 2000), 84–94.

5. Carole Levin and Patricia A. Sullivan, "Politics, Women's Voices, and the Renaissance," in *Political Rhetoric, Power, and Renaissance Women*, ed. Carole Levin and Patricia A. Sullivan (Albany, NY: State University of New York Press, 1995), 2.

6. Lucrezia Marinella, *The Nobility and Excellence of Women, and the Defects and Vices of Men,* ed. and trans. Anne Dunhill, introduction by Letizia Panizza (Chicago: University of Chicago Press, 1999).

7. On Tarabotti, see Elisja Schulte van Kessel, "Virgins and Mothers between Heaven and Earth," in *A History of Women,* 155. Tarabotti's parodies are titled *Inferno monacale* (Nun's Inferno), *Paradiso monacale* (Nun's Paradise), and *Purgatorio delle mal maritate* (Purgatory of the Badly Married).

8. On Sara Copio Sullam, the forthcoming work is projected for publication in the series The Other Voice in Early Modern Europe, ed. Margaret King and Albert Rabil, Jr.: *Sara Copio Sullam: Jewish Poet and Intellectual in Early Seventeenth-Century Venice,* ed. and trans. Don Harrán (Chicago: University of Chicago Press, forthcoming).

9. On Moderata Fonte, pen name of Modesta Pozzo, see Ann Rosalind Jones, "Apostrophes to Cities: Urban Rhetorics in Isabella Whitney and Moderata Fonte," in *Attending to Early Modern Women,* ed. Susan D. Amussen and Adele Seeff (Newark, NJ: University of Delaware Press, 1998), 155–75.

10. See Natalie Zemon Davis, "Women in Politics," in *A History of Women,* 167–83; and Levin and Sullivan, "Politics, Women's Voices, and the Renaissance," 3–4.

11. Eric A. Nicholson, "The Theater," in *A History of Women,* 295.

12. Jane Desmond, "Making the Invisible Visible: Staging Sexualities through Dance," in *Dancing Desires: Choreographing Sexualities on and off the Stage,* ed. Jane C. Desmond (Madison: University of Wisconsin Press, 2001), 3–32.

13. Davis and Farge, "Women as Historical Actors," in *A History of Women,* 3–4. A far darker view of the treatment of cloistered women is given in Carol Baxter's "Repression or Liberation? Notions of the Body among the Nuns of Port Royal," in *Women in Renaissance and Early Modern Europe,* 153–71.

14. Davis and Farge, "Women as Historical Actors," in *A History of Women,* 2. On female discourse in seventeenth-century French theater, see Derval Conroy, "Tragic Ambiguities: Gender and Sovereignty in French Classical Drama," in *Women in Renaissance and Early Modern Europe,* 185–204.

15. Jean-Paul Desaive, "The Ambiguities of Literature," in *A History of Women,* 291–92.

16. See Lynn Matluck Brooks, *The Art of Dancing in Seventeenth-Century Spain: Juan de Esquivel Navarro and His World* (Lewisburg, PA: Bucknell University Press, 2003); and *The Dances of the Processions of Seville in Spain's Golden Age* (Kassel, Germany: Editions Reichenberger, 1988).

17. Sharon E. Friedler and Susan B. Glazer, "Preface," in *Dancing Female: Lives and Issues of Women in Contemporary Dance,* ed. Sharon E. Friedler and Susan B. Glazer (Amsterdam: Harwood Academic Publishers, 1997), xv.

18. See, for example, Corine Schleif, "The Roles of Women in Challenging the Canon of 'Great Master' Art History," in *Attending to Early Modern*

Women, ed. Susan Dwyer Amussen and Adele Seeff (Newark: University of Delaware Press, 1998), 74–92.

19. On the concept of two "cultural realities"—one male and one female—see Ted Polhemus, "Dance, Gender and Culture," in *The Routledge Dance Studies Reader,* ed. Alexandra Carter (London: Routledge, 1998), 171–79.

Patronage and Power

I

Isabella and the Dancing Este Brides, 1473–1514

Barbara Sparti

At the age of sixteen, Isabella d'Este became Marchioness of Mantua after her marriage to Francesco Gonzaga in 1490. She is best known, thanks to her prolific correspondence, as a collector and patron of the arts, a mistress of fashion and elegance, and an able, astute politician.[1] Dance, too, played an important part in her world. Starting with her mother's wedding festivities, continuing with those of her sisters and sisters-in-law, and with Isabella's own narrative threading throughout, this chapter will demonstrate how dance was used by the various Este women to display magnificence and power.

The Ferrara where Isabella grew up was geographically smaller and politically less powerful than the five great states united in the Italian League: the duchy of Milan, the republic of Venice, the republic of Florence, the Papal state, and the kingdom of Naples.[2] (See figure 1.1.) Nonetheless, thanks in large part to her paternal uncles, Leonello and Borso d'Este, who had ruled Ferrara from 1441,[3] the city-state had become a jewel of the Renaissance, renowned for the artists and architects who designed and decorated the city's monuments and palaces.[4] Ercole,

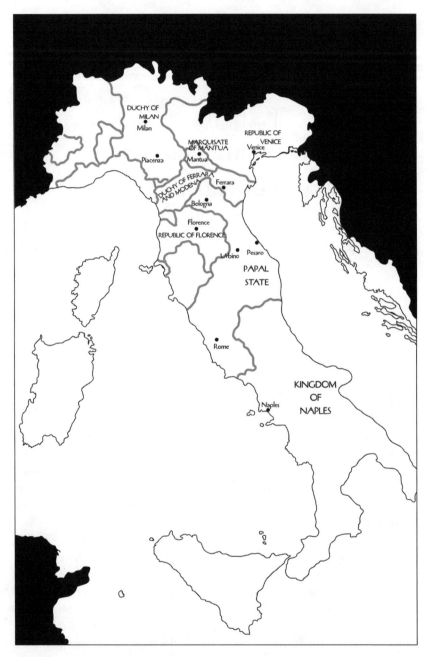

Figure 1.1. Isabella d'Este's Italy (1473–1514). (Map by Patricia Carmo Baltazar Correa; reprinted with permission.)

Isabella's father, succeeding Borso as duke of Ferrara in 1471, continued the tradition and was responsible for a bold and impressive urban reform.[5]

Besides artists, musicians, and scholars, Leonello's court had a dancing master, perhaps the most outstanding of the century. Domenico of Piacenza is known to us today because of an anonymous manuscript that includes descriptions of twenty-three of his choreographies *(basse-danze* and *balli)* and their music, as well as his theory of the dance. Domenico's work, written down somewhat before 1455,[6] is, as far as we know, the first of several extant dance treatises of the period. These others were drafted by his "disciples," the dancing master Guglielmo Ebreo and the poet-humanist-courtier Antonio Cornazano.[7]

Not all fifteenth-century Italian courts had their own dancing masters, as we shall see, and indeed, Domenico's position in Ferrara, where he appears in records as early as 1439, is never specified other than as *"familiaris noster"* (of our household), and as *"spectabilis eques"* and *"spectabilis miles,"* titles of nobility bestowed, for the most part, only on gentlemen.[8] In 1455, he was responsible for three different choreographic productions that took place during the Milanese wedding celebrations of Leonello's sister, Beatrice d'Este, to Tristano Sforza, illegitimate son of the duke of Milan;[9] and at the final ball, Domenico was partnered with the duchess of Milan.[10] Domenico named four of his dances after people and places connected with the Este court: "Leoncello" for Leonello, "Belreguardo" (Beautiful View) and "Belfiore" (Beautiful Flower) for two of the Este country villas, and "Marchesana" (Marchioness) for Leonello's wife.[11] Domenico, though born in Piacenza, is referred to at times as Domenico of Ferrara due to his having remained at the Este court well into the 1470s.[12] It seems unlikely that Isabella, born 17 May 1474, knew him, but his reputation and influence would certainly have been in the air.

Isabella: 1474–81

Someone must have instructed Isabella in the dance, since in 1481, when she was only six years old, she "danced twice with that Ambrosio, formerly a Jew, and [who] is with the most illustrious lord Duke of Urbino as his dancing master." This was reported in a letter written on 24 January by Guido da Bagno, physician to the Gonzaga family.[13] Ambrosio

Niccolò III (Lord of Ferrara and Modena)

Leonello (1407–50)
Lord: 1441–50
m. **Margherita Gonzaga** (d. 1439)
m. **Maria d'Aragona** (d. 1449)

Borso (1413–71)
Lord: 1450–71
Duke: 1471

Ercole (1431–1505)
Duke: 1471–1505
m. 1473 **Eleonora of Aragon**

Beatrice (d. 1497)
m. **Niccolò di Correggio**[1]
m. 1455 **Tristano Sforza**

Sigismondo (1480–1524)
m. 1490 **Angela Sforza** (d. 1501)

Isabella (1474–1539)
m. 1490 **Francesco Gonzaga** (1466–1519)
m. 1491 **Marquis of Mantua** (1478–84)

Beatrice (1475–97)
m. 1491 **Ludovico Sforza** ("il Moro"), Duke of Milan

Alfonso (1476–1534)
Duke of Ferrara: 1505
m. 1491 **Anna Sforza** (d. 1501)
m. 1502 **Lucretia Borgia** (d. 1519)

Ferrante (1477–1540)
Cardinal: 1493

Ippolito (1479–1520)

Some of Isabella's children who lived to adulthood:

Lucretia[2]
m. 1487 **Annibale Bentivoglio**

Eleonora (1493/94–1550)
m. Francesco Maria della Rovere, Duke of Urbino

Federico (1500–40)
future Marquis of Mantua
m. Margherita Paleologa

Ercole (1506–63)
Cardinal: 1527

Ferrante (1507–57)

Note: The genealogy is limited to persons referred to in this essay.
[1] The year of this first marriage is unknown.
[2] Dates of birth and death are unknown. Lucretia was born before Eleonora's marriage.

Figure 1.2. Select genealogy of Isabella d'Este.

was none other than Domenico's former pupil, Guglielmo Ebreo, William the Jew, who some time between 1463 and 1465 had converted to Christianity. In the previous spring, Isabella had become officially engaged to the fifteen-year-old Francesco Gonzaga, future Marquis of Mantua.[14] Visits between the young couple began soon after and continued regularly: Isabella to Mantua and Francesco to Ferrara.[15] It seems that Francesco was in Ferrara with his family attending the wedding of Roberto Gonzaga and Antonia Malatesta, and that Guido da Bagno was in his retinue.[16] Two months after Guido's description of Isabella dancing, in March of that same year, the doctor sent the Marquis of Mantua another letter from Ferrara reporting the recovery of Francesco from an illness that had made it necessary to prolong his stay.[17] It was undoubtedly during the festivities arranged for the wedding and for Francesco's visit that Isabella performed with the dancing master Giovanni Ambrosio. Dancing and declamation (in Latin verse) were often performed by young princes and princesses at courtly gatherings or public ceremonies. Isabella, at six, excelled in both.[18] Besides displaying impressive precocity and grace, the art of oratory was a precious element in the political life of the times.[19]

Guglielmo Ebreo/Giovanni Ambrosio, Domenico's "devoted disciple and fervent follower," carried on the tradition of his master.[20] He, too, composed dances and their music, including them in a treatise that claimed dance to be an art and science, and a pursuit appropriate for a prince. In 1481, when he danced with Isabella, he must have been about sixty years old. He may well have been at the Este court with his patron, Federico of Montefeltro, Duke of Urbino, and it may have been at the request of Isabella's mother, Eleonora of Aragon, that the elderly dancing master was present. Eleanora, or Leonora of Aragon, daughter of the king of Naples, had, together with her sister Beatrice (future queen of Hungary), been taught dancing by Giovanni Ambrosio. In 1466, when Eleonora was sixteen and Beatrice nine, the king of Naples, Ferrante (Ferdinando I), had asked Ambrosio's patron, Alessandro Sforza of Pesaro, to send him the dancing master to instruct his daughters in "the Lombard [style of] dancing."[21] This was probably because Eleonora was then engaged to be married to one of the sons of Francesco Sforza, duke of Milan. Recruiting Guglielmo/Ambrosio to teach Eleonora dances from northern Italy (rather than those of the Spanish sort practiced at the Aragonese court) must have been one of the ways that the king of Naples envisioned preparing his daughter for her future position as the wife of a Lombard lord.[22] It was, however, not until 1473, seven years later, that Eleonora married, and her spouse was not a Sforza but the duke of Ferrara, Ercole d'Este. In the first three years of her marriage, Eleonora/Leonora gave birth to Isabella (17 May 1474), Beatrice (19 June 1475), and Alfonso (21 July 1476).

Eleonora of Aragon's Wedding Festivities: Naples and Rome, 1473

Eleonora's marriage by proxy and the festivities that began in Naples on 16 May and ended in Ferrara two months later are fully documented. What was recorded by princes, chroniclers and ambassadors was, in the fashion of the time, everything that impressed: rich apparel, jewels, gold cloth, the hundred or more elegantly bedecked young women "on view,"[23] precious tapestries, display of gold plate, food covered in gold, the number of people in an entourage or attending an event, the deafening noise, the duration of the banquet or processions, the number of courses, fountains that spilled forth wines, money thrown to the throng, food and sweetmeats *"a saccomano"* (up for grabs), the value of gifts received or donated. Inaccuracy, exaggeration, and flattery were given ample room. The "practice of magnificence" was universally adopted by the Renaissance prince.[24] In many instances, magnificence was indeed used to beautify and benefit the cities. But in the second half of the fifteenth century, the conspicuous display of wealth became, above all, a policy of personal power. It was necessary to impress both rivals and allies with one's wealth; magnificence was used to secure the allegiance of the populace in power struggles with local and foreign lords. Lavish display was also the most obvious gauge for quantifying a prince's status.

Where in this picture of statecraft based on magnificence did dance come in? References to dancing are sparse, and when they do appear they are most often brief remarks, quite outweighed by the long, detailed descriptions of the participants' dress or the hall decorations or the progress of the banquet. On rare occasions we are told who opened the dancing and which illustrious personages danced with whom, another important indication of power and prestige.[25] Otherwise, reports of dancing tended to consist of terse statements such as "and they danced for the duration of two hours," or, "and having returned to the court, they performed many dances 'til nightfall." Even Guglielmo

Ebreo/Giovanni Ambrosio, in the thirty entries of his "autobiography," sets out to impress his readers (would-be aristocratic patrons) with the festivities he has attended and the princes and noble lords with whom he has rubbed shoulders.[26] Going into detail about expensive clothing, the various courses at banquets, the great number of people participating ("10,000 sat down to table"), how much was spent on the festivities (according to hearsay), and the estimated cost of jewels and gifts, he devotes only twelve off-hand references to dancing.

With few exceptions, the chronicles lack any particularized descriptions of princely balls, in part, no doubt, because the dancing was too familiar and obvious to comment on.[27] More to the point, the dancing was *in itself* neither splendid nor costly. Its role, like everything else in the court, was primarily that of enabling the ruling class to display its wealth and power. The dancing at balls offered the perfect opportunity for showing off rich clothing and magnificent jewels. But the actual social dancing engaged in at princely entertainments was, in all probability, considered insignificant. There was, however, another kind of dance whose spectacular nature and symbolism reinforced the prince's image and thus captured the interest of the diarists. Eleonora of Aragon's marriage celebrations included both "social dancing,"[28] in which she herself participated, and a danced spectacle, a kind of ballet, choreographed especially for her.

Eleonora used the occasion of the Neapolitan wedding ceremonies to conspicuously demonstrate her authority and worth during a ball she herself undoubtedly designed. In an open space lined with tiered platforms capable of seating half of the 40,000 inhabitants of the city of Naples (and the entourage of 500 persons from Ferrara), Eleonora opened the "social" dancing with her brother. To duly impress the Ferrarese and other ambassadors, she dressed herself all in gold and with a train "eight arms long." Once the dancing and magnificent *public* display were over, Eleonora changed out of her golden raiment and signed the wedding contract.

On her journey from Naples to Ferrara, where she was finally to meet her husband, Eleonora was feted with balls, pageants, and banquets.[29] The most outstanding festivities were organized in Rome by the nephew of Pope Sixtus IV.[30] Cardinal Pietro Riario was well known for his lavishness and love of spectacle. His seven-hour banquet in honor of Eleonora was one of the most famous and extravagant of its day.[31] The chief steward changed his clothes four times, and the innumerable courses were interspersed with mythological scenes. The poetic texts, sung or spoken in Latin, alluded directly or indirectly to the newlyweds. One of these interludes, performed at the end of the feast, was a kind of "ballet," an allegorical homage to Eleonora's new spouse, Ercole d'Este. The *ballo* portrayed a group of armed centaurs disrupting a wedding celebration and attempting to abduct the nymphs and ladies with whom Hercules (the groom's namesake), Jason, Theseus, and other heroes had been dancing. After the combat, with Hercules victorious, the centaurs fled and the festive dancing recommenced.

Eleonora records the banquet in 135 lines of detailed description, but despite her experience with dancing, she limits her account of the "ballet" to the following three sentences: "The table removed, the *ballo* of Hercules with five men and nine ladies [began]. During the *ballo* the Centaurs came and they performed a fine battle. The Centaurs, vanquished by Hercules, returned and the *ballo* was formed again."[32] A few more details, such as the accompanying musical instruments and the shields and clubs used in the battle, were provided by the Milanese historian, Bernardo Corio. He describes the dancers as being on a stage: "eight men, with eight others dressed as nymphs and their lovers."[33] Since Corio specifies "others" and "dressed" as feminine—"altre vestite"—it would appear that here at least the eight nymphs were female rather than males *en travesti*. Little is known about women dancing women's parts in fifteenth-century private and public performances.[34]

Isabella and Lorenzo Lavagnolo: 1485

In 1485, when Isabella was eleven, she sent a letter, written in her own hand, to her fiancé Francesco Gonzaga, expressing her delight with the dancing master Lorenzo Lavagnolo who had been sent to Ferrara by the marquise of Mantua, Francesco's mother. Lorenzo Lavagnolo, unlike Domenico and Guglielmo, left no written works, and is hence far less familiar to students of dance history today. However, he not only represents the following generation of dancers-choreographers-teachers but he was also considered by Barbara Gonzaga to be "master above all others in the profession of dancing."[35] He was certainly in demand and was sent not only to Ferrara but also to the courts of Mantua, Urbino, Milan, and Bologna. Isabella wrote: "I cannot describe how your

Lorenzo Lavagnolo showed us so much love and diligence in demonstrating the excellences of his dancing to me, but the results that remain with me and my sisters bear witness."[36] Taking lessons with Isabella and Beatrice were, not her nine-year-old brother Alfonso, but an older half-sister, Lucretia, born to Ercole before his marriage. Twenty years later, some time after Lorenzo's death, we find his stepdaughter, the beautiful "Isabella Ballarina" as one of Isabella d'Este's young and favorite ladies-in-waiting.[37]

Lucretia d'Este's Wedding Festivities: Bologna, 1487

The following year, in 1486, Lavagnolo was invited to Bologna to help prepare the festivities for the marriage between the young lord of that city, Annibale Bentivoglio, and Isabella's half-sister, Lucretia. The marriage took place one year later, and among the grandiose celebrations was a remarkable *rappresentazione:* a fable of love, chastity, and marriage. The allegory-spectacle included vocal and instrumental music, dramatic-poetic text (spoken and sung), scenic effects (moveable stage machinery), costumes, mime, and a great deal of dance.[38] Because this kind of documentation is so rare (the succinct résumé of the Roman ballet of Hercules fighting the centaurs being more typical), we cannot even know how exceptional this event was. What is certain is that it anticipates by one hundred years the primacy of *Le Balet Comique de la Royne* as "the first ballet." This designation, together with that of the first *ballet de cour,* was given to the 1581 *Balet Comique* by twentieth-century specialists not only because of its name but especially because of its unification of poetic text, music, scenic decor, and dance around a common dramatic action.[39] These are features evident in the *rappresentazione* of 1487.

The underlying political reason for the splendid 1487 celebrations was Bologna's desire and determination to solidify and perpetuate its own *signoria,* independent of the Papal States and of Este expansionism. Hence, the festive events, which lasted several days, were devised to confer a dignity on the Bentivoglio family equal to that of such magnificent courts as those of the Estes of Ferrara, the Gonzagas of Mantua, and the Medici of Florence. It was undoubtedly Lucretia d'Este, the bride, who suggested Lavagnolo as the "choreographer," since she and her sisters

had taken lessons with him two years earlier. It is also likely that the idea
of having a *rappresentazione* with wonderful scenery, music, verse, and
dance also came from her, thanks to her memories of the numerous *moresche* and productions she had attended in Ferrara.

Dance was present throughout the performance of the fable. The
important stage props—a tower, a palace, a mountain with a cave near
a wood, a rock or crag—each made its appearance "dancing." Diana,
after taming a wild lion (symbol of vice) and presenting it to the lord,
joined her nymphs in a "hunting dance" and in a circular *bassadanza*.
The heroine of the fable, a "lost nymph" (named, like the real bride, Lucretia), was presented to her husband-to-be by Juno. Together they performed the dance (unknown to us today) "Vivolieta" (I live happy). Four
emperors and their ladies emerged from the castle with a celebratory
dance. They were followed by eight blackfaced "moors," adorned with
bells, who danced around a lady holding a flower and a quince (symbol
of fertility).[40] And lastly, couples from the Butcher's Guild, wearing the
device of the Bentivoglios, performed a dance with hooplike festoons of
foliage. In addition, the fable was nicely ensconced between a prelude,
which featured the extraordinary dexterity of a six-year-old Tuscan girl
dancing both alone and with a male partner (her teacher?) to the accompaniment of pipe and tabor, and a postlude, unique for Italy (as far as is
known at present), with circle dancing for all the assembled company.

Lavagnolo is not mentioned, nor is any other choreographer or master of ceremonies, in the various detailed accounts. We do not know
who the performers—the actors, dancers, and singers—in the "Love,
Chastity, and Marriage" allegory were. They almost certainly were not
nobility or they would have been named,[41] and the real Lucretia and
Annibale were, with other important guests, observing all from a raised
tribune. Almost all of the spoken-acted text that took place during the
fable, written by well-known literati, has survived.

Wedding Festivities for Isabella (Mantua, 1490), Beatrice d'Este (Milan, 1491), and Anna Sforza-Este (Ferrara, 1491)

No descriptions of special dance events have so far come to light for
Isabella's own marriage in 1490, which started with her grand entrance

into Mantua, where she was greeted by seven mythological representations in verse and music. Then followed three days of jousts and eight days of fabulous banquets for the 17,000 guests.[42] The next Este bride was Beatrice who was married in Milan in January 1491. Ferrara had decided to strengthen its alliance with Milan, unofficially ruled by Ludovico "il Moro," the unscrupulous and ambitious uncle of the twenty-one-year-old Sforza duke.[43] Thus, not only did Beatrice marry Ludovico, but a few days later, her brother Alfonso married Ludovico's niece, Anna Sforza, the young duke's sister.[44] On 24 January, Ludovico arranged a great ball, in large part to show off the importance of his own bride and his acquired noble relatives. It was opened by the Sforza duchess of Milan (Isabella of Aragon) dancing with a lady-in-waiting. Then came the turn of the Este sisters, Beatrice and Isabella, who were followed by Anna Sforza dancing with her sister, Bianca Maria.[45] Diarists' accounts vary, in part due to memory, to style, and to what they or their patrons thought important. Another account has "the queens"— the Duchess and Beatrice—dancing first, taking as partners two newly dubbed knights.[46] A mimed-danced entertainment featured couples dressed in French, Spanish, Hungarian, Turkish, and Egyptian costumes, recalling the exotic entries for the lavish "Festa del Paradiso" staged by Leonardo da Vinci and presented the year before for the marriage of the young Milanese duke.[47] As with Lucretia d'Este's Bologna entertainment, Milan also produced, after the wedding of Anna and Alfonso, a young Tuscan girl, dancing with grace and agility and with all sorts of turns and body twistings, accompanied by a dancing master.

Anna and Alfonso left Milan for Ferrara, where more festivities awaited them. Here the Milanese ambassador noted that during the ball, the marquis of Mantua (Francesco Gonzaga) danced with the bride, and the groom with the marquise ("our" Isabella d'Este), and that they performed a few *bassedanze*.[48] During a performance of a play by the ancient Roman playwright, Plautus,[49] there were three *intermezzi:* the first was a dance done with torches; the second was sung. The third, a *moresca* in mime and dance, featured a group of "rustics" who, with hoes, spades, rakes, and winnowing fans, alternately "worked the land" and "fought with swords," always keeping in time to the pipe and tabor music and cuffing each other for fun at their exit. As we shall see, this theme will be taken up again in Ferrara, though without the mock battle.

Beatrice d'Este, Duchess of Milan: Politics and Dance (Venice, 1493, and Lombardy, 1494)

Isabella had taken part in the Milanese wedding festivities in the private role of Beatrice's sister, inasmuch as Mantua was then allied, against Milan, with Venice. Two years later, when Milan was once again united with Mantua, Ferrara, Venice, and the Papal State in a new league, Beatrice, now officially Duchess of Milan, was sent to Venice by her husband on an important but delicate political mission, while he, Ludovico Sforza, was attempting negotiations with the king of France (Charles VIII) on one hand and the Holy Roman Emperor, Maximilian I, on the other.[50] Accompanied by her mother, Eleonora, and her brother Alfonso and his wife Anna Sforza, Beatrice was received warmly and with festive ceremony. Writing to her husband, Beatrice describes how, as their galleys and gondolas approached Venice, they were greeted with a danced and mimed "representation" performed aboard a boat. The allegory featured Minerva and Neptune vying for control of Attica, but here the acropolis of the ancient myth was substituted with the coat of arms of the members of the league. Both gods danced alone and then together "with jumps and gambols [capers?]."[51] The crash of Neptune's trident against the mountain brought forth a horse. Venice's message was clear when Minerva was declared the victor after her arrow produced an olive tree, symbol of peace and abundance.

In September of the following year, 1494, the king of France, Charles VIII, invaded the north of Italy on his way to conquering the entire peninsula in four months. Nevertheless, Ludovico Sforza, for his own political gains of the moment, welcomed Charles with due splendor, and he and Beatrice entertained him in one of their Lombard castles.[52] So politically important was the occasion that Beatrice had to abandon her mourning for her mother's death, changing her clothes and taking part in the dancing.[53] According to ambassadorial reports, Charles, following French fashion, kissed Beatrice and her eighty maids of honor, after which he asked Beatrice if she and her ladies would dance for him.[54] This she did, dancing well "in French fashion with several of her ladies."[55] Beatrice, like many Renaissance princesses, including her mother Eleonora, was as much a regent for her husband as was Isabella. She used her dancing skills with the utmost diplomacy. Was it Isabella's personality (or correspondence) that is responsible for her outshining Beatrice's abilities or modern history that has tended to idealize Isabella as *the* Renaissance woman?[56]

Isabella and *Intermezzi:* 1499

Isabella's father, Ercole d'Este, was passionately interested in the theater. Yet we have no comments from Isabella regarding the sung and danced interludes performed between the acts of the plays that he had had staged for the carnivals of 1486 and 1487.[57] If her fiancé, Francesco Gonzaga, was in Ferrara at the time, to whom would she have sent her descriptions? What have survived are a series of letters from her regular informant in Ferrara,[58] which describe in detail the sixteen *intermezzi* offered with the four classical plays performed during the carnival of 1499. Of the plays themselves, not a word. The interludes, termed *intermedi, intermezzi, tramezzi, feste,* or *moresche,* would continue to completely overshadow these classical plays in the accounts of diarists and chroniclers, and later in those of Isabella herself. The nature of the *intermedi* varied, but dance prevailed in all, the most popular characters being peasants, nymphs, and fools.

A 1499 *tramezzo-moresca* recalled the one performed eight years earlier for the wedding celebrations of Alfonso d'Este and Anna Sforza. A group of ten peasants jumped out onto the stage and began to work the land with hoes; they then sowed golden seed that, when grown, they reaped, harvested, bound, threshed, and placed in bags. All ten men moved—each foot, hand, face—as one with the musician. Another description of the same *moresca,* somewhat different in what it highlights, is found in a letter to Isabella by yet another informant.[59] The novelty in this production was that the "farmers" changed costumes as they reappeared for each different season. Besides that performed in Ferrara in 1491 for Alfonso d'Este's marriage, a *moresca* with country folk using gilt implements and golden baskets had already been part of princely wedding festivities in Pesaro in 1471, and the theme would be taken up again in Ferrara in 1502. One of Isabella's early informants explains that the repetition of a subject was unimportant; what counted *were the novelties in actions and gestures, costumes and music, and the general inventiveness of the presentation.*[60] This particular theme was undoubtedly a reflection of the interest in and idealization of the simple country life as exemplified in poetry, music, and pastoral plays from the end of the fifteenth century.[61]

Moreover, the agricultural labors of peasants, culminating in rich har-
vests, symbolically represented the munificence of the prince.

The second *tramezzo* was a wonderful *moresca* by twelve costumed
dancers wearing golden bells, led by a Fool. The *moresca*, Isabella's informant Pencaro specifies, was preceded by the "Chiaranzana," one of the
very rare references to a specific dance to appear in a written record of
the time, whether diary, letter, or ambassadorial or confidential report.
The Chiaranzana, a dance for many couples, often associated with weddings, enjoyed a long popularity in Italy in rural, urban, and courtly
circles from at least 1415 to 1759. Anonymous choreographic descriptions appear in a fifteenth-century treatise and in Fabritio Caroso's *Il Ballarino* of 1581.[62] Another dance mentioned in a *moresca* is a "dordoglione"
(tourdion), played on pipe and tabor to accompany a mad fool who has
jumped out near "a lady Fortuna." She dances with ten youths one by
one. The Fool, in desperation, drags "Fortuna" into a house, at which
the youths, sorrowful, desperate, and furious, take their leave. Another
moresca had dancers with lighted torches creating various figures and designs, once again predating what we have previously known about "fig-
ured" or "horizontal" dance in France. Still another *tramezzo* featured a
bear, which, interrupting an outdoor banquet and "killing" one of the
guests, was finally captured so that the feast could continue "with outward movements full of joy."[63] Then there were the damsels who en-
ticed rich old men to be their lovers, abandoning them for handsome
youths. It is clear, even in these much-abridged descriptions, that not
only were the interludes varied but, with their mime and dance, they
were also early "ballets," that is, danced narratives.[64]

There seem to be no descriptions of *moresche* at Isabella's own court
in Mantua, where theater was a strong presence, especially at carnival.
Considering Isabella's background in dancing and in Ferrarese *intermezzi*, and her detailed epistolary reports of those performed there in
1502, this is difficult to explain. It would also seem, on the basis of a few
letters, that there was no dancing master in residence. On more than
one occasion, Isabella asked her brother, Cardinal Ippolito d'Este, about
"borrowing Ricardetto . . . for a few days [Ricardetto taught dancing
and was a kind of entertainer at the Ferrara court]; I have no doubt I
will shame myself in these balls having forgotten all the French dances
since I have not practiced them for so long."[65] On 23 September 1500
she wrote again answering Ippolito's offer about possibly employing
"Ricardetto, knowing how worthy he is in dancing and in teaching

damsels to be graceful."[66] Whether the initiative was Ricardetto's or Isabella's, times had changed and Isabella was cutting down on staff and further specifies, "I do not have the means to treat him according to his rank." She then adds, referring possibly to political (or personal) events, that "the present times are not suitable for dancing."

Lucretia Borgia-Este's Wedding Festivities: Rome and Ferrara, 1500–1501

In 1500, after heavy political pressures on the part of the Spaniard Alexander VI, an invigorated, expansionist pope, Alfonso d'Este became officially engaged to Lucretia Borgia (Anna Sforza having died three years earlier). Lucretia, the pope's daughter, was also recently widowed, inasmuch as her husband had been conveniently eliminated, thanks to her brother, the infamous Cesare Borgia. Negotiations ensured an immense dowry in money and in various important benefits for Ferrara.[67] Isabella was envious of her future sister-in-law: both Alfonso and Beatrice had married higher and wealthier than she had. To satisfy her curiosity, she dispatched a special informant to Rome, a certain El Prete, who sent her detailed descriptions of the prenuptial festivities at the Vatican. These began with the arrival, on 23 December 1500, of the huge entourage from Ferrara. Isabella, who was known for her elegant dress and expensive jewels, clearly wanted to know all about those of Lucretia, who, furthermore, outdid her in good looks. El Prete informed her at length, supplying her also with several glimpses of different sorts of dancing.[68] On 29 December he reported a private soirée: "That evening [26 December] I went to her room and her Ladyship was sitting next to the bed; and in the corner of the room were about twenty Roman ladies dressed in the Roman fashion. . . . Then there were her ladies-in-waiting, ten in all. The dancing was begun by a gentleman of Valencia with a lady-in-waiting by the name of Nicola. Then My Lady danced elegantly and with particular grace with Don Ferrante. . . . A lady-in-waiting from Valencia, Catalina, danced well; another was seductive."[69] Lucretia was aware of the hostility toward her on the part of her new sister-in-law and even her husband-to-be. She did all she could in making herself attractive physically and socially, including using her dancing skills.

The actual wedding ceremony and signing of the marriage contract took place on the evening of 30 December in the Sala Paolina in the

Vatican, the pope on his throne surrounded by thirteen cardinals and the ambassadors of France, Spain, and Venice. Another letter, written to Isabella three days later, describes the festivities organized in the *Sala dei Papi* for New Year's Day.[70] The pope was seated in his chair while the rest of the guests were on benches or on pillows on the floor, all facing a low stage. Following a pastoral play and an allegorical poem in Latin was a *moresca*. An excellent dancer, dressed as a woman, led forth a group of nine men masquerading as animals. All wore masks and magnificent brocades. One of the dancers was Cesare Borgia, easily recognizable, says El Prete, because both his manner and his gold and velvet brocade attire were "more pompous." Each of the nine dancers then took hold of a silk streamer hanging from a tree in the center of the room, and to the music of shawms (an early type of oboe), and under the direction of a youth who sat on top of the tree reciting verses, they danced round the tree intertwining the ribbons. When the performance ended, at the pope's bidding, Lucretia danced with one of her Spanish ladies-in-waiting, after which the "maskers" danced one couple at a time.

On 6 January 1502, Lucretia left Rome for Ferrara, being feted with banquets and balls at the various cities where the entourage stopped. The entry into Ferrara on 2 February organized by Alfonso's father, the old Duke Ercole, was one of the most splendid spectacles of the day. The wedding festivities began on the next day. During the first ball, the ambassador from Parma reported that Lucretia "danced many dances, in Roman and Spanish fashion, to the music of her pipe and tabor players."[71] Balls were given for the next four evenings, and at one of them, Lucretia danced some French *bassedanses* with a lady-in-waiting. Five plays by Plautus were performed, each with *intermezzi* between the acts. For Isabella, neither the acting nor the verses of the first play, *Epidicus*, were pleasing, "but the *moresche* in between the acts looked very good and had great *galanteria* [elegance, magnificence]."[72] We have her own descriptions of these as well as accounts by Ferrarese chroniclers, and that of the well-known Venetian diarist, Marin Sanudo. Four different *moresche* featured agility and dexterity, dancing with fire, wonderful actions and gestures, beautiful music, and ten "moors" dancing with lighted candles in their mouths. The first of these was the most impressive and received the greatest and most detailed commentary:

Ten warriors presented themselves to the audience one by one, later forming two groups. They were dressed in imitation armor and in helmets with red and white plumes. "Armed after the manner of the ancients," they had large knives, maces, two-handed swords, and daggers.[73] They danced to the music of pipes and tabors and, with quick, aggressive movements expressing a determination to kill their opponents, they fell to blows, which, like their steps, were in time to the music. The maces broken, they drew their swords, stabbing at each other with great dexterity (forward and backward), dancing the whole time. At a given signal, they threw down their swords and, taking their daggers, attacked each other. At another musical signal, half the warriors fell to the ground, as if dead or wounded, while the others, with their daggers drawn, stood over them. The conquerors then bound their prisoners and led them off the stage.[74]

Given Renaissance Italy's interest in antiquity and in the revival of ancient Greek and Roman spectacles, it is hardly a coincidence that this *moresca* closely resembled a mock battle described by Dionysius of Halicarnassus in his *Archaeologica (Roman Antiquities)* in 8 BC.[75] Pantomime (then called "narrative dancing") had been one of the most popular entertainments in ancient Rome, where mythological subjects were frequently used, together with gorgeous costumes, for political purposes.[76] As we have seen, the Renaissance *moresche,* in their lavish costumes, served political purposes as well. The ancient pyrrhic battle dance, which had also been performed as an interlude in plays and other spectacles such as gladiatorial contests and chariot races, was occasionally revived in fifteenth-century spectacles.

Isabella, on one of the next evenings, reported in a letter to her husband that the play, the *Bachide,* was "so long and tedious and without danced interludes. . . . Only two *moresche* were inserted [*tramezate*]."[77] The first began with ten men "who simulated nakedness with a veil across their bodies and heads of tinsel hair" and who held horns of plenty filled with four torches, varnish, and powders that blazed and emanated special perfumes as they moved.[78] In front of them "a young woman appeared, crossing the stage in great fear and without music. A dragon came out and was about to devour her when a knight arrived to defend her. He fought the dragon, captured it and tied it up. The knight then led the dragon around the stage followed by the young woman arm in arm with a youth," and by the "naked dancers," who continued to pour varnish on their fires, everyone doing the *moresca.* (Here, *moresca* seems to be a specific dance type or dance step.)[79] For one modern scholar, it was Isabella's tiredness and boredom and, above all, her being ill-disposed toward her new, acclaimed sister-in-law that prevented her from being able or even trying to interpret the mythological or allegorical significance of this complex pantomime.[80]

And so on for three more evenings when, preceded and/or followed by dancing for the court, each play featured *moresche*, which were reported by diarists and, for some reason, ignored by Isabella. These included scenes with satyrs, with savage men, with a unicorn, and with hunters and wild animals. It was during the performance of Plautus's *Asinaria* on 7 February, the fourth play, that yet another version of the rustics' various labors of the land took place. It introduced six women cooking all sorts of food with pots and casseroles, with flasks of wine for the farm workers, and finished with eight peasants dancing a *villanesca* (country dance) hand in hand with the women to the accompaniment of a bagpipe.[81]

In these fifteen complex danced *moresche* there is no mention ever of a choreographer, a dancing master, a master of ceremonies, or a *corago*, that is, someone who was responsible for the invention of the *moresca* and for the training of the *morescanti* who were, usually, pages of the court. We do have one rather unexpected example of a courtier who composed and directed at least one *moresca*—in Urbino in 1513. This is none other than Baldassare Castiglione, the author of *The Book of the Courtier*, who had served the Gonzagas in his youth and would serve them again, and Isabella in particular, as a brilliant diplomat.[82] While working on the *moresca* production, he expressed the great difficulty he had dealing with "painters, carpenters, actors, musicians and," rather than *ballerini* or dancers, *"moreschieri"* (moreskers).[83]

Isabella: Politics and Dance, 1505–27

Throughout her marriage, Isabella traveled, combining official visits with her own acquisitive interests—political, social, artistic. In her correspondence, carnival festivities and important visits and events would often include a note about having danced until a particular hour. Only a day or two before giving birth to a daughter, Isabella wrote to Francesco about attending a wedding and splendid dinner on 7 November 1503. Dancing took place in the courtyard during the day and after supper in the hall. "I stayed to honor the bride [but] with little pleasure not being able to dance [presumably due to her advanced pregnancy], nor wishing to," because, she explains, of her concerns about Francesco, who, especially at that time, was in serious political and physical danger. She complains that the *festa*, despite the "most sumptuous expense," was very cold . . . except for "the Milanese" who appeared, with three companions, disguised as a nymph.[84]

Ten years later, on 16 January 1513, Isabella wrote Francesco from Milan, where she had been attending a court performance organized by her brother-in-law, the Duke of Milan, with various important ladies and gentlemen, and in particular, the papal ambassador. The play, as usual, afforded Isabella little pleasure, having, she maintained, little to commend it. The supper was copious and laudable, after which there was dancing that lasted the whole night.[85] A few days later, 22 January, she wrote Francesco how Ludovico Sforza, having been taken up with the ambassador and various gentlemen, came to her in the evening with "six or eight of his [courtiers/pages?] in costume. And in order to please him there was dancing until three or four a.m."[86]

Isabella was in Rome for carnival in 1515 and wrote home to Mantua that she "went to dinner with Lorenzo the Magnificent" at his house.[87] After a three-hour bull hunt (in which four bulls were killed), "we danced until nine p.m." Several cardinals were present, most of whom were masked.[88] After a two-hour dinner, there was more dancing until one a.m.

In June of the same year, Isabella was trying to arrange an entertainment for her uncle, the cardinal of Aragon, in the Gonzaga villa at Porto near Mantua.[89] She wrote to Counts Mathia and Francesco of nearby Gazoldo, explaining that the cardinal wished to see dancing in the Lombard style, inviting them and all the good dancers, male and female, they could find.[90] On 13 June she wrote a similar letter to Luigi Gonzaga, a neighbor and a politically important kinsman: "We have decided to give a *festa* on Sunday in our *palazzo* at Porto and we beg your lordship to ask your Maria, as the leader of your fine ballerinas, to invite as many as can come to the fête."[91] It seems likely that these dances were more traditional country dances than urban or courtly ones. Competitions were held in the nearby villages and on the Gonzagas' hunting reserve in which country lads and lasses and members of the court participated. The best "ballarina" won a prize of cloth.[92] At the *festa* in Porto, was it just "a coincidence" or a political message that Luigi Gonzaga won the first prize?

What becomes clear from these and numerous other excerpts is that dancing, especially for Isabella, was often a political tool. During the *festa,* one could meet and talk with important people.[93] In 1530, well after Isabella's husband Francesco had died, Charles V was crowned emperor in Bologna. At the ball organized as part of the reception for the new emperor, Isabella, aged fifty-six, and her daughter Eleonora were among the twenty ladies chosen to open the dancing.[94]

After Francesco Gonzaga's death in 1519, their nineteen-year-old son Federico became the new Marquis of Mantua. As she had done with her husband, Isabella became an active and able regent for her son, helped in many ways by Castiglione, her ambassador in Rome. Isabella would live another twenty years and, as she had since 1514, would continue to spend much of her time, until the sack of the city in 1527, in Rome, seat of the most powerful Italian court of the age. Here she continued to add precious gems and garments to her elegant wardrobe and to seek political favors and benefices, especially a cardinalship for her youngest son. Whenever she could afford to she bought art treasures for her particular collection in Mantua, vying with other princes, including her husband during his lifetime and her brother Alfonso. She mixed with the most fashionable society, including famous literati and influential cardinals, and was received at their palaces with sumptuous banquets, beautiful music, and other entertainments.[95]

Federico Gonzaga, the new marquis, kept up a thick correspondence with Francesco Gonzaga,[96] who reported on various political matters in Rome and included news about Isabella. He even gave an account of dancing, which he found clearly different from that of northern Italy. In 1525, after the baptism of a friend's baby daughter for whom Isabella was godmother, there was dancing to the music of a pipe and tabor player by some ladies and gentlemen of Rome, followed by dancing to shawms "in our [presumably Lombard] style."[97] One year later, Francesco informed the marquis about a wedding celebration held at the home of a cardinal. "As to the dancing, it was done in the following way: whoever wished to dance had to go to an old woman, who was the one chosen to speak to the young women, saying, 'I would like to dance with that one; ask her for me.' If she liked to dance with that young man the agreement was made, if not, too bad. This is the way they dance in Rome."[98]

Two years later Isabella, at the age of fifty-three, lived through the horrific sack of Rome, "giving shelter to some 2200 people besides those of her own household."[99] The grandeur of the Rome she loved so much was a tempered memory in her twelve remaining years of relative retirement in Mantua.

These are some of the dance events in which Isabella, her mother, sisters, and sisters-in-law participated, using dance as a means of displaying their power, whether as performers, patrons, organizers, or honored viewers. The examples not only illuminate various kinds of dance performed between the late fifteenth and early sixteenth centuries, bringing in the contemporary dancing masters and choreographers when known, but they also tell us a great deal about the women involved, princesses connected to the most important courts at the time—Ferrara, Mantua, Milan, Rome, Naples—most of whom were strong personalities, wielded power, and were official and unofficial regents for their husbands. What emerges, among other things, is that despite her background, dance for Isabella was not as important or interesting as jewels and fashionable attire, art treasures, or travel. This disaffection may have begun as a result of Isabella's excess weight (though this did not at all diminish her acquisition of clothes). Undoubtedly, she did not feel up to competing with her sister Beatrice or her sister-in-law Lucretia Borgia, both involved in organizing memorable entertainments and *moresche*, and acknowledged as very fine dancers. Having married less well (in title and dominion) than her sister and brother, Isabella's excess energies went into politics, of which dance seems to have become only an occasionally necessary appendage.

The events recounted above took place during a period just following that of the dancing masters Domenico of Piacenza and Guglielmo Ebreo and almost seventy years before the new Italian style described so minutely in the treatises of Fabritio Caroso and Cesare Negri.[100] The fact that we do not find the names of choreographies or masters with whom most dance specialists are familiar confirms how limited our knowledge of Renaissance dance is, particularly considering how rich was the period in question (1473–1514). Besides Lorenzo Lavagnolo there are the many anonymous "choreographers" who staged the hundreds of *intermezzi* and *balli* for carnivals and weddings.

As to what was danced, we can presume that the opening dances at weddings were *bassadanza*-type dances. Besides these, we have, so far, a few other generic references to the contemporary *bassadanza*, to a "tordiglione" (danced in France and Italy), and to the Chiaranzana. Interestingly, there are several occasions in which Isabella and her sister Beatrice danced "French dances," as did their sister-in-law, Lucretia Borgia, who also performed her native Spanish dances as well as "Roman dances." What all these dances were remains a matter of speculation.

Finally, there are references to local traditional Lombard dancing, in which the younger Este girls joined in with glee whenever the opportunity arose, and the organized festive country entertainments where the guests of the Este-Gonzagas were observers and, on occasion, even participants.

What supersedes all types of dancing in contemporary diaries and chronicles are the mimed and danced *moresche,* presumably performed by pages trained for the occasion. The damsel and dragon, the squadrons fighting squadrons, the peasants reaping gold, Neptune vying with Minerva, and so on, were admired for their novelties (even on old themes), their costumes, stage effects, and general splendor as well as for their allegory and comic and dramatic qualities. And for this type of dancing, which was the most popular at the time of the Este sisters, we have the least information.[101] Here again is a great gap in written dance history—one that is pregnant with rich and varied kinds of narrative dancing and virtuosic leaps and capers.

NOTES

1. A massive bibliography on Isabella was collected by Sylvia Ferino-Pagden, ed., *La Prima Donna del Mondo: Isabella d'Este: Fürsten und Mäzenatin der Renaissance,* Exhibition Catalogue (Vienna: Kunsthistorisches Museum, 1994). Despite its being somewhat outdated, Julia Cartwright's *Isabella d'Este Marchioness of Mantua, 1474–1539: A Study of the Renaissance,* 2 vols. (London: John Murray, 1903), still has some interesting information. See Rose Marie San Juan's article, "The Court Lady's Dilemma: Isabella d'Este and Art Collecting in the Renaissance," in the *Oxford Art Journal* 14 (1991): 67–78, in which she examines the standard assessment of Isabella as a patron and collector and sees gender as a significant factor in social positioning. A more recent article is by Molly Bourne, "Renaissance Husbands and Wives as Patrons of Art: The *Camerini* of Isabella d'Este and Francesco II Gonzaga," in *Beyond Isabella,* ed. S. Reiss and D. G. Wilkins (Kirksville, MO: Truman State University Press, 2001), 93–123, and especially 112, n.4, and 115, n.20.

2. The League was the result of the Peace of Lodi, which lasted from 1454 to 1474.

3. See figure 1.2. Borso, who had no children, raised the dynastic title from Marquis to Duke of Ferrara and Modena.

4. Palazzo Schifanoia (the villa named "Shun Boredom") is only one of these. Its extraordinary frescoes in the "Hall of the Months" were painted by Francesco del Cossa and Ercole dei Roberti, among others. The villa was used for festivities, banquets, weddings, and honoring visiting dignitaries. In 1486,

the law students organized a ball and banquet in the gardens and invited Isabella (aged twelve) and the younger Este siblings. See Marina Nordera, "La Donna in Ballo: Danza e genere nella prima età moderna" (Ph.D diss., European University Institute, Fiesole, Italy, 2001), 73–74, who gives the source as Bernardino Zambotti's *Diario ferrarese dall'anno 1476 sino al 1504*, ed. G. Pardi (Bologna: N. Zanichelli, 1934–37), 172.

5. This was begun in the 1490s under the direction of Biagio Rossetti. See Charles M. Rosenberg, *The Este Monuments and Urban Development in Renaissance Ferrara* (New York: Cambridge University Press, 1997).

6. The title, *De arte saltandj & choreas ducendj / De la arte di ballare et danzare* (On the Art of Dancing and Choreography), was added later. For editions, see D. R. Wilson, *Domenico of Piacenza* (Paris: Bibliothèque nationale, MS ital. 972) (1998; rev. ed., Cambridge: Early Dance Circle, 2006), and A. William Smith, who also provides a translation: *Fifteenth-Century Dance and Music*, 2 vols. (Stuyvesant, NY: Pendragon Press, 1995).

7. For the various treatises, their dates (known or approximate), present locations, publications and/or translations where applicable, see Barbara Sparti, *Guglielmo Ebreo of Pesaro. De pratica seu arte tripudii (On the Practice or Art of Dancing)* (1993; reprint Oxford: Clarendon Press, 1995), chap. 1. For a partial table, see *Dance Chronicle* 16, no. 3 (1993): 374.

8. Domenico married a lady-in-waiting, a Trotto, from the same family that served the Estes as courtiers and ambassadors.

9. Alessandro Pontremoli and Patrizia La Rocca, *Il ballare lombardo* (Milan: Vita e Pensiero, 1987), give a number of sources (23–24, n.9) suggesting that this was the case. See also 206 and the following pages.

10. Pontremoli and La Rocca, *Il ballare*, 155, based on a number of chronicles and ambassadorial diaries. Other noble dancing couples are named.

11. "Belreguardo" is the first of Domenico's choreographies, "Leoncello" the second. Since "Marchesana" is only the tenth dance in his treatise, it would seem likely that Domenico composed it to honor Leonello's second wife, Maria d'Aragona, rather than Margherita Gonzaga, who died in 1439, the same year Domenico presumably arrived at the court of Ferrara.

12. State Archives of Modena. The documents are incomplete but Domenico's name appears starting in 1439 and through 1475. See Sparti, *Guglielmo Ebreo*, 4, n.4.

13. An excerpt of this letter was first published in Alessandro Luzio, *I precettori di Isabella d'Este* (Ancona: A. Gustavo Morelli, 1887), 12. Nordera, in "La Donna" (n. 4 above), 78, n.32, cites the document for the letter in the Archivio di Stato di Mantova, Archivio Gonzaga, busta 1229, E.XXXI.3. All translations, unless otherwise noted, are my own.

14. The engagement ceremony took place in Palazzo Schifanoia on 26 May 1480, in the absence of both Isabella and Francesco.

15. Nordera, "La Donna," reports a visit by Francesco in 1480 in which the youngsters (Isabella, age 6, Francesco, 14) played music and games, sang and danced (83).

16. Nordera, "La Donna," 78 and 84.

17. Daniela Pizzagalli, *La signora del Rinascimento: Vita e splendori di Isabella d'Este alla corte di Mantova* (Milan: Rizzoli, 2001), 30. No date for this letter is given. Though Pizzagalli's sources, as stated on 567–68, are in large part from the State Archives of Mantua, directly or through the works of Alessandro Luzio, she provides no specific documents. However, her book is clearly arranged chronologically, and it should not be difficult therefore to trace documents according to specific dates.

18. Pontremoli and La Rocca, *Il ballare*, 140.

19. Pontremoli and La Rocca, *Il ballare*, 139–44. When Ippolita Sforza (future Duchess of Milan) was four years old, she danced and sang, with her six-year-old brother, before the ambassador of France, who "marveled at their fine dancing and singing considering their tender age."

20. Sparti, *Guglielmo Ebreo*, 89.

21. Sparti, *Guglielmo Ebreo*, 31. Lombardy is a central-northern region of Italy that at this time included, with various political border changes, the Duchy of Milan (as far south as Piacenza) and the Marquisate of Mantua.

22. For dancing at the Aragonese court of Naples, see Cecilia Nocilli, "Dance in Naples: Relations between the Aragonese Court and the Neapolitan Barons (1442–1502)," in *Proceedings, Society of Dance History Scholars 25th Annual Conference* (Stoughton, WI, 2002), 90–95.

23. See Nordera, "La Donna," 70–71, who reports 166 young women invited to two different *feste* organized by Duke Ercole d'Este in Ferrara in 1510. (She gives as her source "Diario ferrarese. Dall'anno 1409 al 1502," in L. Muratori, *Rerum italicarum scriptores*, vol. 24, [Milan, 1738], 244–45.) See also Sparti, *Guglielmo Ebreo*, 51–52 and n.11.

24. Eleonora's wedding celebrations and the "practice of magnificence" are described in detail in my article "The Function and Status of Dance in the 15th-Century Italian Courts," *Dance Research* 14, no. 1 (1996): 42–61. The various chronicles and sources are cited.

25. Such a reference appears in the text above when, in the 1455 ball, Domenico partnered the Duchess of Milan and also below in the descriptions of the dancing at Beatrice d'Este's marriage ball in 1491.

26. In the extant redaction of the treatise *De pratica seu arte tripudii* that bears Giovanni Ambrosio's name (ca. 1474), though it is an almost exact copy of the 1463 original Guglielmo Ebreo version, there are a few extra dances, music, theoretical chapters, and a first-hand account of the festivities in which he participated. All are included in Sparti, *Guglielmo Ebreo*.

27. As I noted in my article, "The Function and Status of Dance" (see n.24), dancing was not one of the liberal arts and was usually ignored "if not scorned" by the humanist educators. Dancing masters were modestly if not poorly remunerated. See especially 52–53.

28. The term "social dancing" is used here not in its later meaning as contrasted to "theatrical dance." First, many of the dances were "art dances" such as those composed by Domenico and Guglielmo. Second, the "social dances" would have been performed by a single couple or group, not only in private rooms for pleasure, but most often in front of or surrounded by large or small numbers of onlookers, whether at magnificent public gatherings or on more intimate occasions.

29. Sparti, "Function and Status," 60. See also Fabrizio Cruciani, *Teatro nel Rinascimento Roma 1450–1550* (Rome: Bulzoni editore, 1983), 151, who, among other things, mentions a private *festa* organized by the citizens of Siena as well as a public ball with fountains of wine.

30. Sparti, "Function and Status," 59–60.

31. Cruciani, *Teatro*, 157–61; and Sparti, "Function and Status," 164, n.12.

32. Reprinted in Cruciani, *Teatro*, 160.

33. Cruciani, *Teatro*, 164. The mythological names of three of the "nymphs" are included.

34. The "nymphs" who danced in the *rappresentazione* for Lucretia d'Este's wedding in 1487 (see below) are referred to as female. If the Hercules *moresca* had taken place elsewhere, it is likely that court ladies would have danced the part of the nymphs. Papal Rome, in theory, could have been a different situation.

35. Barbara of Brandenburg, depicted by Mantegna with her husband Ludovico Gonzaga (Marquis of Mantua, 1444–78) in the famous "Camera degli sposi" frescoes in the palace in Mantua, was Francesco's grandmother. Barbara's recommendation is in a letter sent to the duchess of Milan in 1479. Cited with sources by Pontremoli and La Rocca, *Il ballare*, 64. See also Nordera, "La Donna," 90–94.

36. Alessandro Luzio and Rodolfo Renier, *Mantova e Urbino. Isabella d'Este ed Elisabetta Gonzaga* (Turin-Rome, 1893; reprint, Bologna: Forni, 1976), 41, n.2.

37. Nordera, "La Donna," 89–90.

38. Several documents describing the event have survived, including the composed verses and accounts of the dancing, but except for indications of instruments, no music has been found. See Francesca Bortoletti, "An Allegorical *Fabula* for the Bentivoglio-d'Este Marriage of 1487," *Dance Chronicle* 25, no. 3 (2002): 321–42.

39. See, for one, the musicologist Henry Prunières, *Le Ballet de cour en France avant Benserade et Lully* (Paris, 1914; reprint, New York: Johnson, 1970), 82–86.

Opinions were also based on the claim supplied by the author of the libretto, Balthasar Beaujoyeux, himself.

40. This recalls a similar choreography performed in 1455 at the Milanese wedding at which Domenico da Piacenza was the choreographer. See Pontremoli and La Rocca, *Il ballare*, 207–8.

41. One of the only occasions known in which a prince/courtier danced in a public *moresca* in Italy was in 1502 at the Pope's court in Rome. Cesare Borgia was masked, but was so richly and "pompously" dressed as to be recognized by the chroniclers. See Lucretia Borgia's wedding in the text below as described by Gregorovius. The Bologna dancers were presumably court damsels and pages.

42. Pizzagalli, *La signora*, 43–44, reports on the wedding. Mantua had a reputation for theatrical performances, but extant descriptions regarding these, like accounts of Mantuan festive occasions, are meager compared to those that remain for Ferrara. One wonders if this is due to the quality of the performances or to a different type of "press" or public relations. That Isabella's wedding festivities should have lacked danced spectacles cannot, as yet, be explained. The question of dance in Mantua and Isabella and dance will be discussed in the text below.

43. This duke was Giangaleazzo Sforza. He married Isabella of Aragon one year earlier, in 1490.

44. A third Este-Sforza alliance was arranged with a marriage between Isabella's nephew Ercole (her brother Sigismondo's son) and the eleven-year-old Angela, from another branch of the Sforza family. See *Festa di Nozze per Ludovico il Moro*, ed. Guido Lopez (Milan: De Carlo Editore, 1976), 76.

45. This was the order according to Giacomo Trotto, the Duke of Ferrara's ambassador at the Sforza court in Milan. Bianca Maria Sforza would become the wife of the future emperor, Maximilian. See Pontremoli and La Rocca, *Il ballare*, 235–37.

46. Pontremoli and La Rocca, *Il ballare*, 158–59. This is the account of Tristano Calco, the Milanese historian.

47. A complete published description of the extant chronicle is available in Edmondo Solmi's "La Festa del Paradiso di Leonardo da Vinci e Bernardo Bellincione," *Archivio Storico Lombardo*, 1 (1904): 75–89. Stella Mary Pearce's "The Paradise of Ludovico il Moro," in *Memorable Balls*, ed. James Laver (London, 1954), is a general, not always precise, description, based on Solmi. See also Sparti, *Guglielmo Ebreo*, 51–52.

48. Pontremoli and La Rocca, *Il ballare*, 159.

49. Pontremoli and La Rocca, *Il ballare*, 224–25.

50. Pontremoli and La Rocca, *Il ballare*, 210–11.

51. The original is "scambietti." Pontremoli and La Rocca (*Il ballare*, 211) give the Milanese archival source.

52. At Annona, near Asti. See Pontremoli and La Rocca, *Il ballare,* 163–65.

53. Nordera, "La Donna," 75. Letter to Isabella from her "beloved" secretary, Benedetto Capilupi. (The adjective is supplied by Deanna Shemek in her unpublished paper, *"Machiavelli in gonnella:* Isabella D'Este and the Papal Court," 3, presented at the "Women in Papal Rome" conference at the American Academy in Rome, 1998. Quoted with permission of the author.)

54. In a letter to Isabella, Beatrice reports that in the previous July, at a reception in Asti for Louis of Orléans, she, her maids of honor, and the ladies of quality had already undergone this French practice (Pontremoli and La Rocca, *Il ballare,* 163).

55. Anonymous letter to the Duchess of Bourbon (Pontremoli and La Rocca, *Il ballare,* 165).

56. For another example in which Isabella's primacy is questioned, see William F. Prizer's "Isabella d'Este and Lucrezia Borgia as Patrons of Music: The Frottola at Mantua and Ferrara," *Journal of the American Musicological Society* 38 (1985): 1–33.

57. Nino Pirrotta, *Music and Theatre from Poliziano to Monteverdi,* trans. K. Eales (Cambridge: Cambridge University Press, 1982). See especially 46–55.

58. Isabella had a number of secretaries, like Capilupi, and "hired reporters" (see Shemek, *"Machiavelli in gonnella,"* 2, and Gregorovius below, nn.67, 68) writing to her from other cities, or from Ferrara or Mantua when she was traveling. They kept her abreast of social and political happenings, of fashion in a particular city, and art to be collected. In this case it was Giano Pencaro (Pirrotta, *Music and Theatre,* 49–51). Others will be named in this essay.

59. Bernardino de' Prosperi (Pontremoli and La Rocca, *Il ballare,* 226).

60. Pencaro (Pirrotta, *Music and Theatre,* 51 [my emphasis]). This focus can be seen as part of that long-lasting Renaissance tradition in which an artist would take a genre, a mode, a pattern, that everyone knew and improve or "invent" upon it, so that knowledgeable people (like the nobles watching the performances) would recognize the precedent, the older version, and appreciate the cleverness of the invention.

61. See, for example, William Prizer, "Games of Venus: Secular Vocal Music in the Late Quattrocento and Early Cinquecento," *The Journal of Musicology* 9 (1991), especially 17–37. Prizer points out (18) that the "elite" interest in the popular text resulted in a "popularizing" or "conscious imitation of the popular manner."

62. The anonymous treatise, in the Biblioteca Comunale of Siena (published incompletely by Curzio Mazzi, "Una sconosciuta compilazione di un libro quattrocentistico di balli," in *La Bibliofilia* 16 [1914–15]: 185–209), is based on the Guglielmo *De pratica* but has many more dances than any of the other contemporary treatises, though they are described with far less detail. The "ballecto chiamata chirintana" is on fols. 66v–67r.

63. Pirrotta, *Music and Theatre,* 50. Could this be the same as that described by Pontremoli and La Rocca (*Il ballare,* 228)? They write: "The other intermezzo had some fools, with one dressed up in a bearskin; and they danced the *moresca* and did plenty of crazy things for the laughs."

64. I use the term "ballet" ("ballo" or "balletto" in Italian) not in the Romantic sense but as a narrated story in mime and dance.

65. Nordera, "La Donna," 94.

66. Deanna Shemek generously shared with me a copy and a partial transcription of the original letter from the Archivio di Stato di Mantova (ASMn), Archivio Gonzaga (AG) F.II.9.2993, libro 11, fols. 84v–85r. Translations by Deanna Shemek.

67. Ferdinand Gregorovius, *Lucrezia Borgia* (1874; Italian ed. Bologna: Avanzini e Torraca, 1968), 158–67.

68. Gregorovius (*Lucrezia Borgia,* 179) here refers to El Prete as being, as far as Isabella was concerned, a "Reporter of the 'Times' [the newspaper]"!

69. Gregorovius, *Lucrezia Borgia,* 182. Ferrante was Isabella's and Alfonso's brother. He represented the groom, Alfonso, by proxy at the wedding ceremony. Also accompanying the bride were two other Este brothers, Sigismondo and Cardinal Ippolito who officially presented Lucretia with Duke Alfonso's wedding jewels.

70. Gregorovius, *Lucrezia Borgia,* 184, and document 35, 341–43. (These documents, in the Appendix of the Italian edition, are not available in the English edition.)

71. Gregorovius, *Lucrezia Borgia,* 210.

72. Pirrotta, *Music and Theatre,* 51. This is my translation from the original Italian, and not Eales's.

73. Zambotti, *Diario ferrarese,* 325. See also William Gilbert, *Lucrezia Borgia, Duchess of Ferrara* (London, 1869).

74. See also Margaret McGowan's "A Renaissance War Dance: The Pyrrhic," *Dance Research* 3, no. 1 (1984): 29–38, in which she discusses a very similar armed dance performed in Lyons in 1548 to honor the entry of Henri II of France.

75. Dionysius describes the dress of his warriors, their helmets adorned with plumes, their spears and shields. He explains that the company was split into three divisions, each with a leader who prescribed the figure of the dance for the others and, to the music of flute or lyre, kept time with the beat. Generally, the motions were quick and warlike, and different offensive movements were attempted, at times in single combat, at times one division against another.

76. Karl Toepfer has in preparation "Idolized Bodies: The Imperial Aesthetic of Ancient Roman Dance Drama." He kindly let me view the introductory chapter.

77. Pirrotta, *Music and Theatre*, 51; and Alessandro D'Ancona, *Origini del Teatro Italiano* (Rome: Bardi Editore), vol. 2, 385.

78. The quotation has been translated by K. Eales in Pirrotta, *Music and Theatre*, 51. The chronicler Zambotti (*Diario ferrarese*, 326) used the term "polvere artificiate odorifere" (artificially made perfumed powders). "Artificale" meant "especially created," "made with artistry."

79. As Curt Sachs stated in 1937, the "moresque" was the most frequently mentioned of all the fifteenth-century dances, "yet [it] is one of the most difficult to classify and characterize in all dance history" (*World History of the Dance*, trans. B. Schönberg [New York: Norton, 1965], 333). Indeed, one of the many meanings of "moresca" is a particular step, one related, perhaps, to a saltarello step, which could be danced and improvised.

80. Pirrotta, *Music and Theatre*, 51.

81. Zambotti, *Diario ferrarese*, 330.

82. Castiglione's best-selling *Libro del Cortegiano*, first published in 1528, was already circulating by 1516. For Castiglione as diplomat, see below.

83. One of the *moresche* was about Jason and took place between the acts of a play. See Castiglione's description in his letter reprinted in Bernardo Dovizi, *La Calandra*, ed. Giorgio Padoan (Padua: Antenore, 1985), 205–7.

84. This, and the following documents, were supplied to me by Deanna Shemek from the State Archives in Mantua, Archivio Gonzaga, ASMn, AG F.II.9.2994, libro 16, especially fol. 68r. The daughter of Francesco's secretary-chancellor was the bride. Isabella attended with her two small children. It is not clear who "the Milanese" (the man from Milan) was, but clearly it was someone, a courtier, perhaps, that Isabella and Francesco knew well. I am indebted to Deanna Shemek for sharing this information with me.

85. ASMn, AG F.II.6 busta 2120 fasc. II, especially fols. 77r–v.

86. ASMn, AG.F.II.6 2120 fasc. II, especially fol. 67v. It is not certain who of Ludovico Sforza's retinue would have danced. Pages and young courtiers often peformed in moresche.

87. From a handout supplied by Deanna Shemek with her paper "Machiavelli in gonnella." The document is ASMn, AG F.II.9.2996 libro 31, fols. 69r–v.

88. This could mean "in costume."

89. Porto was the location of one of Isabella's suburban residences. The villa, unfortunately, no longer exists there. It was traditionally occupied by the wives of the Gonzaga rulers. See Bourne, "Renaissance Husbands and Wives," 113, n.9.

90. ASMn, AG F.II.9.2996 libro 32, fol. 11v.

91. Pizzagalli, *La signora*, 384. See also Nordera ("La Donna," 99–102 and nn.85–89) for yet other letters to recruit "ballarine" sent to the vicar and to the local authorities. Nordera furnishes the following sources: ASMn AG busta 2996, F.II.8.32 and F.II.9.32, and busta 1503, F.II.8.

92. Nordera, "La Donna," 98–99, from a letter written in 1524.

93. Pizzagalli, *La signora*, 323 and 331, describes this well with other examples such as the passing through Mantua of the future Duke of Milan, Massimiliano Sforza, for which a ball was immediately arranged. On another occasion, a political rival was invited by Francesco, on Isabella's suggestion, to a carnival costume ball. Aside from the politics, there is an interesting report or letter describing a festa (Pizzagalli, *La signora*, 323). As soon as the instruments began to play, the "most honored [Isabella?] had to dance the first and then the second ballo, after which the ball warmed up intensely, with twenty couples who danced." It has usually been taken for granted that the dances for two, three, or four dancers (the majority composed by Domenico, Guglielmo, Caroso, and Negri) would have been danced by one couple or trio at a time. Since Pizzagalli doesn't give exact references, the interested reader will have to go to the Archives in Mantua and look under 22 January 1512 for confirmation and (perhaps) more information. According to Shemek, in private correspondence, the letter is supposed to be from Lorenzo Strozzi writing, apparently, to Federico Gonzaga.

94. Pizzagalli, *La signora*, 533. Sources for the coronation are Gaetano Giordani's chronicle and the Cronaca del soggiorno di Carlo V in Italia, attributed to Luigi Gonzaga.

95. Shemek, "Machiavelli in gonnella," 5.

96. Pizzagalli, *La signora*, 473; and Nordera, "La Donna," 78–79. It is not clear if Francesco, the Gonzaga ambassador to Rome, was a cousin. According to Cartwright, *Isabella d'Este*, vol. 2, 245, he ultimately replaced Castiglione in this role.

97. Pizzagalli, *La signora*, 476.

98. Pizzagalli, *La signora*, 484. The letter was written on 22 January 1526 when Isabella, too, was in Rome. See also Nordera, "La Donna," 79, n.33.

99. Shemek "Machiavelli in gonnella," 7.

100. The new Italian style was almost certainly being practiced for at least fifty years before Caroso's first publication, *Il ballarino*, in 1581.

101. In terms of written choreographies, libretti, and music.

2

Fabritio Caroso's Patronesses

ANGENE FEVES

In the late sixteenth century, several "how to dance" books were published. Authors carefully described individual steps and then gave complete dance choreographies, often with accompanying music in melodic line and/or lute tablature. Through the intervening centuries, one such book, the *Orchesographie* of Thoinot Arbeau, a French clergyman, has been well known, praised, and often cited as a major source for Renaissance dance style. However, from 1588, when Arbeau's book was published, through the early years of the seventeenth century, it was the Italian dancing masters who were being hired in many courts in France and throughout Europe.[1] Fabritio Caroso and Cesare Negri were among those celebrated and acclaimed professional dance masters of the time. In their books, they named and described the varieties of steps that made up the vocabulary of dance in the mid- to late sixteenth century. Among the imaginative and challenging choreographies that they compiled and taught were newly created dances and dance suites as well as old favorites. Specific melodies accompanied each dance type: *balletto*, *gagliarda*, *passo e mezzo*, or *saltarello*. Many of these dances, dedicated to noble and aristocratic ladies, have been reconstructed and performed in

49

recent years. This chapter investigates the lives of some of the ladies chosen by Fabritio Caroso for special dedications.

Fabritio Caroso of Sermoneta published two tomes on dancing, *Il ballarino* (Venice: Francesco Ziletti, 1581) and *Nobiltà di dame* (Venice: Il Muschio, 1600), but of his personal life we know very little, as yet. Unlike Cesare Negri, who gives copious information about his own background and his students' activities and careers in the first treatise of his book *Le grazie d'amore* (Venice: Pacifico Pontio & Gio. Battista Paccaglia, 1602), Caroso is very reticent.[2]

In his two books, Caroso dedicates dances to more than 120 ladies, but of these, only 5 are singled out as his patronesses. In *Il ballarino* the ladies Caroso names as his patronesses are Olimpia Orsina Cesi, Marchesa of Monticelli, Agnesina Colonna Caetana, Beatrice Caetana Cesi, and Giovanna Caetana Orsina. In *Nobiltà di dame,* Caroso names only one patroness, Felice Maria Orsini Caetana, Duchess of Sermoneta.

Although Caroso did dedicate a handful of dances, preceded by accompanying sonnets, to his "right worshipful" patronesses, Caroso gave no dates of employment, no discussion of stipends and favors, no lists of festivals and ceremonious occasions wherein he must have performed to great applause. However, some information about his life as a dancing master may lie hidden behind these dedications of dances to aristocratic employers. With more information about the lives, activities, and personalities of the ladies Caroso named as his patronesses (and for whom, presumably, he worked), we may find some indication of when he may have been employed (or merely present) as a member of their households.[3] Four of the patronesses share the Caetani family name: Beatrice and Giovanna are members of the family by birth, and Agnesina and Felice Maria are linked to the Caetani through marriage. The Caetani were lords of Sermoneta, a hilltop town south of Rome, which may have been Caroso's birthplace and his family's home. Unfortunately, as yet, specific references to Fabritio Caroso have not been found in the archives of the Caetani family in Rome nor in baptismal and matrimonial archives of the church of Santa Maria in Sermoneta.[4]

In the search for Caroso's patronesses, the exploits of the husbands, uncles, fathers, and brothers of sixteenth-century ladies are recounted far more often than the biographical data (or sometimes even the names) of their daughters and wives. However, the biographical information that can be found often shows that the ladies were brave, resourceful, and self-reliant. There are two major sources of information about the ladies of the Orsini, Cesi, and Caetani families. One source is almost two centuries old, and the other is from recent and ongoing research.

The first of these sources can be found in the sixteen volumes of *Famiglie celebri italiane,* compiled by Pompeo Litta and published in Milan over a period of seven decades beginning in 1819. Litta and his associates in the project gathered as much information as they could about all the members of important Italian families, from the founding of the family to the time of publication, or to the extinction of the family line. They went to the genealogical records and surviving members of the families, investigating family legends as well as family trees. Sometimes these listings of family members are minimal, and sometimes they are accounts that would make soap opera plots seem pale in comparison. Perhaps the biographical details contained in the Litta volumes are precise and accurate, and perhaps they are expanded with backstairs gossip or censored by family pride, but they are a starting place in investigating the lives of Caroso's ladies.

The second important source of information comes from the research of Carolyn Valone, historian of art and architecture, who, for thirty years, has been investigating women's patronage of architecture, altarpieces, and other works of art in sixteenth- and early seventeenth-century Rome.[5] Many of the ladies to whom Caroso dedicated dances were wealthy matrons who may have studied the art of dance in their youth and, as Valone has shown, became patrons of the arts and architecture in their maturity.

Of the five ladies named above, Caroso's favorite patroness seems to have been Olimpia Orsini Cesi. In *Il ballarino,* Caroso dedicates two dances and includes five poems and sonnets to "My most illustrious Lady, and always right worshipful Patroness, the Lady Olimpia Orsina Cesi, Marchesa of Monticelli."[6] She is the only lady to be so honored, except for Bianca Cappello de Medici, Grand Duchess of Tuscany, to whom Caroso dedicated *Il ballarino* itself. Both of the dances in honor of Olimpia, "Le Bellezze d'Olimpia" (fol. 65r) and "Cesia Orsina" (fol. 68r) contain reference to her name in their titles and seem to be choreographed by Caroso himself. "Le Bellezze d'Olimpia," with its tuneful melody full of rhythmical changes, varied floor patterns, and harmonious setting of step combinations to the music, is one of the most delightful of all Caroso's dances.

Messer Battistino is listed as choreographer of the dances for the other three patronesses whom Caroso named in *Il ballarino:* Beatrice

Caetana Cesi, Giovanna Caetana Orsina, and Agnesina Colonna Caetana. This may mean that Battistino was already teaching these dances
ten to fifteen years before Caroso began his career, and that Caroso had
not been the primary dancing master for Beatrice, Giovanna, and Agnesina, even though he called them his patronesses. To date, no details
about Battistino's life have come to light. Therefore Olimpia, Caroso's
"most illustrious Lady," will take precedence in this search. Her relationships to grandparents, parents, aunts, cousins, in-laws, and descendants may reveal a biographical timetable for the dancing moments of
Caroso and the ladies he named as his patronesses.

Olimpia's Grandparents

On her father's side, Olimpia was granddaughter of Camillo Orsini
and his second wife, Elisabetta Baglione of Perugia. Olimpia's grandfather Camillo, according to Litta, was known to have "a surpassing
love for music, and his militias had bands of great fame. . . . He loved literature and art, started factories, opened up streets, but nothing of this
remains, and even the hospital that he founded in the castle of Lamentana [Mentana] was done away with in 1757."[7]

Olimpia's grandmother Elisabetta seems to have been courageous
and valiant. Litta writes: "When in 1520, they had decapitated her
father, and her husband had left the service of Pope Leo X and gone to
Flanders, the commissioners of the Pope and of the Viceroy of Naples
came to assail her at Civitaducale to abduct Grifone da Rieti, from
whom they planned to wrest the secrets of her husband, whose secretary Grifone was. But she, at the head of the women of the countryside,
repulsed force with force and then withdrew to the protection of the Orsini Count of S. Valentino in Abruzzo."

Olimpia's Parents,
Giovanni Orsini and Portia dell'Anguillara

Olimpia's father, Giovanni Orsini, like her paternal grandfather Camillo, was a soldier. At the time of Pope Paul III's death in 1549, he was
a youth but was already in command of a cavalry troop near his father's

regiments in Parma. Giovanni succeeded his brother Paolo to the Marchesate of Lamentana in 1551. By 1569 Giovanni was in France as one of the condottieri fighting for Charles IX against the Huguenots. Litta believes that "then he went to serve the Venetians, and he perished in war against the Turks."

Giovanni Orsini had married Portia dell'Anguillara, Duchess of Cere, in 1553, when she was thirteen years old. A few years later, Portia was already noted in Francesco Sansovino's history of the Orsini family, published in 1565, as "a lady so wise, so kind, great-hearted and worthy of reverence and immortal glory."[8] In 1571 Portia was again praised for her beauty, courtesy, and divine grace, in Gasparo Fiorino's book of verses in honor of Roman ladies, *La nobiltà di Roma*.[9]

Carolyn Valone writes that Portia was "a great heiress and the last of her father's line of the Orsini of Anguillara. . . . Because there were no male heirs to inherit from her father, Giampaolo da Cere, Portia received all his lands including the rich duchy of Cere (near Cerveteri), Bassano Romano, and Magliano Romano Pecorareccio. In 1553, her family, in an attempt to keep this patrimony within the Orsini sphere, married her at the age of thirteen to her cousin, Giovanni Orsini, Count of Lamentana. This ploy failed, however, because Giovanni died young and their only child was a daughter, Olimpia Orsini, born in 1562."[10]

After Giovanni's death, and nine years before publication of *Il ballarino* in 1581, Portia remarried. Valone suggests that "Portia, who was praised by her contemporaries for her goodness and prudence, must have felt the pressure of family tradition weighing heavily upon her; and in the hope of producing a son to inherit her fortune, she married Paolo Emilio Cesi, Marchese of Riano, in 1572 when she was thirty-two years old."

Battistino's *balletto* "Contentezza d'Amore" (*Il ballarino*, fol. 60) is dedicated to "Portia Ceri dell'Anguillara Cesi," Olimpia's mother, and this dance immediately precedes those that Caroso dedicated to Olimpia. "Contentezza d'Amore" ("Love's Contentment") is a *balletto* for lady and gentleman in six sections, or verses. It is a little two-part suite, with the first five verses in moderately slow duple time. The sixth and last verse is a *sciolta* (that is, a loosening of the tempo) in a livelier *saltarello*. The spacing of the dancers' movements seems to be arranged for a very long and narrow ballroom. After the lady and gentleman dance the initial verse at the bottom of the hall, the lady moves in a *passeggiata* or

promenade toward the top of the ballroom in verse two. The gentleman
repeats the same steps and joins her in verse three. They then both
dance the fourth section and return to the bottom of the hall in verse
five. There they dance the *saltarello* together and end the dance. Although the structure of the dance is similar to many other choreographies of the time, with a section for both dancers followed by individual
solo sections and ending with the lady and gentleman dancing together,
this is the only dance in which the lady does her solo first. Indeed, in his
rechoreographed version of "Contentezza d'Amore" in *Nobiltà di dame*,
Caroso writes, "and I say that the Ballo was false" and tells the dancers
not to do as formerly, when the lady led with her *passeggiata* and the gentleman followed. Perhaps the highly unusual precedence given to the
lady in Battistino's version of "Contentezza" from *Il ballarino* may be an
indication of the high esteem in which Portia was held, as well as her social position as sole heir of the Orsini of Anguillara.

Portia's second marriage to Paolo Emilio Cesi lasted fifteen years,
but in spite of the birth of a son, Andrea Cesi, it proved to be unhappy.
She accused her husband of using fraud and violence in his attempts to
gain control of her money and properties. On 2 August 1590, at age 50,
she died. Olimpia and Beatrice Caetani Cesi (another of Caroso's patronesses) were among those present at her bedside.[11]

Among Olimpia's aunts on her father's side was Lucretia Salviati, the
wife of Giovanni's illegitimate brother Latino. Lucretia was the natural
daughter of Cardinal Bernardo Salviati, and another of the Roman ladies praised in verse by Gasparo Fiorino in 1571. Battistino's "Lucretia
Favorita" (Favored Lucretia, *Il ballarino*, fol. 84v) is dedicated to her.

This *balletto* begins with a slow section that is repeated six times and
that contains only a handful of steps in varying patterns. The *riverenza*
ends each verse, following steps that walk forward or sideways *(puntate,
doppi, continenze, riprese)* and (only in the fourth and sixth tempi) some
scurrying *seguiti scorsi*. Then the music changes to a *gagliarda*, played
twice through. Although the *gagliarda* has a reputation as a lively dance,
in this *balletto* the movements remain sedate. A pair of steps *(seguito finto*
and *seguito ordinario)*—neither of which jumps off the floor—round out
those used in the first part of the dance. "Lucretia Favorita" ends with a
return to the opening music and its slower speed. The limited step vocabulary and simplicity of movements in this dance are reminiscent of
bassedanze of the preceding century.

Olimpia's In-Laws:
The Cesi and Caetani Families

On 22 July 1578, Cardinal Niccolò Caetani, known as the Cardinal of Sermoneta, wrote to Paolo Orsini, the head of the Orsini family at that time, about arranging a marriage between Olimpia, daughter of Giovanni Orsini and Portia dell'Anguillara, and Federico, son of Angelo Cesi and Beatrice Caetani Cesi.[12]

This leads us back to the family into which Portia, Olimpia's mother, had married after Giovanni Orsini's death. The Cesi were Roman nobles, and their family chapel in Santa Maria della Pace in Rome had long been attributed (erroneously, according to Valone and other experts in the history of art and architecture) to Michelangelo Buonarroti (whose work as sculptor, architect, and painter Caroso praised in *Nobiltà*, 63). Portia's second husband, Paolo Emilio Cesi, had become Marchese of Riano, a small town north of Rome, when his uncle purchased it for him in 1570, two years before his marriage to Portia. Through Portia's inheritance, the Cesi family became lords of Cere. The Cesi family was also linked to Monticelli and the city of Todi, in Umbria.

Beatrice Caetani Cesi was the daughter of Bonifacio Caetani I (1516–1 March 1574) and Caterina Pio of Savoy (ca. 1515–11 April 1557). Bonifacio and Caterina had married in 1541. As a lad, Bonifacio had been given in hostage to the Spaniards in guarantee of a pact made after the sack of Rome. He was soon liberated and later fought as an ally of the French king, Henry II, against the Spanish. Bonifacio was a member of the legation that Pope Paul IV sent to France under Cardinal Carafa, and he fought for the Pope against the Spaniards and the Duke of Alba after their invasion of the Papal States in September 1555.

Caterina Pio and Bonifacio Caetani had two daughters and a son. Their daughter Beatrice would become Olimpia's mother-in-law; their other daughter, Giovanna Caetani, married Virginio Orsini; and their son, Onorato, would marry Agnesina Colonna. These two daughters (Beatrice and Giovanna) and Bonifacio Caetani's daughter-in-law (Agnesina) are the other three patronesses whom Caroso lists in *Il ballarino*.

Bonifacio's branch of the Caetani family were lords of Sermoneta. In 1555 Bonifacio had discovered a conspiracy instigated by the Caetani from Maenza against Sermoneta. The activities necessary to overcome this plot may have caused Bonifacio to travel more frequently between

Bonifacio Caetani (1516–Mar. 1574), Lord of Sermoneta
m. 1541 **Caterina Pio of Savoy** (ca. 1515–Apr. 1557)

Beatrice Caetani (ca. 1546–1609)
Barriera (Il ball. f. 77v) by Battistino
m. 1561 **Angelo Cesi**, Lord of Monticelli
(d. 14 Jun. 1570)

Onorato Caetani (1542–92)
Lord of Sermoneta
m. 1560 **Agnesina Colonna**
(1538–Apr. 1578)
Bassa Honorata (Il ball. f. 75) by Battistino

Giovanna Caetani (?–1592)
Bassa Romana (Il ball. f. 80v) by Battistino
m. before 1567 as second wife of **Virginio Orsini**,
Duke of Santo Gemine (d. before Oct. 1576)

Federico Cesi (1562–24 Jun. 1630)
Marchese of Monticelli, Duke of Acquasparta,
Prince of S. Polo and S. Angelo
m. 1580 **Olimpia Orsini** (1562–Mar. 1616)
Bellezze d'Olimpia (Il ball. f. 65, Nob. 236)
Cesia Orsina (Il ball. f. 68)

Pietro Caetani (ca. 1562–?)
Duke of Sermoneta
m. June 1593 **Felice Maria Orsini** (1576–Feb. 1647)
Rosa Felice (Nob. 185)

Federico Cesi II (1585–Aug. 1630)
Founder of the Accademia de' Lincei (1603)
(Plus 10 other children. See fig. 2.3.)

Cornelia Orsini (d. 1643)
Alta Orsina (Il ball. f. 71)
m.1) Roberto Altemps,
Duke of Gallese
m. 2) **Andrea Cesi**, Duke of Ceri
Contrapasso Nuovo (Nob. 242)

Giannantonio (1577–1639)
Bassa Honorata (Nob. 223)
m.**Costanza Savelli**
of Castel Gandolfo

Livia Orsini (d. 1619)
Cesarina Balletto (Nob. 229)
m. Giuliano Cesarini,
Duke of Civita Nuova

Figure 2.1. The Caetani Genealogy.

his town of Sermoneta and the Caetani palace in Rome, and at that time he may have chosen Caroso to enter service with his family in Rome.

Perhaps Caroso taught, or helped Battistino teach, the Caetani daughters when they were children in the early 1550s. Caroso himself dates his professional service as a dancing master from 1554: "Now having already passed twenty-seven years in this profession," Caroso wrote in his forward "To the Readers" in *Il ballarino*, published in 1581. Until more records are found, we cannot know exactly when Beatrice, Giovanna, and Onorato's wife Agnesina became Caroso's patronesses, and whether he worked for them all at the same time or consecutively, moving from one family member to another. Agnesina married Onorato in 1560, so it is likely that Caroso's time in service to the Caetani would have extended beyond the year she married into the family.

Many dances in Caroso's books are dedicated to Olimpia's Caetani in-laws and the aunts, spouses, and cousins in their families, so let us look at the branches from the Caetani family trees before returning to Olimpia, her husband Federico Cesi, and their children.

Olimpia's Parents-in-Law, Angelo Cesi and Beatrice Caetani

In 1550, Pope Julius II invested Angelo Cesi as Lord of Monticelli, a title that Federico would inherit. Angelo Cesi had been elected decemvir (one of ten magistrates) of Todi in 1554. (In 1586 Olimpia's husband Federico would also be elected a decemvir of Todi.) Angelo Cesi, a cousin of Paolo Emilio, married Beatrice Caetani in 1561. On 7 May of that year, the Caetani archives record receipt of a wedding gift for them from the city of Todi.[13]

As general for the Holy See, Angelo Cesi took part in the expedition against the Huguenots, sent to France by Pope Pius V in 1569. Olimpia's father, Giovanni Orsini, was also a member of that expedition. Both he and Angelo Cesi distinguished themselves in the defense of Poitiers. Angelo Cesi did not live to see the marriage of his son Federico to Olimpia in 1580. He died in France on 14 June 1570. The following year a doleful *"Vilanella"* with music and poetry in honor of "the happy memory of the most Illustrious S[ignor] Agnolo da Cesi" was included in *La nobiltà di Roma*, Gasparo Fiorino's book of verses honoring Roman ladies (among them, Beatrice Cesi, Portia dell'Anguillara, and Lucretia Salviati).

Beatrice Caetani Cesi survived her husband, living for thirty-nine more years.[14] In 1580 she instituted the Confraternity of the Name of Jesus *(del nome del Gesù)* in Sermoneta. Between 1584 and 1588, she and her sister Giovanna Caetani Orsini, with Portia dell'Anguillara, became patrons of the new Jesuit church in Rome, the Gesù, for which they commissioned the Chapel of Santa Maria della Strada.[15] Beatrice was talented in music and played harpsichord and viola da gamba.

The "Barriera" (*Il ballarino*, fol. 77), a dance that was to maintain its popularity for at least four decades, was dedicated to Beatrice Caetani Cesi. Although Battistino's choreography of the "Barriera" for Beatrice is for one couple, extant sources contain no fewer than seven additional settings of this *balletto*, often for three or more couples. In *Il ballarino*, there is a "Barriera Nuova" for three couples by an unnamed choreographer (*Il ballarino*, fol. 171v), which may mean that the dance had become popular years before and was already a favorite. In *Nobiltà di dame* Caroso reworked "Barriera" (190) and "Barriera Nuova" (139) in accord with the "fine rules and perfect theory" he had developed. Negri gives his Milanese version, "La Barriera messa in uso in Milano" (which, he says, can be danced by two or more persons), in the third treatise of *Le gratie d'amore* (122–24). The dance master Ercole Santucci includes a "Barriera" with choreography by the Roman dancing master Oratio Martire in his manuscript, dated 1614, for four, six, eight, or more dancers.[16] It was performed at the Medici court in Florence in 1617, when all those who had taken part in a festive tournament, including combatants, lords, and pages—numbering forty gentlemen and forty ladies—joined in a final dance. "And even though the great number [of participants in the dance] led one to fear major confusion, in any case there was nothing that did not present delight and almost admiration, since the *ballo* was to the music of the "Barriera," which is customarily danced, and according to the same rules."[17] It is fitting that the "Barriera" be danced at a tourney, since originally it was a depiction of tilting at barriers in jousts. But the only explicit remnants of jousting in the choreography occur in the *saltarello* section, when the dancers move forward toward each other in mock confrontation, alternately clapping their right and left hands.

The music for the "Barriera" begins with several repeats of a lively duple melody and continues with frequent changes in tempo and dance style. A solemn *sciolta grave* danced to each side is interspersed with lively repeats of phrases from the initial duple time. Then follows a *sciolta* into *saltarello*, and the dance ends in a *gagliarda*. The tuneful melodies, coupled with the variety of styles of dance and music, may account for the long popularity of "Barriera" in Rome, Florence, Milan, Perugia, and other cities throughout Italy.

Olimpia's Aunt-in-Law, Giovanna Caetani Orsini

Olimpia's aunt by marriage and Caroso's patroness, Giovanna Caetani Orsini, was the second wife of Virginio Orsini, Duke of Santo Gemine, whom she married prior to 1567. Battistino's "Bassa Romana" (*Il ballarino,* fol. 80v) is dedicated to her. The first part of this dance often features *doppi* (double steps) or traveling *seguiti ordinari* performed in groups of three. This resembles the *bassedanze* of the fifteenth century, when it was fashionable to group one, three, or five double steps together. However, the *sciolta* in *gagliarda* in this two-part dance uses combinations of two and four *seguiti,* rather than three *seguiti* one after the other. This *gagliarda*'s balanced structure of steps repeating equally to each side points toward Caroso's increasing use of more symmetrical step patterns, which, in 1600, he would advocate as a necessity for a dance made with "perfect theory."

Giovanna was widowed in 1586 and died in September 1592. Caroso seems to have remained in close contact with members of Giovanna's family as her descendants attained adulthood, married, and remarried over the years. Two of Giovanna's daughters, Cornelia and Livia, her daughter-in-law Costanza Savelli, and her stepdaughter Beatrice, all have dances dedicated to them in *Il ballarino* and *Nobiltà di dame.*

Giovanna's daughter Cornelia, like Olimpia, has a dance dedicated to her in each of Caroso's books. "Alta Orsina" (*Il ballarino,* fol. 71), dedicated to Cornelia Orsina Altemps, Marchesa of Gallese, is a nod to Cornelia's maiden name. In this short dance, an initial duple section is followed by a lively *saltarello.* Throughout both parts of this dance, the step combinations and patterns are symmetrical, and the dancers often touch or take right hands, then repeat the same steps joining or touching left hands.

After the death of her first husband, Roberto Altemps, Duke of Gallese, Cornelia married Andrea Cesi, Duke of Cere (Olimpia's half-brother, from her mother Portia's second marriage). "Contrapasso Nuovo" (New Contrapasso) for six dancers (*Nobiltà di dame,* 242) is one of four versions of this dance to appear in Caroso's books, and he boasts that this setting of the dance, which he dedicated to Cornelia, is "a *Ballo* made with true Rules, perfect Theory, & Mathematics."[18]

"Cesarina" (*Nobiltà di dame*, 229), a lively *gagliarda*, is dedicated to Giovanna's daughter Livia, who married Giuliano Cesarini, Duke of Civita Nuova. Giovanna's son Giannantonio (1577–1639), Count of Nerola and Duke of Santo Gemine, married Costanza Savelli of Castel Gandolfo (a hilltop town near Rome, now famed as the Pope's summer retreat). "Bassa Honorata" (*Nobiltà di dame*, 223) is dedicated to her as, a generation before, it had been dedicated to Agnesina Caetani, Giovanna's sister-in-law. Except for a few minor changes,[19] the *Nobiltà* dance is almost exactly the same as that in *Il ballarino*.

Giovanna's stepdaughter Beatrice, wife of Federico Sforza, Count of Santa Fiora, is the dedicatée of "Gratia d'amore" (*Il ballarino*, fol. 82). Although this dance is described for one couple only, its music and choreography reveal that "Gratia d'amore" is another setting of "Chiaranzana" (*Il ballarino*, fol. 176v), which was often danced at weddings by an unlimited number of couples and could be traced back to the fifteenth century or earlier.

Olimpia's Uncle-in-Law
Onorato and His Wife Agnesina

Olimpia's uncle by marriage, Onorato Caetani, brother to Beatrice Caetani Cesi and Giovanna Caetani Orsini, was born in 1542 and died 9 November 1592. He became governor of Borgo (an area in Rome near the Vatican) and Lord of Sermoneta. Onorato's travels included a trip to Spain in 1573 or 1574 to "kiss the hands of the King." This custom (rather like taking the Grand Tour) was usual for Italian noblemen at that time, depending on the shifting alliances between the Papal States, France, and Spain. Onorato must have traveled with a great retinue, since in a note written in 1592, Onorato's son Pietro recollected that his father had spent forty thousand *scudi* (an amount equivalent to Olimpia's entire dowry) on the Spanish trip.[20] Perhaps Caroso also traveled to Spain with Onorato, since Pietro Pantanelli, in his book about the history of Sermoneta, wrote that he had in his keeping "two curious letters from him [Caroso] to Onorato Caetani, from which one can recognize the degree of familiarity to which he was admitted."[21] Unfortunately, these letters seem to have disappeared.

On 26 July 1558, a nuptial contract was drawn up between Onorato Caetani and Agnesina Colonna, and they were married in 1560. Agnesina, born in 1538, was the daughter of Ascanio Colonna and Giovanna of Aragon. Battistino's dance "Bassa Honorata" (*Il ballarino*, fol. 75) is dedicated to Agnesina. Its five verses of the *bassa* and the *sciolta* in *saltarello* were so near to the "true rules & perfect theory" that Caroso later described in *Nobiltà* that he made few changes or corrections to the choreography. Agnesina's death on 26 April 1578 may have occurred while he was preparing *Il ballarino* for publication, as he calls her his patroness "of blessed memory."

Agnesina's sister Girolama Colonna married Camillo Pignatelli, Duke of Monte Leone, near Rome, and a collection of poems in her honor was published in Padua in 1568. Girolama (or Hieronima, the spelling of her name that Caroso uses) was, according to Litta, addicted to astrology.[22] The "Passo e mezo" (*Il ballarino*, fol. 45) dedicated to her in *Il ballarino* was a dance "of uncertain origin" with new *mutanze* (variations or diminutions) and *passeggio* by Caroso.

Olimpia's Cousins by Marriage: Pietro Caetani and His Wife Felice Maria Orsini

Pietro Caetani, first-born son of Agnesina and Onorato Caetani, married Felice Maria Orsini in June 1593. According to Litta, Felice Maria was the daughter of Ferdinando Orsini, Duke of Gravina, and Costanza Gesualdo, daughter of Luigi Gesualdo, Prince of Venosa.[23] Felice Maria's paternal grandfather Antonio Orsini was the brother of Giovanna Caetani's husband, Virginio Orsini. So she is doubly Olimpia's cousin: through her marriage to Pietro Caetani and through her Orsini parentage. With her marriage, the seventeen-year-old Felice Maria became Duchess of Sermoneta. (Pietro had succeeded his father as Duke in 1592.) She is the only patroness that Caroso lists in *Nobiltà di dame*.

The inset portrait of Caroso on the title page of *Nobiltà* depicts him at the age of seventy-four, so he was at least sixty-seven at the time of Felice Maria's marriage to Pietro and had been a professional dance master for forty years. The dance Caroso dedicated to Felice Maria Orsini, "Rosa Felice" (*Nobiltà di dame*, 183), is a *balletto* containing ten *tempi* (or verses) set to a twelve-measure phrase of music. This short musical strain must be repeated twenty or more times before the dance ends.

Ferdinando Orsini married as his second wife **Maria**, daughter of **Vernai Castriota-Scanderbach**

Virginio Orsini (d. before October 1576)

m. 1) **Ersilia**, dau. of Nicolo Orsini, Count of Pitigliano

m. 2) **Giovanna** (d. 1592), dau. of **Bonifacio Caetani**, Duke of Sermoneta

Bassa Romana (Il ball. f. 80)

Antonio Orsini

m. 1545 **Felice Sanseverina** of Bisignano

Giulia   Lelio   **Ferdinando Orsini**, Duke of Gravina

m. **Costanza**, dau. of Luigi Gesualdo, Prince of Venosa

Felice Maria Orsini (1576–February 1647)

Rosa Felice (Nob. 185)

m. June 1593 **Pietro Caetani**, Duke of Sermoneta

from Viginio Orsini's first wife, Ersilia:

from his second wife, Giovanna Caetani:

Beatrice

m. 1) Federico Sforza,
Count of Santa Fiora

Gratia d'Amore (Il ball. f. 82)

m. 2) Periteo Malvezzi of Bologna

Cornelia (d. 1643)

m. 1) Roberto Altemps,
Duke of Gallese

Alta Orsina (Il ball. f. 71)

m. 2) **Andrea Cesi**, Duke of Ceri

Contrapasso Nuovo (Nob. 242)

Giannantonio (1577–1639)

m. **Costanza Savelli** of Castel Gandolfo

Bassa Honorata (Nob. 223)

Livia (d. 1619)

m. Guiliano Cesarini,
Duke of Civita Nuova

Cesarina Balletto (Nob. 229)

Figure 2.2. The Orsini Genealogy: The Line of the Dukes of Gravina.

Each verse is full of complex step combinations and ends with a *chiusa* (a sequence of three jumped steps), similar to the ending of a *Pavaniglia*, also known as the Spanish Pavan. If indeed she ever danced "Rosa Felice," young Felice Maria (and the gentleman dancing with her) must have had a good memory, strong dance technique, and agile legs.

Apparently Felice Maria's marriage to Pietro Caetani was not a happy one. Her husband was almost twice her age when they married, and her life as described by Litta portrays a pious princess who may have been more devoted to religion than to music and dance. Litta says:

> Wife without desiring it, she soon was left a widow without offspring; she dedicated herself to piety. One of her kinsmen wanted to force her into a second marriage, and upon her refusal, came to tell her that he would so arrange matters that she would find a new husband in her bed. But she let him know that she did not lack the spirit to have him killed. She retired for some time to a convent of lay-sisters. . . . In Rome she was the founder of the Madonna of Santa Maria in Portico di Campitelli, a church wherein she passed all her hours. When her only brother [Michele Antonio] died the 26th of January, 1627, she had to travel to Naples. There in 1631 she erected at Chiaja a church, laying the foundation stone March 4th, 1631. . . . She succeeded to the title of Duchess of Gravina in 1627. . . . But because of debts owed to creditors of her brother, Gravina was auctioned off and sold in 1629 to Pietro Orsini Prince of Solofra, to whom in 1635 she ceded the ducal title. . . . She died February 2, 1647, in Naples, and was entombed in the habit of the lay-sisters of Santa Francesca Romana, the church she had founded.[24]

Olimpia's Husband, Federico Cesi, and Their Children

And what of Olimpia and her husband Federico Cesi? Like his father, Angelo Cesi, Federico became Marchese of Monticelli, and in 1586, was elected a decemvir of Todi. In 1588 Pope Sixtus V elevated the territory of Acquasparta to a duchy, thus making Olimpia a duchess and Federico a duke. In 1613 they moved another step up the nobility ladder when Pope Paul V elevated the marquisates of San Polo and Sant'Angelo near Rome (which Federico had acquired in 1594) into principalities. Thereafter they became Princes of San Polo and Sant'Angelo.

In *Nobiltà di dame,* a rechoreographed version of "Le Bellezze d'Olimpia," with more complex and ornamented steps, was dedicated to Olimpia, Duchess of Acquasparta. (And, as in *Il ballarino,* the dance was musical, varied, and inventive.) Thus, although Caroso no longer named her as his patroness, Olimpia was still alive. What had she been doing during those intervening years?

Carolyn Valone has found that, like her mother, Portia dell'Anguillara, her mother-in-law, Beatrice Caetani Cesi, and her aunt by marriage, Giovanna Caetani Orsini, Olimpia was one of the patrons of the new Jesuit church, the Gesù, consecrated in 1584. Olimpia Orsini Cesi's "wish to be identified with the women in both her families prompted her to choose a chapel which is the twin of Santa Maria della Strada [the chapel in the Gesù that had been commissioned a few years earlier by Portia, Beatrice, and Giovanna]."[25] Both Portia and Olimpia supported the Capuchin order, and Olimpia's chapel was dedicated to Saint Francis of Assisi.

Not only was Olimpia a patroness of religious architecture and art (as she had been of dance), but she was also the patron of Francesco del Soto (or Sodo), who dedicated his fourth book of musical *Laudi Spirituali* to her.[26] In 1591 the historian Antonio Gallonio praised Olimpia and dedicated to her his *Historia deli sante vergini romane,* a book about Christian women in ancient Rome.

In addition, Olimpia was bearing six sons and five daughters. Three of her daughters survived. Her eldest daughter Portia became a nun in the Dominican order in Santa Maria Maddalena at Montecavallo. Olimpia's daughter Maria married Giannangelo, Duke of Altemps. Caterina married Marchese Giulio della Rovere. After her husband's death, Caterina founded the Carmelite house of Santa Teresa of Avila in 1627.[27] Four of Olimpia's sons survived to adulthood. Her eldest son Federico and her second son Giovanni inherited family titles. Her youngest son Angelo entered the Church and was appointed bishop of Rimini by Pope Urban VIII and was Apostolic Nunzio to the Venetian Republic for Pope Innocent X.

Problems between her husband Federico and her first-born son Federico seem to have grown as the years passed. Litta says: "She loved her son Federico and always tried, although with little profit, to curb the animosity of her husband toward him."

What were the young Federico's activities that his father so opposed? Litta states:

Camillo Orsini
m.1) Brigide, dau. of Napoleone Orsini, Lord of Bracciano
m. 2) **Elisabetta**, dau. of **Giampaolo Baglione** of Perugia

from Camillo's first wife:

Paolo
m. Lavinia Franciotti

Giulia (d. 1598)
m. Count Baldassare Rangoni

from Camillo's second wife:

Maddalena (1534–1605)
m. Lelio da Ceri
Beatified in 1668

Latino (illeg.)
m. **Lucrezia**, dau. of
Cardinal Bernardo Salviati
Lucretia Favorita (Il ball. f. 84v)

Giovanni Orsini
m. **Portia dell' Anguillara,**
dau. of Giampaolo Lord of Ceri
Contentezza d' Amore (Il ball. f. 60)

Olimpia Orsini (1562–12 Mar. 1616)
m. 1580 **Federico Cesi** (d. Jun. 1630)

Federico Cesi II (1585–1630)
Porzia (nun)
Maria — m. Giannangelo, Duke of Altemps
Enrico
Isabella
Francesco (died young)
Giovanni (d. 1656)
Firmino (d. 1627)
Caterina — m. Giulio della Rovere
Beatrice (d. 1604)
Angelo (d. 1646) at age 5

Plus Federico Cesi's illegitimate sons: Ottavio and Giangiacomo

Figure 2.3. The Orsini Genealogy: the Line of the Marchesi of Mentana.

He was barely 18 years old, when, the 17th of August, 1603, he founded the celebrated Accademia de' Lincei, one of the most vast and daring projects of which human genius can conceive. . . . The scope of the institute was the progress and the propagation of Natural Science, not only in one city, but throughout the world. . . . The academicians, among them Galileo, aimed to use scientific methods of experience and verification until then almost unknown. Distinguished scientists quickly began to honor the institution and Federico. All of this led one to expect great progress in the natural sciences. Federico had done much work investigating the fluidity of the heavens, but his masterwork was a botanical treatise. He laid a foundation for the botanical sciences that became the basis for all later botanical works, well before Linnaeus and others who used his tables without citing him.[28]

But the academicians were called heretics, magicians, and necromancers. The schools of the Academy in Rome were sacked, and Federico had to flee. He was called before the tribunals of the Papal government and the Inquisition. In 1610 he was finally able to open a branch of the Academy in Naples. His father, Olimpia's husband, "was the greatest persecutor of the Accademia de' Lincei [and its members] and left nothing untried in the most vile attempts against them. Oppressed by debts because of continual squandering, in 1609 he [Federico senior] left all his goods to his son Giovanni, the better to harm his first-born son Federico. . . . An attempt was made to pay off the debts, but it was unsuccessful. In 1618 he burdened his son Federico with the administration of this perturbing patrimony, in hopes that this would also distract him from his interest in the Accademia de' Lincei."[29]

Adding to young Federico's concerns was the illness of his mother Olimpia. In her will,

> she instructed her heirs to bury her in the chapel of the Gesù should she die in Rome, or in a Capuchin church should she die outside of Rome; in either case she was to be buried without pomp, dressed like a Capuchin nun in an old habit and barefoot, wearing a white cloth over her head and shoulders, in keeping with the rules of the Capuchin Third Order. She made numerous bequests to various churches and organizations, but the two main religious beneficiaries were the Jesuits in Rome, and Capuchin friars and nuns both in Rome and in Porcaria, near Acquasparta. She also specified 100 *scudi* for an oil lamp to burn perpetually at the tomb of Saint Francis in Assisi.[30]

Olimpia died at age fifty-four on 12 March 1616. Litta says that Federico "mourned for a long time a mother who had been so loving."

Olimpia's husband, Federico Cesi, died in Rome 24 June 1630. Their son Federico did not long survive his father. He died less than six weeks later, on 2 August, at age 45. Federico's Accademia de' Lincei was disbanded by the middle of the seventeenth century. As the centuries passed, the Academy was reinstituted three times, and today Italy's most prestigious scientific academy, refounded in 1875, is named the Accademia dei Lincei in honor of Olimpia's son Federico and his vision.[31]

And what of Caroso? Certainly the dances for these ladies, all in a close interconnected circle of Orsini, Caetani, and Cesi family members, suggest that Caroso's early professional life was spent in Rome and its environs. Was he a member of Onorato's great retinue that made the trip to Spain in the early 1570s? Did his career then expand as a result of this exposure to other noble families? Are there any records in Spain (in archives, letters, or diaries) that allude to Caroso creating dances or taking part in performances? And most tantalizing to contemplate, are there any letters from Olimpia to Caroso hidden in some forgotten archive . . . ?

NOTES

I would like to thank three graceful and gracious ladies who would surely have been among Caroso's favorites, had he met them: Sandra Hammond, Carolyn Valone, and (to use Negri's words in praise of Caroso) "la mai abbastanza lodata" Barbara Sparti.

1. See my article "Italian Dance Masters at the French Court," *Pro Musica Magazine* 1, no. 1 (January/February 1976): 3–6. Throughout this article, my use of the terms "dance master" and "dancing master" will be based on my impression that a "dancing" master is only concerned with movement, teaching steps and dances, whereas a "dance master" is a true *Maestro da Ballo:* a master of the art of dance. The dance master not only gives information about the execution of steps and dances but also is concerned with theories of movement and/or choreography.

2. In addition to the autobiographical details included in Negri's *Le gratie d'amore*, see the article by dance historian Katherine Tucker McGinnis, "At Home in the 'Casa del Trombone': A Social-Historical View of Sixteenth-Century Milanese Dancing Masters," in *Reflecting our Past; Reflecting on our Future*, Proceedings of the 12th Annual Conference, Barnard College, New York, NY,

19–22 June, comp. Linda J. Tomko (Riverside, CA: Society of Dance History Scholars, 1997).

3. Recently, Michael Lutz ("Continuity and Change within the Two Dance-Treatises of Fabritio Caroso," in *On Common Ground 2: Continuity and Change*, Proceedings of the Second DHDS Conference, 14 March [London: Dolmetsch Historical Dance Society, 1998], 33–42) and Marina Nordera ("Maestri e allieve/i a Roma nella seconda metà del XVI secolo" from "La donna in ballo: danza e genere nella prima età moderna," Ph.D. diss., Istituto Universitario Europeo [Fiesole, Italy, 2001]) have also been investigating the dedicatées in Caroso's books.

4. See Paolo Raponi, "Fabrizio Caroso e il Ducato di Sermoneta nel XVI Secolo," in Caroso, *La danza italiana tra cinque e seicento, studi per Fabritio Caroso da Sermoneta*, ed. Piero Gargiulo (Rome: Bardi Editore: 1997). Although Raponi found information about the Caroso and Carosi families in Sermoneta, he found no records or dates pertaining to Fabrizio/Fabritio Caroso, the dance master.

5. I am indebted to Barbara Sparti, who introduced me to the work of Carolyn Valone. Not only has Valone unearthed information about many of Caroso's sixteenth-century women and their patronage of art and architecture, she has also found archival details about their marriages, lawsuits, and wills.

6. Unless otherwise noted, this and all other translations from Italian in this article are my own.

7. Pompeo Litta, *Famiglie celebri d'Italia:* "Orsini di Roma," Dispensa 118, table XXVI, contains the information quoted about Camillo, his wife Elisabetta, their son Giovanni, and Giovanni's wife Portia dell'Anguillara.

8. Francesco Sansovino, *L'historia della casa Orsini* (Venice, 1565), 17.

9. Gasparo Fiorino, *La nobiltà di Roma, versi in lode di cento gentildonne romane* (Venice: Girolamo Scotto, 1571), 8.

10. Carolyn Valone, "Mothers and Sons: Two Paintings for San Bonaventura in Early Modern Rome," *Renaissance Quarterly* 53 (2000): 108–32.

11. See Valone, "Mothers and Sons," for details about Portia's lawsuits and wills, her efforts to ensure an inheritance for her daughter Olimpia, and her endeavor to thwart Paolo Emilio Cesi's attempts to gain control of all her wealth.

12. Archives of the Caetani family, Palazzo Caetani, Rome (hereafter cited as Arch. Caet.) #16312.

13. Arch. Caet. #147874.

14. Carolyn Valone notes (in personal communications, 2003) that official birth and death dates for Beatrice are lacking in the archives. Pio Pecchiaio, chronicler of the Gesù, wrote of her death in 1609 "at the age of 53" setting her birth in 1556. This would make her five years old when she married in 1561, fourteen when she was widowed in 1570, and twenty-four when Olimpia married her grown son. Like Carolyn Valone, I suspect that her birth date was at

least a decade earlier, in 1546 or as early as 1540–44, and her death in 1608 or 1609.

15. See Valone, "Architecture as a Public Voice for Women in Sixteenth-Century Rome," *Renaissance Studies* 15, no. 3 (2001): 312–14, for more details of their patronage.

16. Ercole Santucci, *Ercole Santucci Perugino, Mastro da Ballo (1614)* (facsimile reprint, Hildesheim: Georg Olms Verlag, 2004), 428–33. This volume includes a substantive introduction by Barbara Sparti. In addition, Barbara Sparti writes about the "Barriera" in two lesser-known sources: "There are seven known versions of 'Barriera' if we include the version in the anonymous Chigi manuscript, and the 'Barriera' by Messer Antonio di Fiorenza (dated 1601) found in the antiquarian bookstore in Basel which is complete with tablature and with all the musical-choreographic sections clearly noted. Despite the intervening twenty years, the choreography is Battistino's—though described in Messer Antonio's own words—and not Caroso's later couple version" (Sparti, private correspondence, July 2003).

17. Gioseffo Casato, *Viaggio et nozze del Duca di Mantua Ferdinando*, quoted in Angelo Solerti, *Musica, ballo e drammatica alla corte Medicea dal 1600 al 1637* (Florence, 1905; facsimile reprint, London: Benjamin Blom, 1968).

18. *Nobiltà di dame*, 243. There is also a "Contrapasso da farsi in Ruota" (Contrapasso to be done in a Circle, *Nobiltà di dame*, 284) for several couples, and in *Il ballarino*, the "Contrapasso," a *balletto* of unknown origin for one couple (fol. 173) and "Contrapasso Nuovo" for six dancers (fol. 147v).

19. For example, every time they occur, a pair of *riprese* in Battistino's *Il ballarino* version became a *destice* in Caroso's *Nobiltà* choreography.

20. Arch. Caet. Misc. #903, 153–56.

21. Pietro Pantanelli, *Notizie istoriche appartenenti alla terra di Sermoneta in distretto di Roma*, vol. 1 (Roma, 1911), 603.

22. Litta, *Famiglie celebri*, "Famiglia Colonna," Dispensa 56, Table VII.

23. According to research by Marina Nordera ("Maestri e allieve/i a Roma"), Felice Maria's mother, who died in childbirth, was Virginia, daughter of Guidobaldo della Rovere, Duke of Urbino, and widow of Count Federico Borromeo (the brother of Saint Carlo Borromeo).

24. Litta, *Famiglie celebri*, "Orsini di Roma," Dispensa 118, Table XXVIII.

25. Valone, "Architecture as a Public Voice," 312–14.

26. *Il quarto libro delle laude a tre e quattro voci* (Rome: Alessandro Gardano, 1591).

27. Carolyn Valone, "Women on the Quirinal Hill: Patronage in Rome, 1560–1630," *The Art Bulletin* (March 1994): 140.

28. Litta, *Famiglie celebri*, "Cesi di Roma," Dispensa 7, Table II.

29. Litta, *Famiglie celebri*, "Cesi di Roma," Dispensa 7, Table II.

30. Valone, "Architecture as a Public Voice," 324–26.

31. For more information about Federico Cesi II and the Accademia de' Lincei, see Maria Luisa Altieri-Biagi, *Scienziati del Seicento* (Milan: Rizzoli Editore, 1969); Domenico Carutti, *Breve storia della Accademia dei Lincei* (Rome, 1883); and Baldassare Odescalchi, Duke of Ceri, *Memorie istorico critiche dell'Accademia de'Lincei e del Principe Federico Cesi* (Rome, 1806).

3

At the Queen's Command: Henrietta Maria and the Development of the English Masque

ANNE DAYE

The Queen commanded Inigo Jones, surveyor of her majesty's works, to make a new subject of a masque for herself, that with high and hearty invention might give occasion for a variety of scenes, strange apparitions, songs, music, and dancing of several kinds, from whence doth result the true pleasure peculiar to our English masques, which by strangers and travelers of judgement are held to be as noble and ingenious as those of any other nations.[1]

With these words, William Davenant prefaced the libretto of *Luminalia,* the queen's masque of 1638, paying tribute for posterity to the French princess's mastery of the English dance theater and her ambitions for it. This discussion will elucidate Davenant's assertion through analysis of the queen's early program for masques. Modern scholarship has privileged the art of the professionals, headed by Inigo Jones and Ben Jonson, so that the monarchs' personal contributions to the masques they performed in has been neglected. However, investigations from the viewpoint of dance scholarship reveal a marked and intimate involvement by the royal protagonists. King Charles and Queen Henrietta Maria developed the masque form on the foundations laid by their predecessors,

James and Anne; the masque was an arena of equality for men and women, so a focus on Henrietta Maria's policies sheds light on those of her husband, the king.

When Henrietta Maria came to England in 1625 as the young bride of King Charles I, she brought a rich heritage of dancing from the French *ballet de cour.* Although similar to the masque in the broad sense of being a form of theater dance, it differed significantly from the English genre. As court theater dance was, at this time, an outgrowth of social dancing, it was shaped by the decorum prevalent in each country. The French court was habitually open and accessible and therefore saw nothing amiss in the mingling of noble and professional dancer in ballet entries. The English court was closed, maintaining a distinct separation between those of noble rank and the degrees below them.[2] This produced the division of court performances into antimasque by professionals and the main masque by courtiers. The French were happy to see the king and his nobles take on comic and grotesque roles, as well as the heroic and divine. The English court abhorred the assumption of any expressive or histrionic mode by their nobility, hence the entrenchment of that aspect into the antimasque section. In France, dance expertise formed part of the professional profile of the court musical establishment, particularly the violinists, and from these emerged the *baladins,* the first dance professionals. In England, the court violinists choreographed dance entries and undertook the duties of dancing master, but there is little evidence of them as dance performers. The English dance profession was growing out of the acting profession at this time, and the term "antimasquer" began to denote a dance specialist. English professionals were exclusively male, whereas in France, and on the continent as a whole, there was an acceptance of female professionals in dance, drama, and music. Nevertheless, Anne of Denmark had established the right of a queen to dance in a masque at the outset of the Stuart reign, and ladies' masques were received as seriously as gentlemen's masques. Ladies and gentlemen would occasionally combine in a double masque for a suitable occasion such as a wedding, while in France at this time separate performances were maintained for ladies and gentlemen.

Among the differences in the common structure of each genre, a significant one was the placing of the social dancing: in France, *le bal* followed the conclusion of *le ballet;* in England, the revels were integrated into the action of the masque. The French court drew on larger resources than did the English and presented ballets more frequently. A ballet was presented through song and dance with complex stage machinery, including fireworks. There was also a greater emphasis on fantasy and spectacle with an episodic structure, featuring the *ballet à entrées*. In England a masque included speech, with a "through-written" text by a poet, and an emphasis on verisimilitude and character in the antimasque. A synopsis of Henrietta Maria's life in France will reveal her first experiences of dance theater in Paris, before her removal to England.

Childhood and Marriage

Henrietta Maria was the last-born child of Henri IV of France and Marie de Medici, as her father was assassinated in 1610 when she was six months old. Nevertheless, she had a happy and privileged upbringing, based at Saint Germain, with periods at the center of power at the Louvre in Paris. Excellent personal skills in dancing were highly valued by French society, but as the youngest of three princesses of France, Henrietta Maria's education was not a matter of detailed record. Yet from daily records kept by the court doctor, Héroard, of her brother Louis's diligence in practicing and his increasing participation in ballets from the age of eight, the importance of dance training in the education of the royal children is clear.[3] Henrietta Maria not only gained excellent accomplishments in dancing and singing but also developed into a confident horsewoman, unusual in France, but an activity she would later share with her English husband. Her first dance lessons may have come from the leading master of the French court, Jacques Cordier, also known as Bocan.[4]

Louis came of age in 1614 and was betrothed to the Infanta of Spain, Anne of Austria, in 1615, while his sister Elizabeth was married to Philip, the future king of Spain. Although Louis's marriage was not a happy one, the appearance of unity was propagated through the presentation of paired ballets by Louis and Anne, commencing in 1616.[5] Each offered a ballet to the other. In Louis's *Ballet dansé par le Roi pour la Reine*, he declared his devotion to his wife. Anne's rhetoric was more reticent, as befitted a woman. The paired ballets were presented close to each other in the Christmas season and were planned to use the same stage and scenic construction as well as the same team of artists. They formed the central events of a full cycle of ballets by the king, the queen mother, and other nobles. In 1619, the paired ballets were the chief festival for the nuptials

of Princess Christine to Victor Amadeus of Savoy. The king presented
Le Grand Ballet du Roy . . . sur l'aventure de Tancrède en la Forest enchanté, and
the detailed records of this performance confirm the attendance of
Henrietta Maria at age nine. The queen presented her work as *Le Ballet
de la Reyne tiré de la fable de Psyche*, taking the role of Juno, so we can be rea-
sonably sure that Henrietta Maria saw this work too. Indeed, she may
have had a small part as Amour Celeste.[6]

The first positive record of Henrietta Maria's participation in a ballet is that of *Le Grand Ballet de la Reyne représentant les fêtes de Junon la Nopcière*
of March 1623, in which she danced the role of Iris. Now aged thirteen,
this is likely to have been her first proper role as dancer. By a coincidence
that has resonated throughout her story, she was observed in rehearsal at
the Louvre by Prince Charles and the Duke of Buckingham incognito
en route to Spain to woo Anne of Austria's sister Maria. Their point of
interest was to gain an idea of Maria's looks from those of her sister, and
they took no special notice of Henrietta Maria. The performance, which
they did not see, was well received. The fifteen goddesses were revealed
enthroned on high, surrounding the queen as Juno. Their final grand
ballet was impressive. According to one historian, "These earthly goddesses danced their *grand ballet* which lasted a long time, without missing
a single measure, although it was necessary to make many variations in
the figures, including a chain figure which linked from hand to hand
most ingeniously."[7] In February 1624 Queen Anne presented another
ballet, *Le Ballet de la Reyne dansé par les Nymphes des Jardins*, in which Henrietta Maria danced. By this time Henrietta Maria was being courted by
Prince Charles, following the failure of the Spanish match.

The wedding negotiations were complicated by the religious difference and dragged out across the whole of 1624, then suffered a hiatus
with the unexpected death of James I in March 1625. Henrietta Maria
was finally married by proxy at age fifteen to Charles I on Sunday, 11
May 1625. There is no record of extensive celebrations at the French
court: ballets were danced to mark the nuptial treaty in November 1624,[8]
so the subsequent complications of the negotiation, and the untimely
season of the final ceremony may have precluded such celebrations.
Henrietta Maria arrived in England on 12 June to meet her bridegroom
and consummate the marriage. During the courtship, conducted by
proxy by leading nobles of James's court, Henrietta Maria's vivacity and
dance skills were immediately in the forefront. The first report by the
wooing ambassador, Lord Kensington, Earl of Holland, noted, "She

dances (the which I am witness of) as well as I ever saw any creature."[9] Holland was a sound judge, being a masque dancer himself. Indeed, the nuptial negotiations brought key figures to the French court, who would later support Henrietta Maria's first ventures—Holland himself, Sir George Goring, and George Villiers, Duke of Buckingham.

This is not the place for a full treatment of her life and character,[10] but important sources of information for her dance activities are the reports of the Venetian ambassadors and the Florentine agent Amerigo Salvetti.[11] As independent observers, writing secretly and often in cipher to their masters, they are the least biased commentators to hand. They convey great respect for Henrietta Maria's wisdom and shrewd negotiation of the political difficulties she faced, despite her extreme youth and vulnerability in a foreign country. Her energy and courage are revealed by them, supporting what all historians agree developed into a passionate and enduring relationship with her husband. They chart her health and condition and pay respect to the role of a wife and sister in contributing to diplomacy. They are ready with praise for her performances in masques and plays, writing without any need to flatter or any expectation that their words would be read by anyone except the doge or the grand duke and their advisers.

First Steps, 1625–31

Arriving in England in June, Henrietta Maria was in good time to make plans for the Christmas season of 1625–26. She came with expectations of ballets as an integral part of court entertainment, into a court that shared a similar routine. The previous Christmas of 1624–25 had seen Charles dance in *The Fortunate Isles* on 9 January, attended by James I before he fell into his last illness. However, no full court masque was presented until Christmas 1631, and after that the pattern was intermittent. Investigation of the chronological pattern reveals that the presentation of masques was directly related to the queen's childbearing. When she was tied up with a pregnancy or complications, plus the lying-in period, court masques were curtailed. Two other factors were the illness of Charles I with smallpox at the end of 1632 and the installation of the Rubens ceilings in the Banqueting House in 1636. Poverty and political problems were ever present, so they did not impinge on masque productions as directly as one might expect.

The years 1625 to 1631 were eventful ones for the young queen, and sufficient evidence of her cultural activities remains to deduce a pattern of development. She arrived at a court experiencing humiliating financial hardship, so much so that the coronation festivities were reduced. The wedding celebrations were also overshadowed by mourning for James and the outbreak of plague in London. While limiting festivities at this time, the lack of proper celebration of both the wedding and the accession haunted the couple and their well-wishers, motivating later masques.[12] The fact that she was able to present a pastoral play in French with the assistance of her own ladies is astounding. *Artenice* was presented at Somerset House (the queen's own residence) on Shrove Tuesday 1626, with perspective scenery and costumes by Inigo Jones, concluding with a masque by gentlemen.[13] If she was not aware of the potential scandal to the English court in presenting herself as an actress in a play, then Charles and his advisers were. His support of her venture was quite clear, and the participation of gentlemen in the masque lent tacit support too. He took pains though to emphasize the privacy of the occasion, and to restrict the audience. Objections were voiced but not pursued,[14] so Henrietta Maria succeeded in a major innovation within months of arrival in England. This early collaboration with Inigo Jones was also a foundation for the future.

The relationship between Charles and Henrietta Maria quickly became contentious in the spring and summer of 1626, centering on issues relating to her French entourage. Their difficulties were exacerbated by the meddling of the Duke of Buckingham, who had retained his position of dominance after James's demise. Charles took impetuous action by marching in on Henrietta Maria in her apartments, where her French ladies were "unreverently dancing and curvetting before her."[15] He demanded a private interview to inform her that the French train would be dismissed and English ladies and servants substituted. This action undermined the marriage treaty, so Louis XIII sent a special ambassador to negotiate a new settlement. Fortunately, François Le Maréchal de Bassompierre was an experienced diplomat, who successfully engineered compromises acceptable to all, including the problematic area of religious practice. Henrietta Maria had to accept in principle the loss of her French entourage and learn to live with the distinguished English noblewomen who were now her daily companions. It is interesting to note that her French musicians were retained in their entirety, and their number later increased.

With negotiations concluded, Bassompierre was fêted by the court, notably with an important invitation to York House, where the Duke of Buckingham entertained the king, queen, and the ambassador to a full evening of music, dinner, and a ballet led by Buckingham, followed by country dancing. Bassompierre noted that this was "the most magnificent celebration of my life";[16] praise indeed from a principal performer in Louis XIII's ballets, including *Tancrède*. The ballet included a spectacular representation of the Queen Mother of France surrounded by her married children, plus Charles's sister and her husband, indicating the role of marriage in international peace.[17] The records do not indicate whether this was a tableau vivant or a painted scene, but it was so lifelike as to move Henrietta Maria to tears. The Venetian ambassador noted that "Buckingham himself danced, as he excels in posturing and agility."[18] The queen followed this with hospitality at Somerset House, inviting Bassompierre to a masque of her own on the occasion of her birthday. The few records for this indicate a strong comic and grotesque vein, with contributions by Jeffrey Hudson, the queen's dwarf, the Duke of Buckingham, Lord Holland, and Sir George Goring.[19] They were roundly censured for taking on histrionical roles, with severe criticism for Buckingham as a privy councillor.[20] The financial records indicate a fairly lavish expenditure by the king for this event led by the queen and her ladies.[21]

With Bassompierre on his way home, the court prepared for the Christmas season and Henrietta Maria's first masque presentation at Whitehall. Salvetti, the Florentine agent, records her demeanor at this time. "Her Majesty the Queen in this extremity of animosity between the two countries, while no doubt she feels the difficulties of her position, acts with perfect calmness and is at this moment occupied with fourteen ladies of her court preparing a ballet which is to be performed at Christmas."[22] He continues to note her rehearsals, and the delay occasioned by a bout of toothache, until the performance on 14 January 1627. Another correspondent noted the king's contribution: "The king took much pains in placing the ladies' gentlewomen with his own hand. The masque ended, his majesty, with the duke, and fourteen others of the noblemen and knights, led, the queen being one, and the rest of the masquers, a dance. Doubtless it cost abundance."[23] Despite being a significant occasion,[24] there is no surviving libretto, suggesting that no poet was commissioned. It seems highly likely that the masque was devised by Inigo Jones, shifting the emphasis to the visual rather than the verbal, in the manner of France.[25] Henrietta Maria will have had valuable guidance in masquing practice from members of the court musical establishment. First, her own musicians included Louis Richard, Camille Prevost, and Pierre de la Mare, former members of Anne of Denmark's French musicians, who had returned to France at her death in 1619. Henrietta Maria was also served by Jacques Cordier, commonly known as Mr. Bocan. He was included in a list of servants who did not accompany the queen in 1625 but received payments between then and 1633 as free gifts from the king and queen, initiated by the Duke of Buckingham. Bocan had also served Anne of Denmark in her masques in a residency between 1608 and 1614. This circumstantial evidence suggests that Buckingham argued for Bocan's usefulness to Henrietta Maria in embarking on her masque career in England, leading to a special invitation as a freelance artist rather than as a member of the ensemble. Bartholomew de Montagut, a French dancer, was in Buckingham's household at this time, and it is possible that Nicholas Confesse, who had choreographed for Anne of Denmark between 1610 and 1613, was employed briefly by the queen.[26]

Although the evidence for these three early masques—one by Buckingham and two by Henrietta Maria—is sparse, nevertheless it is revealing. It shows that Buckingham, Holland, and Goring dared to take on dance roles more suitable to professional dancers as was the norm for the nobility in France, but in defiance of English decorum. The brief records also indicate the placing of the social dancing at the end of the masque at York House and Whitehall, according to French practice rather than English. The cluster of courtiers sympathetic to French taste seems to have created a milieu within which she negotiated her own plans for the masque, with the professional advice of the deeply experienced Inigo Jones and leading musicians, but also with the full support of the king.

This burgeoning artistic movement was put on hold as the turbulent political and personal scene erupted. The records for Christmas 1628 show both the king and the Inns of Court planning masques, but no firm evidence that they were performed. Shortage of cash was a formidable problem at this time, forcing Charles to recall Parliament to vote subsidies. Buckingham had begun to develop aggressive attitudes toward the French treatment of the Protestant Huguenots. This brought England to the brink of outright war with France, and Buckingham's failed military expeditions led to his deep and increasing unpopularity across England. The seething hatred climaxed in his assassination in August 1628.

Meanwhile Henrietta Maria's concern was her failure to conceive after three years of marriage: the production of an heir was her primary function. The continuing strained relationship between her and Charles did not promote intimacy and was the subject of court gossip and international diplomacy. However, the death of Buckingham removed an intrusive figure, and all the court noted with amazement how the king and queen began to warm to each other in the following months. This warmth developed into an enduring love affair, and their union was blessed with a conception by October that was made public in March. Sadly, the child was premature and died, but the queen was pregnant again the following autumn, resulting in the successful delivery of an extraordinarily bouncing boy, Prince Charles, on 29 May 1630, the first of eight children. The timing of these two pregnancies prevented Henrietta Maria from dancing in masques in 1629 and 1630. However in 1631, with a fresh impetus from a consolidation of power and the dynastic future,[27] their majesties presented the first state masques of the reign.

The Masques of 1631

The season of 1631 launched a cycle of paired masques by Charles and Henrietta Maria, modeled on those of Louis XIII and Anne. With no precedent for masquing by both a king and a queen in England, it is not surprising that the French practice was adopted. The evidence across the period 1631–40 suggests that the use of the same poet and other artists for each pair of masques was followed as well as the use of the same stage and scenic structure. Each masque was planned for a key festival day in the Christmas season: the king's for Twelfth Night (the end of the first twelve days of Christmas) and the queen's for Shrovetide (the end of the second cycle of Christmas from Candlemas to Lent). Hand in hand with this was the presentation of the theme of the joys of royal married love as fundamental to the security of the nation. Ben Jonson won the commission for 1631 and brought to the task his lengthy experience and an interest in paired masques.[28] However, it is clear that Inigo Jones was now taking the lead in devising masques, as the visual elements of the king's masque, *Love's Triumph through Callipolis*, dominate at the expense of the verbal. This masque was delivered entirely through song and dance in the French style and featured an opening *ballet à entrées* of commedia dell'arte characters that was clearly designed to appeal to the queen.[29] *Chloridia: Rites to Chloris and Her Nymphs,* "wherein her Majesty with the like number of her ladies purposed a presentation to the king,"[30] was based on Ovid, according to Jonson's libretto. The masque commenced with a meeting between Zephyrus and Spring to announce and enact Jupiter's decree that the earth should be covered with flowers like the stars in the heavens, and to relate how Cupid, unhappy with his neglect by the gods, had gone to hell to stir up Jealousy. This is delivered in full song, accompanied by "the Naiades, or Napaeae, who are the nymphs, fountains and servants of the season."[31] The soloists and chorus approached the state (king's throne) with their singing, and "the song ended, the nymphs fall into a dance to their voices and instruments, and return into the scene."[32] This episode of delightful dancing by professional performers, outside the antimasque section, was an innovation and, furthermore, was clearly executed in the dancing space in front of the state, the region belonging to the court dancers, rather than on the stage.

Then followed the antimasque, labeled as such in the libretto. This commenced with the arrival of a dwarf postilion from hell accompanied by two lackeys. In a racy monologue, he narrated the amusing scene of hell falling into merrymaking under Cupid's influence. These three then danced, before leaving the stage. Inigo Jones's designs make plain that the postilion was an actor on a tourney horse with false legs, his own forming the beast's legs, ending in claws. The lackeys wore tabards and had clawed feet.[33] This first entry, a scene of familiar English antimasque, was followed by a series of mute dance entries, which in their length were more in the style of the *ballet à entrées.* The second entry brought on Cupid with Jealousy, Disdain, and Dissimulation. The third entry was presented by the queen's dwarf, Jeffery Hudson, "apparelled as a prince of hell, attended by six infernal spirits; he first danceth alone, and then the spirits, all expressing their joy for Cupid's coming among them."[34] Changing to a scene of horrid storm, the fourth to eighth entries represented the weather by the dancing of Tempest and the four winds, three Lightnings, one Thunder, five persons as Rain, and seven as Snow and Hail.

Juno calmed the tempest, and the scene was changed to reveal the bower of Chloris. Here sat Henrietta Maria as the Queen of Flowers surrounded by her nymphs in a rich arbor of gold and flowers, with a rainbow in the distant sky. Once again Spring and the Napaeae appeared with the Rivers and Floods to celebrate in song the arrival of Chloris and the defeat of Cupid and Jealousy, interspersed with the descent of the masquers to dance their first and second entries. The theme of praise then shifted into the celebration of Chloris's virtues in a wider sphere through Fame. Juno, now joined by Iris, began a sung celebration of Charles and Henrietta Maria. As they did so, the scene changed to reveal a hill arising out of the earth, supporting the figure of Fame mounted on a globe. On the hill were placed four symbolic personages whose voices enriched the full chorus of water gods: Poetry, History, Architecture, and Sculpture. Their words explained that they were agents of eternal Fame. Fame concluded by rising into the heavens, singing. Only when the masque ended and the scene had closed did the revels commence, in the manner of *le grand bal* at the French court. This was in contrast to the king's masque, which had kept the revels within the action.

Analysis reveals that the masque has five sections: a prologue, the antimasque, the main masque, an apotheosis, and the revels. Jonson's assertion that the masque was based on the story of Chloris as given by Ovid is embellished with two quotations from the *Fasti*.[35] This work concerned the calendar festivals of the Romans, so Ovid's poem briefly tells of Zephyrus's rape of Chloris, followed by a love leading to his conversion of her into Flora.[36] This is unlikely to have been Henrietta Maria's choice for a masque celebrating her chaste marriage. Jonson has thus deflected posterity from seeking other sources.[37] It is possible that a key source for this version of the story was the opera *La Flora,* presented as part of the 1628 nuptials between Margherita de' Medici, daughter of the Grand Duke Cosimo II and Odoardo Farnese of the leading family of Parma.[38] It was sung in recitative, with a *ballo* concluding each of five acts. The libretto by Andrea Salvadori was published in Florence, with designs for five scenes by Alfonso Parigi. Scholars of Inigo Jones's sources of design suggest that he drew on this at least three times for later masques, so his access to the libretto is already accepted.[39] The dedication by Salvadori to the couple stresses the appropriateness of the story to their own youthful love, and that the fruits of their marriage will ornament Italy just as the flowers ornament the earth. These are sentiments to appeal to Henrietta Maria as a theme of her masque. The plot developed by Salvadori out of the bare bones of Ovid concerns the love of Zephyrus for Chloris and Cupid's thwarting of its happy fulfillment.

This led him to go down to hell to bring back Jealousy. The stormy feelings he engenders in Zephyrus were mirrored in the outbreak of a natural storm represented in stage effects and dance. The storm was calmed by Neptune, and with Jupiter's help, Cupid was restored to his proper function of promoting love. When Zephyrus wept with joy at gaining the love of Chloris, his tears turned to flowers. As the final scene, Chloris appeared in the heavens, transformed into the goddess Flora, by the command of Jupiter.[40] The libretto emphasized the dynastic symbolism of the flowers, denoting the Medici as rulers of Florence, allied with Parma. "Here the entire stage is to be filled with flowers, particularly with the lilies of Florence and Parma."[41]

Henrietta Maria's presentation of herself as Chloris and Flora can now be seen to refer to her descent from the Medici dynasty through her mother Marie de Medici. This is confirmed by identification of the source for the apotheosis section, which has no concordance in the opera. The figure of Fame is common enough, and Jones's source for this representation has been attributed to *Il Guidizio di Paride* by Parigi[42] and to Ripa,[43] although Stephen Orgel and Roy Strong note that the globe base is unusual. This is found, however, in the opera *Il Rapimento di Cefalo* of 1600, offered as part of the celebrations for the proxy wedding in Florence of Marie de Medici herself to Henri IV. "Dame Fame with great wings and flowing hair, holding the traditional trumpet and an olive branch. . . . One of her feet was planted on the globe, the other raised as if to dance. Beneath her sat sixteen women representing the eighteen cities subject to the Grand Duke Ferdinando. . . . As the chorus of cities extolled Ferdinando, Fame was whisked away on a cloud into the heavens."[44] Jones interpreted these words into his design and stage action (figure 3.1). This same opera later inspired the presentation of Night and the wonderful aerial ballet that concluded *Luminalia*. The leadership of Inigo Jones, fluent in Italian, in devising this masque becomes apparent, particularly as Jonson chose to mock this scene in a later poem.[45] That Jones drew on Italian and French visual sources is discussed at length by scholars of his designs.[46] Orgel and Strong identify three libretti as sources for his art from 1625: *Il Guidizio di Paride*, 1608; *La Flora*, 1628; and *Le Nozze degli Dei*, 1637. While forty-five books of Jones's library are held by Worcester College, no texts for these are present.[47] The books may be lost, or Jones could have borrowed copies from diplomats in contact with Italy. Equally, these texts could have been in the possession of Henrietta Maria, sent by her mother. Each work was planned to honor an important Medici wedding, of great significance to

Figure 3.1. The Devonshire Collection, Chatsworth. Reprinted by permission of the Duke of Devonshire and the Chatsworth Settlement Trustees. Photograph: Photographic Survey, Courtauld Institute of Art.

all members of a powerful family, for whom the libretti were an important souvenir.

There are further personal resonances contained in the masque *Chloridia*. Salvadori's plot concerning the love of Zephyrus and Chloris is eliminated, so that Cupid and Jealousy are explained away in general terms. However, the court would know of the pairing of the two, from

Ovid if not from Salvadori. Furthermore, Charles and his companions would remember that he danced as Zephyrus at age nine, supported by noble girls as naiads, in his mother's masque *Tethys' Festival* in 1610. This is emphasized by giving Zephyrus a train of Napaeae only (nymphs of the dells, lifted from the Napee of the opera) and dropping the silvani and satiri of *La Flora*, while also calling them naiads. The audience was therefore invited to consider Zephyrus and Chloris as representative of Charles and Henrietta Maria, in the veiled rhetoric typical of female expression.

With the rainbow above Chloris on her first appearance, and the later arrival of Iris, a reference was also made to Henrietta Maria's first appearance as Iris in 1623, for which Charles saw a rehearsal. It is worth noting that the calming of the storm is done by Juno in *Chloridia* rather than Neptune, and that Juno and Iris lead the apotheosis rather than Neptune and Jupiter, who make restoration at the end of *La Flora*. While Juno is a common enough goddess in these performances, she was strongly associated with the queen of France, Anne of Austria, as the wife of the king, for whom Jupiter was a common designation; she took that role in *Psyche* and in *Junon la Nopcière*. There is also a strong possibility that Henrietta Maria danced as a Napean nymph of the flowers to Anne's Diana in *Le Ballet de la Reyne dansé par les Nymphes des Jardins* in February 1624, according to Malleville's verses, and that the marriage between herself and Charles was also anticipated in terms of the rose and the lily.[48] This ballet was attended by the Earl of Holland, who had come to test the waters for the marriage, according to Bassompierre. This was an important opportunity for him to see the princess in action and forward the favorable report (see above) about her to Charles.[49]

Putting these details together, it seems that a cluster of associations plays around Henrietta Maria's role of Chloris. As goddess of flowers, her uniting of the rose of England and the lily of France would be obvious to contemporaries and had been stated in *Love's Triumph through Callipolis*.[50] The emblem of flowers for Florence, and again the lily specifically, would be well understood by the English court. The freshness of spring and the celebration of May was evoked, too, both still celebrated in England and Italy. Her proxy marriage took place on 11 May (French new style), which was 1 May in England; Prince Charles was also born in May. Jones heightened the spirit of youthful and feminine beauty by presenting most of the female characters bare breasted, including the vices from hell; this was explored for Chloris and her nymphs, although the final design (figure 3.2) is of a revealing décolletage that just covers

Figure 3.2. Choris: The final design. The Devonshire Collection, Chatsworth.
Reprinted by permission of the Duke of Devonshire and the Chatsworth Settlement
Trustees. Photograph: Photographic Survey, Courtauld Institute of Art.

the nipples.[51] Jonson developed the evocation of the Roman festival of Floralia in May by entitling the masque *Chloridia: Rites to Chloris and Her Nymphs*. Finally, there is the allusion, known to her close circle, to the floral ballet of the courtship months.

It seems likely that Henrietta Maria drew on vivid memories of the two great ballets presented for her sister's wedding in 1619, for which she may have retained the libretti.[52] Her brother's work, *Tancrède*, included entries by creatures from hell. "Le Ballet des Monstres Armez" performed "devilish steps," and "Le Ballet des Puissances d'Enfer" performed "steps, gestures and attitudes suitable to their condition";[53] this latter accords closest with Hudson's entry accompanied by six infernal spirits. There is no *ballo* for the inhabitants of hell in *La Flora*. More significantly, the penultimate section of the work was a "Ballet des Anges," for which twenty *anges musiciens* sang to accompany eight *anges baladins* dancing. They descended on a cloud, then approached the state singing; there the dancers performed to song. This is replicated in the prologue to *Chloridia* in the song and dance of the Napaeae after procession to the state. The chorus at the end of each act of *La Flora* performed a dance: act 1 finishes with "chorus of Tritons, Naiads and with *ballo*," implying dance performed to song. *Le Ballet de Psyche* included two ballets relating to the presentation of the storm in *Chloridia:* "Le Ballet des Hyperborées" (people of the far north) with "brisk steps and movements like soldiers" and "Le Ballet des Vents" by eight little boys as winds "imitating the changeability of the winds."[54] Again, the libretto of *La Flora* described "chorus of Tempests with stormy *ballo*" to conclude act 4. The *baladin* and *maître à danser* Bocan was another link with the ballets of 1619.[55]

Finally, this first state masque by Henrietta Maria seems to have recycled elements from an earlier performance—the masque at Somerset House of November 1626. The financial records feature the costumes and therefore the characters performing: "A suite, and cloke and horsecloth for a Postilian. . . . Two suites and Cloakes for two Pages," which matches exactly with the postilion and two lackeys of *Chloridia*, a detail that owes nothing to the opera; also "a suite for Ieffry the Dwarfe . . . fower suites with Clokes and cassoks for foure Dwarfs"[56] showing Hudson making an entry with colleagues, and reminding us that his entry as prince of hell was accompanied by six infernal spirits, who are likely to have been of the same stature.

The private and remembered features of *Chloridia* are a distinct indication of Henrietta Maria's close personal supervision of the masque.

The adaptation of the texts of two libretti synthesized with other elements suggests the closest collaboration of Jones, Jonson, and court music and dance experts in the fulfillment of her commission.

1631 and Beyond

The technical demands of the masque led Inigo Jones to develop the fly gallery for the first time, to allow Fame to soar upward from stage level. From now on, the curtain was raised at the beginning of the masques, rather than being lowered to the floor to reveal the first scene. Jones was also able to engineer a change of weather within a scene to create the storm, an effect also created in the opera. "The verdant scene changed to one of horror," according to the libretto; "Then falls rain, hail, with lightning and thunder."[57] The storm itself was developed by the expressive dancers of the antimasque. For the first time, specific designs were made for the costumes of the antimasque dancers for both the king's and queen's masques, with the implication that these performers were now being treated with greater respect. Jones also continued to consult the queen closely over her dress as Chloris, as revealed by the six preparatory sketches to the finished design. With Henrietta Maria pressing him to realize the scenic effects of the French stage, he developed the art of perspective scenery and the manipulation of aerial effects to an astonishing degree. As the English Civil War broke out, he was poised to embark on a new era of technical mastery with the Masquing Room replacing the Banqueting House as a designated dance theater. Nevertheless, his achievements were developed by his successors in the indoor theaters of the Restoration.

In *Chloridia*, her inaugural masque, Henrietta Maria was supported by fourteen ladies of high rank, drawn from her immediate circle and other great families. A large proportion of them were to dance in her subsequent masques. She had now been surrounded by English ladies for a good five years, which would have assisted her acclimatization. However, before her arrival, no ladies' masque had been presented at Whitehall since 1613, following the departure of Princess Elizabeth to the Palatine and the cessation of Anne of Denmark's performance. The whole court must have anticipated a new era under their young queen, still only twenty-one. These ladies were also links to key aspects of Anne of Denmark's masque policy. It is interesting to note that she adopted an eponymous role in Chloris, closely identified in the published title by the naming of her rite: Chloridia. As in France, masque titles were often unspecific, but in 1610 and 1611 Queen Anne and Prince Henry had taken on eponymous and fictional roles as Tethys and Oberon in the radical period surrounding the celebrations for his creation as Prince of Wales. While only a subtle shift in identification, it gave a singular prominence to the royal protagonist. Royal dancers did not progress to making solo performances in England, and even Louis XIV did not attempt this until 1655.[58] Although the convention was for the noble masque dancers to form a uniform group, Henrietta Maria retained a prominent identity in role and costume. She also maintained some degree of leadership in the dancing: as the choreographed entries were based on symmetrical geometrical figures, the use of herself plus fourteen ladies would result in figures based on two sevens plus one, as well as absorbing her into groups based on multiples of three or five.

Each masque ended with a celebration of the virtues of Charles and Henrietta Maria in order to emphasize the benefits to the state of their union. Formerly, the masques had celebrated the power of the watching King James. This dynastic statement was also part of Anne of Denmark's policy and was communicated to Henrietta Maria in Buckingham's masque of 1626. Having presented herself as Flora, descendant of the Medici of Florence in 1631, she appeared as the Chief Heroine in *Salmacida Spolia* of 1640, daughter of the warrior king Henri IV, in the presence of her mother. The portraiture of Charles and Henrietta Maria pursued the same dynastic theme, emphasizing the marriage and children, who were too young as yet to be included in the masques.

Another of Anne of Denmark's strategies adopted by Henrietta Maria was the use of the antimasque. Anne of Austria's ballets maintained an overall tone of beauty and charm, lacking the grotesque and bizarre dimensions of Louis XIII's ballets. The ballets of the cold and the wind in *Psyche* are charming rather than disturbing, and the work excludes the descent into hell that forms an important part of the classical story. It is therefore revealing that Henrietta Maria embraced the grotesque dimension of the antimasque in her works and that, in 1631, *Chloridia* had a more typical comic and grotesque entry than that of Charles, with a lively verbal induction. Seen initially as a useful foil to the splendor of the main masque, the antimasque provided a forum for experimentation in dance theater, which Henrietta Maria exploited fully in her later masques. She also raised the status of this section, so that by

1638 noblemen were accepted in antimasque roles. It is likely that French dancers assisted in this as choreographers and occasionally performers, although the records are sparse. Among her own musicians, four were dance specialists: Jacques Gaultier, George Turgis, Simon Hopper, and Simon de la Garde. Among the king's musicians were the highly respected father and son, Sebastian and Guillaume La Pierre. Independent artists assisting from time to time were Bocan (Jacques Cordier), a guest for periods between 1625 and 1633, and Bartholomew de Montagut, who was admitted as groom of her chamber on the death of Buckingham, and who danced in *Chloridia* and *Luminalia*. Other French dancers and dancing masters practiced in London, such as Monsieur de la Gay and Michel Robinson. However, most antimasques required at least twenty dancers, so the growing body of English specialists was intrinsic to development. The cast list for *Salmacida Spolia* provides at least twelve English names. The later development of dances of action and character may well have grown out of the expressive skills of a dance profession emerging as a specialist branch of the acting profession.

Outside the court, Henrietta Maria's patronage stimulated the expansion of dance in the public theaters, leading to the emergence of a new genre, the moral masque, featuring dance as the key mode of expression. This ran alongside her active support of the drama and her innovations in female performance that paved the way for major change at the Restoration. (See figure 3.3.)

Henrietta Maria also laid a foundation for the future in the dance education of her children. Her precocious son, Charles, was able to present a masque at age six, although not expected to embark on the formidable challenge of the revels, just as Henrietta Maria's brother danced his first ballet at age eight. Despite the grave interruption to their education by the war and exile, James, Duke of York, was competent enough to dance in ballets with Louis XIV, as was his youngest sister Henrietta Anne. She continued in her mother's footsteps, first of all by dancing as Erato in *Les Nopces de Pelée et Thétis* at age nine in 1654, then by an important career in the ballets between 1661 and 1666, as Madame, wife of the king's brother.[59] She developed a close relationship with her brother-in-law, which gave rise to scandal, but their partnership in dance graced the main period of Louis's performances, leading to the inclusion of noble females in the king's ballets. His withdrawal from the stage occurred in the same year as Henrietta Anne's early demise at age twenty-six. The return of Henrietta Maria's French musicians to Paris

21 February 1626 Somerset House	*Artenice* Pastoral play by Racan, performed by Henrietta Maria and her ladies, followed by a masque by gentlemen of the court
24 November 1626 Somerset House	untitled masque By Henrietta Maria with antimasques by Buckingham, Holland, Goring, and others
14 January 1627 Whitehall	untitled masque Led by Henrietta Maria with her ladies
22 February 1631 Whitehall	*Chloridia* Masque, poet Ben Jonson, paired with the king's masque
14 February 1632 Whitehall	*Tempe Restored* Masque, poet Aurelian Townshend, paired with the king's masque
9 January 1633 Somerset House	*Shepherd's Paradise* Pastoral play by Montagu, performed by Henrietta Maria and her ladies, probably followed by a masque
19 November 1634 Somerset House	*Love's Mistress, or, The Queen's Masque* A moral masque by Heywood, first presented in The Phoenix, Drury Lane; performed with scenery by Inigo Jones for the king's birthday
10 February 1635 Whitehall	*The Temple of Love* Masque led by the queen and her ladies, poet Davenant, incorporating noblemen as an antimasque
21 December 1635 Whitehall	*Florimène* Pastoral play by French actors and actresses, with danced *intermedii* and antimasques by Townshend to conclude
12 September 1636 Richmond Palace	*Entertainment at Richmond* Masque led by Prince Charles, age six
12 January 1637 Whitehall	*The Royal Slave* Play with dancing, first performed before Their Majesties at Oxford, restaged at court by King's Men with dancers
6 February 1638 Whitehall	*Luminalia* Masque with antimasques by mixed groups of noblemen and professionals, poet Davenant, paired with the king's masque
21 January 1640 Whitehall	*Salmacida Spolia* Double masque by the king and queen, poet Davenant

Figure 3.3. Masques, pastorals, and moral masques commissioned by Henrietta Maria.

must also have influenced the growth of Louis XIV's ballets in their crucial period, 1653–70. This is a field still awaiting research, but an indication is the evidence for Guillaume La Pierre, who, with his son, danced alongside the king with Jean Favier, Pierre Beauchamp, Jean-Baptiste Molière, and Jean-Baptiste Lully and helped to inaugurate the new era of professional ballets with *Le Bourgeois Gentilhomme* 1670 and *Psyche* 1671.[60]

This study of Henrietta Maria's masque practice in *Chloridia* reveals not only a close supervision of the genre, but also a high degree of innovation and a synthesis of French, Italian, and English elements in the exploration of a dance genre that yet remained essentially English. Placed briefly in the context of her achievements between 1625 and 1640, Henrietta Maria can indeed be seen to have promoted "dancing of several kinds" in the service of "our English masques, . . . as noble and ingenious as those of any other nations."

NOTES

1. Stephen Orgel and Roy Strong, *Inigo Jones: The Theatre of the Stuart Court* (London: Sotheby Park Bernet, 1973), 706.

2. The Stuarts brought Franco-Scottish attitudes to the English court in 1603, which sometimes put them into contention with the English system. The masque was a forum for negotiation. David Starkey et al., *The English Court from the Wars of the Roses to the Civil War* (London: Longman, 1987), 173–225.

3. Jean Héroard, *Journal de Jean Héroard sur l'enfance et la jeunesse de Louis XIII*, vols. 1 and 2 (Paris: Didot, 1868).

4. Margaret McGowan, drawing on French histories, states that Bocan taught all the princesses of France, England, and other countries (*L'Art du Ballet de Cour en France, 1581–1643* [Paris: Centre National de la Recherche Scientifique, 1963], 152, 236–37). Andrew Ashbee's lists of payments provide information to support Bocan's movements, placing him in France at the right time to teach Henrietta Maria. *Records of English Court Music*, vols. 3 and 4 (Snodland: Ashbee, 1988, 1991).

5. Paul Lacroix, *Ballets et Mascarades de Cour de Henri III à Louis XIV*, vol. 2 (Geneva: Gay, 1868–70); McGowan, *L'Art du Ballet*, 279–91.

6. "A diminutive female figure dressed in a flowered headdress and frock" called Amour Celeste is one of three costume designs for *Psyche*. This character is not noted in the printed sources available for the work. Cupid is accompanied by twelve little boys as cupidons or Génies d'Amour, so she is not part of his train. The elevated aspect of Love, and the resemblance to a nine-year-old girl, suggests a role for Henrietta Maria, possibly as part of the opening tableau

of goddesses (Margaret McGowan, *The Court Ballet of Louis XIII* [London: Victoria and Albert Museum, n.d.], 18).

7. Lacroix, *Ballets et Mascarades*, vol. 2, 206. Translation from the French is my own.

8. McGowan, *L'Art du Ballet*, 290.

9. Alison Plowden, *Henrietta Maria: Charles I's Indomitable Queen* (Stroud: Sutton Publishing, 2001), 12.

10. Henrietta Maria has been the subject of biographies throughout history, most painting a picture of a frivolous woman who interfered with matters of state. Her love of dancing is always used against her! Recent biographies tend to present a more measured view (Carola Oman, *Henrietta Maria* [London: White Lion Publishers, 1976]; Rosalind K. Marshall, *Henrietta Maria: The Intrepid Queen* [London: Her Majesty's Stationery Office, 1990]; Plowden, *Henrietta Maria*). There is still a gross neglect of the cultural achievements of Charles and Henrietta Maria, due to the substantial loss of their property during the English Civil War and the focus on assessing their responsibility for these events. Erica Veevers undertakes a serious review of the queen's religious and cultural program of Neo-Platonism (*Images of Love and Religion* [Cambridge: Cambridge University Press, 1989]). Karen Britland has recently examined Henrietta Maria's contribution to the English stage in *Drama at the Courts of Henrietta Maria* (Cambridge: Cambridge University Press, 2006).

11. *Calendar of State Papers Venetian* (hereafter cited as *CSPV*), vols. 19–24 (London: Her Majesty's Stationery Office, 1864–1940); Amerigo Salvetti, *Salvetti Correspondence*, MSS Henry Skrine, Hist. MSS, Commission 11th Report (London: Her Majesty's Stationery Office, 1887).

12. A case study of *The Triumph of Peace* (as part of my doctoral research) makes plain that the Inns of Court wished to offer a triumph in compensation for the inability of the country to afford one at Charles's coronation or on return from his coronation in Scotland in 1633. They also regretted the lack of a masque at the wedding, as they had offered two to Princess Elizabeth's nuptials. The rhetoric of the paired masques is that of former nuptial masques, culminating in the double masque *Salmacida Spolia* of 1640, a form strongly associated with the celebration of weddings.

13. Orgel and Strong, *Inigo Jones*, 383–85.

14. "On Shrove Tuesday, the queen and her maidens represented a pastoral, followed by a masque, with rich scenery and dresses, and remarkable acting on her part. The king and court enjoyed it, those present being picked and selected [then, in cipher] *but it did not give complete satisfaction, because the English objected to the first part being declaimed by the queen*" (*CSPV,* 488; emphasis in the original).

15. Thomas Birch, *The Court and Times of Charles the First* (London: 1848), 119.

16. Maréchal de Bassompierre, *Journal de ma Vie* (Paris: Renouard, 1870), 274. Translation is my own.

17. Salvetti makes plain the interpretation put on the tableau, which was "to put an end to all the discords of Christianity. A fanciful and mystical conceit which indicates a desire that such a peaceful result might be attained by the instrumentality pointed out in this fiction" (Salvetti, *Salvetti Correspondence*, 94).

18. *CSPV,* no. 34.

19. Orgel and Strong, *Inigo Jones,* 389–92.

20. "His grace took a shape upon him the other Thursday night, which many thought too histrionical to become him . . . yet never before then did any privy counsellor appear in a masque." (For "masque" read "antimasque.") Birch, *Court and Times of Charles the First,* 175.

21. Malone Society Collections, "Dramatic Records: The Lord Chamberlain's Office," *Collections,* vol. 2, part 3 (Oxford: Oxford University Press, 1931), 332–34, 413–15.

22. Salvetti, *Salvetti Correspondence,* 95.

23. Birch, *Court and Times of Charles the First,* 168.

24. "On Sunday last the queen performed her masque, which was very pretty. The king had the ambassadors invited, adding that they should have a place apart. As the first at the Court, and following what was done about Bassompierre a few weeks ago, I thanked his Majesty for the honour, saying I expected a place near his person" (*CSPV,* 29 January 1627).

25. John Peacock suggests that Inigo Jones wrote occasional verse, so he may have supplied what was needed (*The Stage Designs of Inigo Jones: The European Context* [Cambridge: Cambridge University Press, 1998], 10).

26. Ashbee, *Records of English Court Music,* vols. 3 and 4; Barbara Ravelhofer, ed., *B. de Montagut: Louange de la Danse* (Cambridge: Renaissance Texts from Manuscript Publications, 2000).

27. Some historians also link the onset of state masquing with Charles's new mode of rule without Parliament, now labeled the period of Personal Rule. However, at this time, it was a temporary state, with no awareness of the long-term consequences, and a strategy also adopted by his predecessors Elizabeth and James.

28. Anne Daye, "Ben Jonson: Choreographer of the Antimasque," in *Proceedings,* Proceedings of the 22nd Annual Conference, University of New Mexico, Albuquerque, NM, 10–13 June, comp. Juliette Willis (Riverside, CA: Dance History Scholars, 1999).

29. Orgel and Strong, *Inigo Jones,* 404–15.

30. Stephen Orgel, *Ben Jonson: The Complete Masques* (New Haven, CT: Yale University Press, 1969), 462.

31. Orgel, *Ben Jonson,* 464.

32. Orgel, *Ben Jonson,* 465.

33. Orgel and Strong, *Inigo Jones,* 434–35.

34. Orgel, *Ben Jonson,* 468.

35. "Unius tellus ante coloris erat" (Till then the earth had been of one color); "Arbitrium tu, dea, floris habe" (You, goddess, have dominion over flowers). (Orgel, *Ben Jonson*, 462). See also *Ovid's Fasti*, trans. James G. Frazer (London: Heinemann, 1967), 276–77.

36. The *Fasti* may have been less well known in England than other poems by Ovid, but Ovid in Latin was widely read by educated men. The poems were first translated into English by John Gower around 1640 (Christopher Martin, ed., *Ovid in English* [London: Penguin 1998], 164). The marriage of Chloris and Zephyrus was a commonplace for educated men, and certainly the goddess Flora was often depicted in art and literature (Betty Radice, *Who's Who in the Ancient World* [Harmondsworth: Penguin, 1973], 116).

37. No one has questioned this until recently, from Charles Herford, Percy Simpson, and Evelyn Simpson on. See Herford, Simpson, and Simpson, *Ben Jonson*, vol. 10 (Oxford: Clarendon Press, 1932–66). Some aspects of the use of *La Flora* in *Chloridia* are discussed in Britland, *Drama at the Courts of Henrietta Maria*, 75–89.

38. Alois M. Nagler, *Theater Festivals of the Medici, 1539–1637* (New York: Da Capo Press, 1976), 139–42.

39. Orgel and Strong, *Inigo Jones*, 41–42.

40. In Ovid, Zephyrus made Chloris the queen of flowers. Ben Jonson gives his real source away by stating that she was transformed by a council of the gods and the command of Jupiter.

41. Nagler, *Theater Festivals*, 142.

42. Enid Welsford, *The Court Masque* (Cambridge: Cambridge University Press, 1927), 218.

43. Orgel and Strong, *Inigo Jones*, 451.

44. Nagler, *Theater Festivals*, 100.

45. "'Th' ascent of Lady Fame which none could spy / Not they that sided her, Dame Poetry / Dame History, Dame Architecture too, / And Goody Sculpture, brought wth. much adoe / To hold her up" (Herford, Simpson, and Simpson, *Ben Jonson*, vol. 8, "Ungathered Verses," no. 34).

46. Orgel and Strong, *Inigo Jones;* Peacock, *Stage Designs of Inigo Jones.*

47. John Harris, Stephen Orgel, and Roy Strong, *The King's Arcadia: Inigo Jones and the Stuart Court* (London: Arts Council of Great Britain, 1973), 64.

48. Concerning the 1624 *Pour la Reyne, representant Diane qui alloit trouuer les Napées. Au Roy,* Sieur De Malleville, in the last verse, refers to her companions as "les nymphes des fleurs" and "ces Lys" (*Poésies du sieur de Malleville* [Paris: Courbe, 1870]). The accompanying verses, *Vers presentez par Diane à la Reyne Mere du Roy, pour le Balet de la Reyne d'Angleterre,* conclude with praise of Henrietta Maria, who will adorn the banks of the Thames and "Va faire un mariage / De la rose & du lis." The confidence of the title is puzzling, as discussions about the marriage were at an early stage and James I was still alive and Charles the heir

only. However, the verses were published posthumously, so the title may have been added later. McGowan, but not Lacroix, lists this as a separate work.

49. Bassompierre, *Journal de ma Vie*, vol. 3, 84–85.

50. "Beauty and Love, whose story is mysterial / In yonder palm tree and the crown imperial / Do from the rose and lily so delicious / Promise a shade shall ever be propitious / To both the kingdoms" (Orgel, *Ben Jonson*, 461).

51. Orgel and Strong, *Inigo Jones*, 445.

52. The case study of *The Triumph of Peace* reveals elements in the scenario that can also be traced back to the ballets viewed by Henrietta Maria in France.

53. Lacroix, *Ballets et Mascarades*, vol. 2, 124–31.

54. Lacroix, *Ballets et Mascarades*, vol. 2, 206.

55. Translations from French and Italian are my own.

56. Malone Society, *Collections*, 332.

57. Andrea Salvadori, *La Flora o vero Il Natal de' Fiori* (Florence: Cecconcelli, 1628), 79. Translation from the Italian is my own.

58. Marie-Françoise Christout, *Le Ballet de Cour de Louis XIV, 1643–1672* (Paris: Picard, 1967), 78.

59. Christout pays tribute to Madame's frequent role as dancer and patroness of the ballet de cour (Christout, *Le Ballet de Cour*, 119).

60. From the detailed records gathered in Christout, *Le Ballet de Cour*, one can discern the repertoire of Henrietta Anne and La Pierre. Discussions of cross-cultural influences between France and England are also pursued in Marie-Claude Canover-Green, *La Politique-spectacle au grand siècle: les rapports franco-anglais* (Paris: Papers on French Seventeenth Century Literature, 1993).

PROFESSIONAL PERFORMANCE

4

The Female Ballet Troupe
of the Paris Opera from
1700 to 1725

Nathalie Lecomte

Translated by Régine Astier

It was not until 1681 that female dancers first appeared on the stage of
the Royal Academy of Music, during a revival of the *Triomphe de l'Amour*.
There were four: Mesdemoiselles Caré, Pesant, Leclerc, and La Fontaine. The Opera dance company, which had so far been exclusively
composed of men, was at long last opening up to professional female
dancers. Their growing presence became rapidly and increasingly felt
and the first female celebrities of the prestigious Parisian troupe were
soon to hold their own under the leadership of ballet master Guillaume
Louis Pécour.

Rare are the surviving sources allowing us to know the composition
of this company and assess its bylaws. To make up for this lack of information, the only recourse is to methodically analyze the cast of every
production given by the troupe on the Parisian stage.[1] The present study
of the Opera's female dance troupe in the first quarter of the eighteenth
century is based on investigation of a corpus of 145 libretti (from the
Ballet des Saisons on 31 July 1700 to *Atys* on 23 December 1725).[2] The collected data has been compared and cross-checked with other available

data whenever feasible to present information about the troupe's composition as well as its organization.

Index of Female Dancers

Between 1700 and 1725, a total of eighty-seven female dancers appeared on the Opera stage, as shown in figure 4.1. For better legibility, names are listed in alphabetical order, taking into account the length of their careers: on the left side, forty-five dancers with careers of less than four years, and on the right, forty-two whose careers amounted to or were greater than four years.

Before analyzing this list further, two preliminary points should be made. First, the spelling of surnames is not fixed in the eighteenth century; a performer's name can be written differently from libretto to libretto, indeed, from act to act within the same libretto. Examples include Mademoiselle La Ferriere/La Feriere/Laferiere/De la Feriere/ De la Ferière; Mademoiselle Du Fort/Dufort; Mademoiselle Le Roy/Le Roi/Leroy; Mademoiselle Menés/Menès/Menez; Mademoiselle Prévost/Prevôt/Provôt; Mademoiselle Le Comte/Lecomte/Le Conte; or, Mademoiselle Thybert/Tibert/Thibert/Thybere. For the sake of convenience, one spelling, that most commonly found at the time, is given in the chart—for example, La Ferriere, Du Fort, Le Roy, Menés, Prévost, Le Comte, and Thybert.

Second, the first names of female dancers are never mentioned in casts of libretti.[3] When two sisters are part of the same production, their names are traditionally accompanied by initials, "L" meaning the elder and "C" meaning the younger.

Comparison for the same period of both the women's and men's indexes reveals the existence of many namesakes, such as Mesdemoiselles and Mrs. Dangeville, Delisle, Dupré, Duval, Guillet, Guyot, Javillier, Joly, Le Comte, Le Roy, Mion, Paris, Rameau, Richalet, Rose, Ruelle, and Saligny. The current level of research does not permit establishing a blood relationship between most of these artists. We may nevertheless surmise that the Salignys were brother and sister, since they were cast in roles meant for young performers in 1703. Less clear is the case of Marie-Catherine Guyot and Jean-Baptiste Guyot (who was dancing in the ballet troupe in 1699 and again from 1712 to 1722): were they just namesakes, brother and sister, or husband and wife? The same goes for

CAREERS LESS THAN FOUR YEARS LONG	CAREERS EQUAL TO OR MORE THAN FOUR YEARS LONG
Antié/Lantié 1721–22	Binet 1724–25*
Bassecour 1704–6	Brunel 1714–19
Basset 1704	Carré [aînée] 1703, 1705–9
Beaufort 1711–12 *[1715]*	Chaillou 1707–12
Bertin 1703–4	Chateauvieux 1714–16, 1718–20
Blin 1704	Corail 1718–23
Boulogne 1704	Dangeville (Michelle) 1699–1706
Boyer 1721	Defrêne 1706–12
Briere 1712	Delastre (Jeanne Edmée Camus, married)
Caré cadette 1708	1719–23
<u>Chapelle</u> 1700	Delisle [aînée] 1712, 1720–25*
<u>*Clement*</u> 1700–1701 *[1705]*	<u>Desmâtins</u> (Marie-Louise) 1700–1703
Corbière 1713–14	*Dimanche* [aînée] 1708–9, 1711–14 *[1715]*
Delong 1703	<u>Du Fort</u> (Elisabeth) 1700–1702
Deseschaliers 1715–17	*Dupré* 1714–16, 1718–24 *[1726]*
<u>Desplaces</u> 1700	Duval 1713–25*
Dimanche cadette 1713–14 *[1715]*	<u>Freville</u> (Marie Buard, married) 1700–1702
Doflise 1711–12	Guyot (Marie-Catherine) 1705–22
Douville 1708–9	Haran (Anne Julienne) 1710–19
Duplessis 1703–4 *[1695–1705]*	Isec (Marie-Louise) 1710–17
Dupressoy 1712	La Ferriere 1702–4, 1713–25*
Emilie 1710, 1718–19	La Martinière 1723–25*
Fleury (Renée Julienne) 1712–13	Le Comte 1704–8
Gautier 1724	Le Roy [aînée] (Anne) 1708–9, 1713–22
Goblain 1725*	<u>Lemaire</u> (Anne) 1702, 1709–10, 1712–25*
Guillet 1702–4	Mangot (Françoise) 1705–22
Guyerville 1708	Maugis 1709–12
Javillier 1722	Menés (Madeleine) 1708–25*
Joly 1699	Milot 1708–11
La Fargue 1702, 1706–7	Petit (Marie-Antoinette) 1721–25*
Lacroix 1708–9	<u>Prévost</u> (Françoise) 1700–1725*
Le Brun 1700–02	Rameau 1712–17
Le Fevre 1704, 1706–7	*Rey* 1722–25 *[1715]*
Le Roy cadette 1717–19	Richalet 1723–24*
Lizarde 1719–20	Rochecourt 1703–4, 1706, 1708–10
Manon 1699	Roland 1721–24
<u>*Minette*</u> 1700–1701 *[1705]*	Rose 1700–1704, 1706–8, 1712, 1716, 1718–19
Mion 1712	<u>Subligny</u> (Marie Thérèse Perdou de) 1700–1705
Morancour 1704–5	Thybert (Jeanne Eleonore) 1722–25*
Nadal 1705, 1713	Tiery 1706, 1722–24
Noisy 1703–4	Tissard 1699, 1703–4, 1707

(figure 4.1 continues on page 102)

Figure 4.1. Female dancers listed at the Paris Opera between 1700 and 1725.

(figure 4.1 continued)

CAREERS LESS THAN FOUR YEARS LONG	CAREERS EQUAL TO OR MORE THAN FOUR YEARS LONG
Paris 1708	Verdun 1725*
<u>Ruelle</u> 1700	Victoire 1700–1704
Saligny 1703, 1705–6	
St. Léger (Catherine) 1723–24	

Note: Each name is followed by the female dancer's active years in the company. <u>Underlined names</u> indicate the female dancers who were already in the company prior to 1699. Names followed by an asterisk (*) indicate dancers who continued their opera careers beyond 1725. *Italicized names* are given for female dancers with identical names who appeared in Brussels at that time. [Dates for these appearances are quoted between brackets.]

the Sieur and Demoiselle Rameau, whose blood relationship with Pierre Rameau,[4] the author of *Le Maître à danser*, cannot be established with certainty. Family links might have existed between several female dancers and members of the current or earlier troupe. Thus, if we rely on the Parfaict brothers,[5] the "petite Caré" who danced in the last *entrée* of the *Muses* at its first production on 28 October 1703 was none other than the daughter of one of the first four women who danced upon the Paris Opera stage in 1681. Elisabeth Du Fort was Claude Balon's sister-in-law.[6] We also find homonymous ties with musicians of the orchestra: was Mademoiselle Paris related to Claude Paris (a *basse de violon* listed in 1704, 1713, and 1719), and what of Françoise Mangot and Jacques Mangot (an oboe player in 1713)?

Figure 4.1 reveals the presence of three pairs of sisters—the Caré, the Dimanche, and the Le Roy—who appeared together in the company in 1708, in 1713–14, and in 1719, respectively. Siblings are indeed frequently found, and among the men, we need only mention the two Javilliers, the three Malters, the two Marcels, or the four Dumoulins, who were most famous at that time. To these may also be added, from 1700 to 1706, the Dangeville family, consisting of two brothers and one sister, Michelle.[7] While Antoine François, known as "Dangeville l'aîné" (the elder), and Jean-Baptiste, known as "Dangeville le cadet" (the younger), continued their careers at the Opera, Michelle, as the Parfaict brothers reported, abandoned hers on Easter 1706, for the sake of engagements "in foreign troupes."[8] Last, if we trust a comment made by the same Parfaicts, Mademoiselle Dupré would be the sister of Louis, the famous *Grand Dupré*.[9]

Outline of Careers

Figure 4.1 indicates the active period of each female dancer in the troupe. The average length of a woman dancer's career at the beginning of the eighteenth century can be established: for 61 percent of women, their careers were less than five years long; for 22 percent, from five to nine years; for 9 percent, from ten to fifteen years; for 5 percent, from sixteen to twenty years; and for only 3 percent, more than twenty years. Seven dancers can boast of having performed more than fifteen years on the Opera stage: Mademoiselle La Ferriere (sixteen years, up to 1730), Marie-Catherine Guyot and Françoise Mangot (seventeen years), Mademoiselle Duval (eighteen years, up to 1730), Madeleine Menés (twenty-one years, up to 1728), Anne Lemaire (twenty-three years, up to 1729), and Françoise Prévost (thirty-two years, up to 1730). The last named started at that theater as a child, and after her long career, her fame lasted into posterity. According to the Parfaicts, she "had appeared so young on the stage of the Royal Academy of Music, and had stood out there so early, on account of her gift for the dance, that the public continued to mindlessly call her *la petite Prévost* until her retirement in 1730. It seems pointless to recall how much she excelled in her profession: her name is, in itself, high praise."[10] The dancer is indeed listed in Opera libretti as *la petite Prévost* until the first production of *Ulysse*, on 21 January 1703. From the revival of *Psyché*, on the following 8 June, and thereafter, she is referred to as Mademoiselle Prévost. Other children—girls as well as boys—did appear on the stage of the Opera.[11] The *petite Caré* already mentioned (in 1703) and the *petite Rochecourt* (from 1703 to 1706) began their careers in the same way as Françoise Prévost but did not meet with so brilliant a destiny.

Sadly, there is little information about how these female dancers were trained and what motivated their debuts in the company. Note that Françoise Prévost was the daughter of "a *piqueur* of Opera performers"[12] (a supervisor who calls the roll), which may explain her early engagement. We may also speculate that the Opera dance school, founded in 1713 to perfect young artists destined to the corps de ballet but not to train children, could have seen the likes of Mesdemoiselles Binet, La

Matinière, Petit, Roland, Thybert, and Verdun pass through its ranks.[13] Mademoiselle Richalet might also have attended this so-called *école du Magazin*. Be that as it may, Richalet did make her debut in the third act of the *Fêtes grecques et romaines*, on Thursday, 26 August 1723, that is to say, a few weeks after its first night. Very exceptionally, the *Mercure de France* reported the event,[14] revealing on this occasion the interesting detail that Mademoiselle Richalet was Françoise Prévost's student[15] and offering this additional information: "This young woman has a very small waist and a graceful figure. . . . She is not yet fifteen." This debut must have been effective since Richalet's name appears again in the next production and was regularly listed in the corps de ballet thereafter.

Dancer and/or Singer: The Case of Mademoiselle Desmâtins

As a rule, a woman took up a career at the Opera as either a dancer or a singer. This distinction is, however, less rigid than one might think. In the dance school's first set of regulations issued on 19 November 1714 (article 29),[16] one rule seems to suggest that not only the company's female dancers but also its female singers were requested to take classes three times a week from the ballet master. For the period under study, no singer's name was found in the cast of choreographed divertissements. On the other hand, the *Mercure de France* reported at least two female dancers who occasionally performed as singers: Mademoiselle Dimanche, on 24 August 1721 (in the airs added to the *Fêtes vénitiennes* and Mademoiselle Lizarde, on 29 August 1721 (as *Aeglé* in *Thésée*).[17]

One artist led a double career as both a dancer and a singer: Marie-Louise Desmâtins. Daughter of the *violon du Roi*, Claude Desmâtins, she was also the famous Pierre Beauchamps's niece. According to the Parfaict brothers, she "made her debuts at the age of twelve in the opera *Persée* (in 1682)[18] as both a dancer and a singer, but soon gave up her first talent to concentrate on the second in which she reached the highest level, being equally well endowed to express tender or raging passion. Mademoiselle Desmâtins was beautiful, tall and shapely. To be honest, a little plumpness was to spoil her figure."[19]

Casts corroborate Desmâtins's alternation of sung and danced roles until 8 June 1703, in a revival of *Psyché*. In this production, she sang the title role of the Quinault-Lully lyrical tragedy and danced the part of a grieving woman in the first act and that of Apollo's attendant in the fifth and last act. She may have acceded to title roles in singing, but in the matter of dancing, she was to remain in the corps de ballet. From 27 November 1703 (*Armide*'s revival) to November 1707, she would focus solely on her vocal career. According to the Parfaicts, she died "in 1708 from a liver ulcer at the age of thirty-eight."[20]

Life Outside the Opera

If a handful of young women seem to have spent their entire careers at the Opera, others were obviously only passing through. Did they belong to those couples (husband and wife, brother and sister) who moved from theater to theater wherever engagements were taking them? Did they come from the countryside as did Mademoiselle Emilie,[21] or from a foreign country as was the case for la Camargo in 1726? Did they return home once they had spent some time on the Parisian stage? Were they often invited abroad for foreign engagements, like Michelle Dangeville or Marie Thérèse de Subligny, who had the honor of dancing in London in 1701–2,[22] or like Mademoiselle Deseschaliers, who appeared in several operas in Hamburg in 1724–25?[23] How did the various Parisian troupes relate to one another, notably that of the Comédie Française? Thanks to the Parfaict brothers we learn, for instance, that Mademoiselle Freville had been hired at the Comédie Française as both musician and actress from 4 December 1684 to 12 December 1688 before "moving" to the Opera as a dancer.[24] All these topics are worthy of further research.

Information on hundreds of Paris Opera artists is included in the *Dictionnaire des danseurs de Bruxelles de 1600 à 1830*.[25] Six homonyms are found through that source and are reported in figure 4.1, but no evidence proves that these dancers were one and the same person: Mesdemoiselles Beaufort, Clement, Dimanche, Duplessis, Dupré, Minette, and Re/Rey. Two *demoiselles* Clement appeared in Bruxelles in 1705. One of them (nicknamed "the dumb girl" by Quesnot de la Chesnée in his *Parnasse belgique*) could have gone through Paris before returning to the Théâtre de la Monnaie, as could Mademoiselle Minette, whose portrait was sketched by Quesnot de la Chesnée and titled "the brazen one."[26] Louise Dimanche, who appeared at La Monnaie in Danchet's and Campra's *Nouvelles fêtes vénitiennes* in 1715 before leaving for Lille in 1718, could well have been one of the two sisters listed in the Parisian troupe between 1708 and 1714; Louise Duplessis, described by Quesnot de la Chesnée as "not too practiced in her art"[27] did not seem to have what it took to make a career at the Paris Opera. As for Mademoiselle Dupré, it seems strange that she would have been a mere walk-on in Lille in 1718 but dancing in *Pirithoüs* at the Théatre de la Monnaie on 2 September 1726.

The Female Dancer's Reputation

Few documents have turned up to give us any idea of the daily life of the Opera's female dancers at the beginning of the eighteenth century. Unhappily, satirical couplets and some scant testimonies tend to dwell on some of these young ladies' easy virtue and on their lovers. In this respect, the portraits by Quesnot de la Chesnée of female dancers in Brussels are revealing. Given the times, the Royal Academy of Music's women dancers, as well as singers, benefited from an attractive and enviable freedom by virtue of Lully's privileges, which emancipated them—be they minors or married—from all parental or marital tutelage, and they lived as they pleased. During the regency of Philippe d'Orléans, who was appreciative of good-looking Opera dancers, and in the context of a greater freedom of morals, it was acceptable for some women to multiply the gallant adventures that sometimes brought them notoriety, thanks to more or less influential protectors. Other women led virtuous lives, as did Anne Haran who lived with her parents, or Mademoiselle La Ferriere who retired after marrying a militia officer who "fell in love with her and took her with him to Fontainebleau."[28]

Two dancers in particular were the talk of the town. The first one was Emilie Dupré, who made a career under the stage name of Mademoiselle Emilie. She successively granted her favors to the duc de Melun; to the regent, Philippe d'Orléans, whose mistress she remained for six months; to the duc de Mazarin; and to a Monsieur Fimarcon (a colonel belonging to the comte de Charolais). In 1720, according to Barbier, "the little Emilie, an Opera woman who is very pretty and is known by all the young men (who haunt the Palais Royal)" was the object of a quarrel between Fimarcon and the comte de la Roche-Aymon that ended in a duel.[29]

The second much-talked-about dancer was the elder of the Delisle sisters (born around 1696, died 22 June 1756). She was the comte de Charolais's mistress[30] and was seen on stage in May 1723 "dressed in a costume of pure silver that cost two thousand *écus*, to dance a solo in the current opera [*Philomèle*]. This creature is pretty with a very beautiful figure. Before being at the Opera, she was a fifty-*sous* whore. She is very gratified now; the prince[31] entertains in her house and she lives in great style. Admittedly, there would be reason to be sorry, for the man is brutal, and moreover, often drunk."[32] She had born him a son who had died at about age seven and, according to Barbier, "had been the darling of all the Condés, none of whom had ever been married."[33]

Other members of the dance company also had illegitimate children. Thus, Françoise Prévost gave birth on 1 January 1718 to Anne-Auguste de Valjoly,[34] daughter of Alexandre Maximilien Balthazar de Gand, Count of Middelbourg. Jeanne Edmée Camus, who spent her career under her husband's name, Mademoiselle Delastre, was delivered of a daughter, Jeanne Michelle Delastre, baptized on 1 November 1720. Fruit of an adulterous liaison with the famous dancer Michel Blondy, the child was brought up by one of his colleagues, Claude Javillier and his wife.[35]

Three Records Pertaining to the Female Troupe

Three records pertaining to the female troupe, drawn in 1704, 1713, and 1718, have so far surfaced. These were cross-examined with the index of women dancers whose names, for these years, are listed in the production casts. (See figure 4.2.) The 1704 record (drawn in October) was found in a collection of archival documents intended for the evaluation of debts due to the Opera staff by its director, Francine. That of 1713 was among the documents appended to the new set of theater bylaws issued by Louis XIV on 11 January of the same year.[36] That of 1718 was published in 1719 by Nicolas Boindin.[37]

In these three documents, the number of female dancers (ten, ten, and twelve, respectively) is always fewer than that found in the index (seventeen, thirteen, and sixteen). Should we conclude that the theater was hiring supernumeraries? It appears that Mesdemoiselles Basset, Bertin, and the young Rochecourt were called in very occasionally in 1704. Mesdemoiselles Corbière and Rameau, on the other hand, were

1704 Bylaws (October)	Index for 1704 (3 January–5 October)
Subligny	Bassecour
Dangeville	Basset
Rose	Bertin
Victoire	Blin
Prévost	Boulogne
Le Fevre	*Dangeville*
Duplessis	*Duplessis*
La Ferriere	Guillet
Tissard	*La Ferriere*
Noisy	*Le Fevre*
	Noisy
	Prévost
	Rochecour
	Rose
	Subligny
	Tissard
	Victoire

1713 Bylaws (January)	Index for 1713 (27 December 1712–24 April 1713)
Prévost	Corbière
Guyot	Dimanche
Menés	*Fleury*
Lemaire	*Guyot*
Isec	*Haran*
Haran	*Isec*
Fleury	*Lemaire*
Mangot	*Le Roy*
Le Roy	*Mangot*
Nadal	*Menés*
	Nadal
	Prévost
	Rameau

1718 Bylaws	Index for 1718 (11 January–4 December)
Prévost	Brunel
Guyot	Chateauvieux

(figure 4.2 continues on page 109)

Figure 4.2. Bylaws and index comparison.

(figure 4.2 continued)

1718 Bylaws	Index for 1718 (11 January–4 December)
Dupré	Corail
Duval	*Dupré*
La Ferriere	*Duval*
Haran	*Emilie*
Lemaire	Guyot
Mangot	*Haran*
Le Roy cadette	*La Ferriere*
Rose	*Lemaire*
Emilie	*Le Roy aînée*
Le Roy aînée	*Le Roy cadette*
	Mangot
	Menés
	Prévost
	Rose

Note: Names in italics are common to both bylaws and index.

regularly employed in 1713. Corbière, who made her debut in *Médée et Jason* on 24 April 1713, remained until the first production of *Arion* on 10 April 1714. Rameau, who first appeared at the premiere of *Callirhoé* on 27 December 1712, was seen for the last time in *Tancrède* on 8 June 1717. We may infer that Mademoiselle Rameau was hired as a supernumerary before being engaged in the troupe. The 1718 record might have been drawn before Mademoiselle Corail's arrival, since her name only appeared in the corps de ballet on 4 December in the second act of *Sémiramis*, which would explain her absence in Boindin's census. Mesdemoiselles Brunel and Chateauvieux had, nevertheless, been active in the company since 1714 and contributed to fill out the female corps de ballet. The case of Mademoiselle Menés is more puzzling: casts confirm her presence in the *Fragments de M. de Lully* from 19 September 1708 onward. She was a great success in 1718, first in *Amadis de Gaule* on 26 April, then in the *Jugement de Pâris* on 21 June, and once more in *Acis et Galatée* on 18 August. She was not cast in the first production of the *Ages* on 9 October or in *Sémiramis* on 4 December, but she reappeared in the revival of *Iphigénie en Tauride* on 15 January 1719. This suggests that Boindin had either forgotten her name or else had drawn his list around October 1718.

The Hierarchy: Principals and Corps de Ballet

The way performers' names were laid out on a page and the typographical setting of casts in libretti permit study of role assignment within the company. Celebrities' names stand out from those of the corps de ballet's *demoiselles* by either being capitalized or set apart on a single and higher line than the rest of the female dancers.

Over the course of time, the solo dancers were Mesdemoiselles Du Fort, Desplaces, de Subligny, Dangeville, Prévost, Guyot, Le Fevre, Chaillou, Menés, Petit, Corail, and Delisle-the-elder.[38] Regretfully, they are rarely mentioned in testimonies, with the exception of Françoise Prévost—and not even much in her case. Pierre Rameau, in his preface, is pleased to see women on the Opera stage and praises Mademoiselle Subligny and Mademoiselle Guyot, whom he calls "excellent dancers," Mademoiselle Menés, who "never fails to embellish the spectacle and be greeted with applause from the public," and of course, Mademoiselle Prévost, whom he compares to Terpsichore.[39] The *Mercure de France*, which reported Marie-Catherine Guyot's retirement, called her "one of the most excellent female dancers ever to be seen on the theater stage. She had a noble appearance imbued with infinite graces."[40] For the Parfaict brothers, Mademoiselle Guyot "had ranked among the most excellent dancers of her time. She was forced to retire in 1722 at the closure of the theater, because her weight no longer allowed her to exercise her art with the same agility. She was much missed."[41]

The music composer Destouches, in his correspondance with Antoine de Grimaldi, prince of Monaco, is somewhat harsher on her: "Your former friend,[42] Mademoiselle Guyot," he wrote to him, "has grown too fat and has retired; she is uglier and more wicked than any one of the others in that house of ill fame [the Opera]; as such, she does not deserve regrets." But about Prévost, he admitted in the same letter that "her worth still stands supreme."[43]

Only a few choreographies composed for these artists have been notated in the Feuillet system. Of those, four concern Mademoiselle Guyot and one, Mademoiselle Victoire.[44] They testify to the high technical level reached by these two artists.

The methodical study of casts through the pages of libretti enables us to appraise the amount of dancing by women within a given production. The size of the corps de ballet varies in importance but remains sensibly constant, with an average of four to eight dancers and up to ten when an *entrée* entirely danced by women was required, as for example, in the prologue of *Canente* on 4 November 1700. Principals are showcased in three ways: in trios, duets, and solos. Trios may be mixed and composed of two men and one woman (as in *Aréthuse*, act 3, on 14 July 1701), or vice versa, two women and one man (*Polyxène et Pyrrhus*, act 5, on 21 October 1706; *Alceste*, act 5, on 16 January 1716; *Les Ages*, act 1, on 9 October 1718 and 10 October 1724). They may also consist entirely of women, as was the case in the first act of *Thétis et Pélée* on 13 May 1712 and in the fifth act of that work on 4 November 1723. But these types of trios are especially used to introduce the Graces. (See figure 4.3.) Female duets, like couple duets or solos (*entrées seule,* to use the period terminology), are found in great number throughout the work, giving the best artists an opportunity to shine and attract the public's esteem.

Graces (3)	Desplaces, Dangeville, Victoire	1700	*Hésione* (act 2)
Graces (3)	Du Fort, Dangeville, Victoire	1701	*Omphale* (Prologue [Pr])
Graces (3)	Victoire, Guillet, La Ferriere	1703	*Europe galante* (Pr)
Graces (3)	Dangeville, Rose, Tissard	1703	*Muses, 2e version* (Pr)
Graces (3)	Victoire, Dangeville, Rose	1704	*Didon* (Pr)
Graces (3)	Saligny, Morancour, Nadal	1705	*Triomphe de l'Amour* (Pr)
Graces (3)	Prévost, Guyot, Saligny	1706	*Europe galante* (Pr)
Graces (3)	Prévost, Guyot, Le Fevre	1706	*Polixène et Phyrrus* (act 2)
Graces (3)	Rose, Chaillou, Le Comte	1708	*Hippodamie* (Pr)
Graces (1 + 3)	Guyot/Chaillou, Lemaire, Menés	1710	*Diomède* (Pr)
Graces (1 + 3)	Guyot/Chaillou, Menés, Lemaire	1711	*Manto la fée* (act 4)
Graces (3)	Lemaire, Haran, Isec	1711	*Nouveaux Fragments* (Pr)
Graces (3)	Lemaire, Menés, Maugis	1712	*Idoménée* (Pr)
Graces (3)	Prévost, Guyot, Isec	1712	*Achille et Polyxène* (act 1)
Graces (3)	Haran, Isec, La Ferriere	1713	*Télèphe* (Pr)
Graces (3)	Lemaire, Mangot, Duval	1714	*Arion* (Pr)
Graces en matelottes	Mangot, Dimanche cadette, Corbière	1714	*Amours déguisés* (Pr)
Graces (1 + 3)	Guyot/Isec, La Ferriere, Haran	1715	*Plaisirs de la Paix* (Pr)
Graces (1 + 3)	Menés/Haran, Chateauvieux, Brunel	1715	*Europe galante* (Pr)
Graces (1 + 3)	Guyot/Menés, Isec, La Ferriere	1716	*Fêtes de l'été* (Pr)
Graces (1 + 3)	Prévost/Menés, Isec, Dupré	1717	*Vénus et Adonis* (act 3)
Graces (3)	La Ferriere, Dupré, Brunel	1719	*Carnaval et la Folie* (Pr)
Graces (3)	Dupré, Delisle, Antié	1722	*Renaud* (Pr)
Graces (3)	Dupré, Duval, Delisle	1723	*Philomèle* (Pr)
Graces (3)	Richalet, Petit, La Martinière	1724	*Europe galante* (Pr)
Graces (3)	Delisle aînée, La Ferriere, Petit	1725	*Eléments* (Pr)

Figure 4.3. Female dancers cast as Graces from 1700 to 1725.

Henry DUMOULIN	1712	*Médée et Jason*
Henry DUMOULIN	1713	*Psyché*
Henry DUMOULIN	1713	*Armide*
Henry DUMOULIN	1714	*Arion*
Henry DUMOULIN	1714	*Armide*
François Robert MARCEL	1715	*Europe galante*
François Robert MARCEL	1716	*Alceste*
François Robert MARCEL	1716	*Mort Alcide*
François Robert MARCEL	1716	*Hypermnestre*
François Robert MARCEL	1716	*Roland*
François Robert MARCEL	1717	*Fragments*
François Robert MARCEL	1717	*Ariane*
François Robert MARCEL	1717	*Tancrède*
François Robert MARCEL	1717	*Vénus et Adonis*
François Robert MARCEL	1717	*Isis*
François Robert MARCEL	1718	*Amadis de Gaule*
François Robert MARCEL	1718	*Jugement de Pâris*
François Robert MARCEL	1718	*Acis et Galatée*
François Robert MARCEL	1719	*Iphigénie en Tauride*
François Robert MARCEL	1719	*Carnaval et la Folie*
François Robert MARCEL	1719	*Issé**
François Robert MARCEL	1720	*Polidore*
François Robert MARCEL	1720	*Amours de Protée*
François Robert MARCEL	1720	*Scylla*
François Robert MARCEL	1721	*Omphale*
Michel BLONDY	1721	*Fêtes vénitiennes*
François Robert MARCEL	1721	*Phaëton* (act 3)
François Robert MARCEL	1721	*Phaëton* (act 4)
François Robert MARCEL	1722	*Renaud*
François Robert MARCEL	1723	*Pirithoüs*
François Robert MARCEL	1723	*Philomèle*
François Robert MARCEL	1723	*Fêtes grecques et romaines*
MION	1724	*Amadis de Gaule*
François Robert MARCEL	1724	*Europe galante*
François Robert MARCEL	1724	*Armide*
MION	1725	*Eléments*
MION	1725	*Télégone*

*A Feuillet choreography exists for this duet (a Zephyr and a Nymph, act 4): *Saraband compos'd by M. Pécour and danc'd by M. Marcell and Mlle. Menais at Paris, 1720* [*sic*] (see Lancelot, *La Belle Dance*, FL/Ms13.1/07; *Little Ellis and March*, LM/7640).

Figure 4.4. Madeleine Menés's male partners.

Partnerships

The layout of casts also brings into evidence the existence of favored partnerships. Some couples are very conspicuously brought together. Such are Marie-Thérèse de Subligny and Claude Balon, who became her almost exclusive partner. When Subligny retired in 1705, Balon turned to Françoise Prévost, until his own retirement in 1710. She would subsequently share herself between the two brothers Dumoulin, François and David, as did Marie-Catherine Guyot, who also paired off at times with Michel Blondy. Mademoiselle Chaillou tended to dance with the elder Dumoulin, Henry, as did Madeleine Menés early in her career. But later, from 1715 to 1724, as Pierre Rameau remarked, she would form a popular partnership with François Robert Marcel, the elder of the two Marcels (see figure 4.4).[45] Mademoiselle La Ferriere was less exclusive, apparently dancing most with François Dumoulin, but from 1716 to 1718 almost exclusively with Guillaume Louis Pécour, who seemed to have returned to the stage to appear by her side.[46] In 1723 Mademoiselle Corail found a regular partner in Antoine Laval, just as Mademoiselle Delisle did in Mion between 1723 and 1725.

The preferential partnering of female dancers is less predictable, if one excepts the numerous duets involving the two stars Marie-Catherine Guyot and Françoise Prévost between 1715 and 1718. A good number of choreographies published by Feuillet and Gaudrau trace these partnerships: eleven for the couple Subligny-Balon; five for Guyot-David Dumoulin and two for Guyot-François Dumoulin; three for Chaillou-Henry Dumoulin; one for Menés-Marcel; and five for Mesdemoiselles Guyot-Prévost.[47]

Size Comparison of the Male and Female Troupes

In order to compare the numbers of male and female dancers, and to evaluate them proportionally over the course of time, seven years of reference are used: 1700, 1704, 1708, 1713, 1717, 1721, and 1725. A diagram reviewing the data presents a synthesis of this evolution. (See figure 4.5.)

A first point of evidence is apparent: during these years, the size of the female ballet troupe is always smaller than that of the male. The most frequently recurring differences between the two groups amount to a deficit of three female dancers (20 percent), of four female dancers

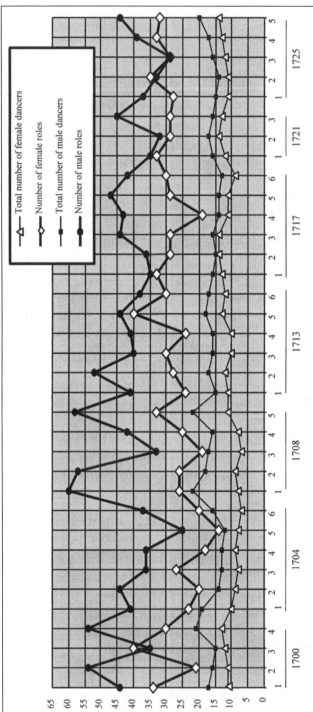

Titles of works corresponding to the graph numbers: **1700:** 1. Les Saisons; 2. La Grotte de Versailles and Le Carnaval Mascarade; 3. Canente; 4. Hésione. **1704:** 1. Le Carnaval et la Folie; 2. Isis; 3. Iphigénie en Tauride; 4. Didon; 5. Acis et Galatée; 6. Télémaque. **1708:** 1. Hippodamie; 2. Thétis et Pélée; 3. Les Fragments de M. de Lully; 4. Issé; 5. Atys. **1713:** 1. Médée et Jason; 2. Psyché; 3. Les Amours déguisés; 4. Médée et Jason; 5. Télèphe; 6. Armide. **1717:** 1. Fragments; 2. Ariane; 3. Tancrède; 4. Vénus et Adonis; 5. Isis; 6. Camille reine de Volsques. **1721:** 1. Omphale; 2. Les Fêtes vénitiennes; 3. Phaéton. **1725:** 1. La Reine des Péris; 2. Les Eléments; 3. Les Fêtes de l'été; 4. Télégone; 5. Atys.

Figure 4.5. Evolution of the male/female ratio.

(22 percent), and of five female dancers (17 percent). The smallest gap is of one female dancer (a unique occurrence, *Ariane,* on 6 April 1717); the largest one is of fourteen (also a unique occurrence, in *Hippodamie,* on 6 March 1708).

The total number of female dancers in works is relatively stable during the whole period, amounting to a minimum of seven (in the *Fragments de M. de Lully* on 19 September 1708) and reaching a maximum of fourteen (in *Ariane,* in *les Fêtes vénitiennes,* on 10 July 1721 and in *Atys,* on 23 December 1725). From 7 August 1717 *(Vénus et Adonis)* onward, the gap stabilizes and the relationship between the two groups—male and female dancers—evolves in a parallel manner.

To complete this analysis, we must pay attention to the number of roles that were covered, since the same artists could appear several times within the same work and in act after act. Thus, Mademoiselle Rose undertook as many as six characters in *Canente* on 4 November 1700, performing in the prologue *divertissements* and in each of the tragedy's five acts. On average, a female dancer was seen three times per show. In the diagram, the graph curve indicating the number of female roles is noticeably lower than that representing the number of male roles, with three exceptions. The two curves merge in the *Fêtes de l'été* on 28 August 1725 (twenty-nine women's roles, as many as for men). The curve is higher on two occasions: in *Canente* (forty female roles to thirty-five for men) and in the *Eléments* on 29 May 1725 (thirty-five to thirty-three). A balance is almost achieved twice: in *Omphale* on 21 April 1721 and in the *Fragments* on 8 February 1717 (thirty-three roles for women to thirty-five for men). Finally, note that a small number of female dancers were, at times, called on to perform numerous characters: in *Canente* there were twelve of them to share forty roles (five each for Mesdemoiselles Dangeville and Freville); in *Télèphe* on 28 November 1713, thirteen would cover forty characters (Mesdemoiselles Haran, Isec, and Rameau interpreted five each); and in the *Eléments,* thirty-five roles were shared among eleven dancers.

Comparison of Women's and Men's Wages

The comparison of wages paid to women and men dancers is possible thanks to the 1704 and 1713 bylaws, which listed salaries. As a rule, women were paid somewhat less than men.

In 1704, aside from Claude Balon, who came under a separate stat-ute,[48] and Guillaume Louis Pécour, who held a combined position as both dancer and ballet master (thus receiving 3,000 livres in salary), the annual wages amounted to 800 livres for four of the male soloists and 700 livres for the other two. Two of the male corps de ballet dancers were paid 500 livres and the other two, 300 livres. On the women's side, the company principal, Marie Thérèse de Subligny, earned 1,500 livres, which was about the same amount as what Pécour was receiving as a dancer. This being said, she was not granted the special statute enjoyed by her colleague, Claude Balon. Each of the other soloists (Mesdemoi-selles Dangeville, Rose, and Victoire) earned 700 livres, as did two of their male counterparts. The demoiselles of the corps de ballet were ei-ther at the same level as the gentlemen or slightly under and were enti-tled to 500 livres (Mademoiselle La Ferriere), 450 livres (Mademoiselle Tissard), 400 livres (Mademoiselle Le Fevre and Françoise Prévost, then at the beginning of her career), and last, 300 livres (Mesdemoiselles Du-plessis and Noisy).

In 1713 the significant increase in the combined Opera personnel was followed by a decrease of the highest salaries (especially those of sing-ers), but they were more equitably distributed. Pécour (who no longer performed but continued to hold the position of ballet master) still re-ceived 1,500 livres yearly. The two main principals earned 1,000 livres and the four others, 800 livres. Four of the male dancers in the corps de ballet earned 600 livres and the other two, 400 livres. The sliding scale of female wages is narrower: Françoise Prévost and Marie-Catherine Guyot, by now celebrities, each received 900 livres, somewhat less than Michel Blondy and François Dumoulin. Four of the corps de ballet's young women (Madeleine Menés, Anne Lemaire, Marie-Louise Isec, and Anne Julienne Haran) who, at times, took on prominent roles, re-ceived 500 livres each, which is less than male dancers of the same rank. Finally, the last four dancers (René-Julie Fleury, Françoise Mangot, Anne Le Roy, and Mademoiselle Nadal) earned the same amount as their male colleagues, 400 livres each.

Types of Roles and Performers' Specializations

The listing of performers' names with each role adds yet further interest to the study of libretti casts. We can thus evaluate the various types of roles and determine which were available to both women and men, which were exclusively reserved to women, and which were withheld from them.

Among the mythological characters, Venus, Diana, and Flora were the three main goddesses supplied with large corteges of followers such as priestesses, who were called in at times to celebrate their cult. Venus's retinue might combine the two sexes, but on the whole, her suite, like that of Diana, Astrea, and Minerva, was largely or exclusively female. On the other hand, Eros's suite (with one exception in the *Mort d'Alcide* on 18 August 1716) and that of Zephyrus were solely composed of men. In reverse, characters such as vestals, Amazons, or Graces,[49] had no male equivalent. Nymphs, bacchantes, dryads, nereids, mermaids, priestesses, and huntresses, which complete this female typology, typically had their matching male counterparts (fauns, satyrs, tritons, sacrificers, hunters). The same went for the vast range of Greek women and other female inhabitants of the cities or regions of the antique world (Athenians, Cretans, Ionians).

In respect to allegorical characters, Dance could be personified by either a male or a female dancer, as was the character of Folly. If women had no place in the wake of Jealousy, Victory, Hatred, Fury, or Destiny, they were, in return, alone in following Virtue. They found their place in the mixed cortege that followed Youth, Peace, Wisdom, and the four continents. The part of the Hours was reserved to them, that of the Arts, forbidden them. The personification of Games and Pleasures began to be theirs around 1709, after having been exclusively male.

In general, roles associated with the destructive power of nature, such as winds, or those conjuring up the sulphurous infernal world, were male specialties. Of course, women could incarnate fairies (the female equivalent of enchanters, their usual companions), but there was no female elf or genie. Roles of witches and furies were, moreover, always imparted to men in female guise.

The Pastoral yielded countless *entrées* of country or shepherd girls paired with suitors, just as exotic themes led to the portrayal of women from distant countries such as Chinese ladies or Sultanas. On the whole, female dancers had access, as did men, to colorful roles, notably in the numerous nautical fêtes (lady sailors and even gondoliers) or in masked balls and carnival scenes, where they had the opportunity to perform *commedia dell'arte* characters such as Arlequine, Scaramouchette, and Pantalone (but not Pulchinella)—roles traditionally reserved to men.

Through the study of casts we see that some performers were allowed to specialize in certain types of roles, but that, in this respect, women specialists were noticeably fewer than men. Mademoiselle Du Fort, for example, was often cast in typed characters—Arlequine[50] (*Les Saisons*, 1700), lady sailor (*Aréthuse*, 1700), and peasant girl (*Acis et Galatée*, 1702)—as was Mademoiselle Petit later on. Among the dancers portraying the Graces (see figure 4.3), we notice four times the names of Mesdemoiselles Victoire, Dangeville, Haran, and Prévost; five times, the names of Mesdemoiselles Lemaire, Menés, and Guyot; and six times those of Mesdemoiselles Isec and La Ferriere. The latter first appeared as Arlequine in the *Fragments de M. Lully* and on six more occasions later on, between 1714 and 1722. Madeleine Menés, as well as Marie-Catherine Guyot and Françoise Prévost, took on a broader range of roles. The last two seemed to have been particularly suited to roles of nymphs and shepherdesses, and in the case of Mademoiselle Prévost, to those of lady sailors.[51] Françoise Prévost also owed part of her success to her ability to perform vastly different characters, as Pierre Rameau pointed out: "She has all the advantages of Proteus in the fable. She, at leisure, assumes all manner of shapes, with this difference only, that Proteus oftentimes made use of them to frighten curious mortals that came to consult him, and she enchants the greedy eyes of those who look on her, and gains the applause of everybody, which excites a noble emulation among the other women dancers."[52]

Conclusion

If male dancing was still predominant at the beginning of the eighteenth century, female professional dancing was nonetheless of high quality, and this, long before the arrival in the early 1730s of two emblematic figures, Mesdemoiselles Sallé and Camargo. Marie Thérèse de Subligny, then at the end of her career, and Françoise Prévost, in the full and irresistible swing of hers, have ascended to posterity and to the honor of figuring in every dance dictionary. It is a pity that personalities such as Elisabeth Du Fort, Michelle Dangeville, Marie-Catherine Guyot, Madeleine Menés, and so many of their colleagues, who so brilliantly marked their epoch with their talent, are now forgotten. Fortunately, with this research, a sizeable slice of dance theater history, which women have so enlivened, has come to light.

Notes

1. From 31 July 1699 (the revival of Quinault and Lully's *Proserpine*), libretti sold at the theater doors began to mention performers' names. For the preceding period, unfortunately, the Parisian productions' programs do not list casts. This is not the case for court productions, which, on Louis XIV's request, list casts from *Thésée* (1675) to *Issé* (1697); this allows us to have a glimpse—albeit partial—of the troupe's composition at the time of Lully and Pierre Beauchamps. My colleague and musicologist Jerôme de la Gorce and I will shortly publish the results of our joint work concerning singers and dancers in *La troupe de l'Opéra d'après les distributions des livrets, 1699–1733*.

2. A libretto was published on the first night of each production, either on the opening night of a lyrical creation or on that of its revival. Consequently, the libretto never mentions the eventual alternation of performers for a given role or, needless to say, last minute replacements of sick performers.

3. The first names of only eighteen of the eighty-seven female dancers appearing on the Opera stage are known (see figure 4.1). Therefore, the terms "Mademoiselle" and "Mesdemoiselles" will be used in this text when first names are unknown. The first names mentioned in figure 4.1 were established thanks to several archival documents, the information gathered by Claude and François Parfaict in their *Dictionnaire des théâtres de Paris*, 7 vols. (1756; reprint, Geneva: Slatkin, 1967), and by Émile Campardon in *L'Académie Royale de Musique au XVIIIe siècle* (Paris: Berger-Levault, 1884).

4. None of the archival documents concerning Pierre Rameau states or alludes to his belonging to the troupe of the Royal Academy of Music. This leads me to think that he is not the Rameau who appears between 1711 and 1717.

5. Claude Parfaict and François Parfaict, "Histoire de l'Académie Royale de Musique," Bibliothèque nationale, Paris, MS nouv. acq. fr. 6532.

6. In 1696, Balon had married Elisabeth Du Fort's sister, Marie Du Fort, herself a dancer in the Opera troupe.

7. They are related to the famous dynasty of Comédie Française actors bearing the same name.

8. Parfaict and Parfaict, *Dictionnaire des théâtres de Paris*, 2:247. Mademoiselle Dangeville is indeed listed for the last time in *Alcione* (Première, 18 February 1706), where she was cast as a shepherdess (prologue), an Eolienne (act 1) and a priestess (act 4).

9. Parfaict and Parfaict, "Histoire de l'Académie Royale de Musique," fols. 136–37.

10. Parfaict and Parfaict, "Histoire de l'Académie Royale de Musique," fol. 98.

11. Children were sometimes hired for just one production: such were the young Baptiste, Clement, and Paris in the first production of *Sémiramis* on 4

December 1718, and later, the young Gilon and Rabodon in the revival of *Atys* on 23 December 1725. Since they were never hired again, their names have not been retained in the index of figure 4.1.

12. Parfaict and Parfaict, "Histoire de l'Académie Royale de Musique," fol. 98.

13. On the subject of the Opera dance school in the eighteenth century, see Nathalie Lecomte, "Maître à danser et baladins aux XVIIe et XVIIIe siècles: quand la danse était l'affaire des hommes," in *Histoires de corps: à propos de la formation du danseur* (Paris: Cité de la musique, 1998), 153–72.

14. *Mercure de France*, September 1723, 582.

15. This tends to confirm that women, without the title of dancing mistress, taught other women dancers, or at any rate, perfected them in their training.

16. Archives nationales, Paris, France, AD VIII. On the subject, see Nathalie Lecomte, "Maître à danser," 160.

17. *Mercure de France*, August 1721, 108 and 133.

18. Both debuts are also mentioned in the preface to the first volume of the *Recueil général des opéras* (Paris: Ballard, 1703), 10.

19. Parfaict and Parfaict, "Histoire de l'Académie Royale de Musique," fol. 51

20. Parfaict and Parfaict, "Histoire de l'Académie Royale de Musique," fol. 51.

21. According to Jean Hervez, *La Régence galante* (Paris: Bibliothèque des curieux, 1909), 61, she was from Rennes in Brittany.

22. Two choreographies by G. L. Pécour published by Feuillet in 1704 and by Gaudrau in 1713 indicate that she danced there. See Francine Lancelot's catalog, *La Belle Dance* (Paris: Van Dieren, 1996), FL/1704.1/06 and FL/1713.2/32; and Meredith Little Ellis and Carol G. Marsh, *La Danse Noble: An Inventory of Dances and Sources* (Williamstown, Mass.: Broude Brothers, 1992), LM/5020 and LM/6560.

23. I thank Marie-Thérèse Mourey, author of the thesis "Danser dans le Saint Empire germanique aux XVIIe et XVIIIe siècles" (Paris 4-Sorbonne: 2003), for bringing this piece of information to my attention.

24. Parfaict and Parfaict, *Dictionnaire des théâtres de Paris*, 2:539.

25. Jean-Philippe Van Aelbrouck, *Dictionnaire des danseurs à Bruxelles de 1600 à 1830* (Liège: Mardaga, 1994).

26. Quesnot de la Chesnaye, *Parnasse belgique, ou portraits . . . may 1706*, Cologne, 1706. "La Sotte" and "l'Impudique" are quoted in Van Aelbrouck, *Dictionnaire des danseurs à Bruxelles*, 90 and 183.

27. Quoted in Van Aelbrouck, *Dictionnaire des danseurs à Bruxelles*, 112.

28. Parfaict and Parfaict, *Dictionnaire des théâtres de Paris*, 2:539.

29. This anecdote is reported by E. J. F. Barbier in *Journal historique et anecdotique du règne de Louis XV*, vol. 1 (Paris, 1847), 116–18.

30. Paul Colin, *Le comte de Charolais et la Dlle Delisle danseuse de l'Opéra* (Paris, 1895).

31. Charles de Bourbon (1700–60), comte de Charolais, was prince of the blood, being the son of Louis, Prince de Condé, and Mademoiselle de Nantes.

32. Barbier, *Journal historique et anecdotique*, vol. 1, 175.

33. Barbier, *Journal historique et anecdotique*, vol. 1, 174.

34. She was to marry the music composer François Rebel in 1733. On Prévost's personal life and on her daughter, see Régine Astier's article in this volume, "Françoise Prévost: The Unauthorized Biography."

35. About this young woman, who entered the Opera in 1740 under the name Mademoiselle d'Azincourt, see Campardon, *L'Académie Royale de Musique*, vol. 2, 11.

36. Archives nationales, Paris, France, minutier central XXVI-219 (18 March 1705) and AJ 13 1. About these two documents, see Jérôme de la Gorce, *L'Opéra au temps de Louis XIV* (Paris: Desjonquères, 1992), 127 and 159. One page of the 1713 record was reproduced in Marian Hannah Winter, *The Pre-Romantic Ballet* (London: Pitman Publishing, 1974), 69.

37. Nicolas Boindin, *Lettres historiques sur tous les spectacles de Paris* (Paris: Pierre Prault, 1719), 14.

38. About Mesdemoiselles Guyot, Prévost, and Subligny's careers, see Paige Whitley-Bauguess, "The Search for Mademoiselle Guyot," in *Proceedings of the Eleventh Annual Conference, Society of Dance History Scholars*, North Carolina School of the Arts, 12–14 February (Riverside, CA: Society of Dance History Scholars, 1988), 32–67; Régine Astier, "Prévost, Françoise" and "Subligny, Marie-Thérèse Perdou de" (two entries in the *International Dictionary of Ballet* [Detroit: St. James Press, 1993]); Régine Astier, "Françoise Prévost: The Unauthorized Biography," in the current volume; and Moira Goff, "Surprising Monsters: The First Female Professional Dancers, Terpsichore 1450–1900," in *Terpsichore 1450–1900*, Proceedings of the International Dance Conference, Ghent, Belgium, 11–18 April, ed. B. Ravelhofer (Ghent: Institute for Historical Dance Practice, 2000), 179–87.

39. Pierre Rameau, *Le Maître à danser* (Paris: Jean Villette, 1725), xiv–xvii.

40. *Mercure de France*, April 1722, 119.

41. Parfaict and Parfaict, *Dictionnaire des théâtres de Paris*, 3:55.

42. Before becoming prince of Monaco, Antoine de Grimaldi had lived a long time in Paris and had attended the Royal Academy of Music, where he could have been taken by Mademoiselle Guyot's talent.

43. André Tessier published Destouches's letter of 6 February 1724 in *La Revue Musicale* (1 December 1926): 110.

44. See Lancelot, *La Belle Dance*; Little Ellis and Marsh, *La Danse Noble*.

45. "Mademoiselle Menese [*sic*] who is almost always partnered by Marcel

in duets of a very special character . . . ," according to Rameau, *Le Maître à danser*, xvii.

46. It cannot be George Pécour, who was confined to the corps de ballet between 1706 and 1718 and never achieved major roles. Since Mademoiselle La Ferriere and Monsieur Pécour were listed in *entrées* prominently displayed in the cast of ballets, it apparently can only refer to the famous dancer and ballet master, Guillaume Louis Pécour.

47. See Francine Lancelot, *La Belle Dance;* Little Ellis and Marsh, *La Danse Noble.*

48. He, indeed, received fourteen livres on "every day of performance" and seven livres "when he was sick."

49. The Graces appear very often in the Opera prologues. (See figure 4.3.)

50. According to the Parfaict brothers, she was "the first to dance the role of Arlequine" (*Dictionnaire des théâtres de Paris*, 2:344), and she was "an excellent dancer especially as an Arlequine" ("Histoire de l'Académie Royale de Musique," fol. 86).

51. About the roles undertaken by these two dancers, see Whitley-Bauguess, "The Search for Mademoiselle Guyot;" and Astier, *Françoise Prévost.*

52. Rameau, *Le Maître à danser*, xvi–xvii.

5

Françoise Prévost:
The Unauthorized Biography

Régine Astier

To Wendy Hilton (1931–2002),
Francine Lancelot (1929–2003), and
Germaine Prudhommeau (1923–2007)

Among the first professional female dancers who entered the Paris
Opera at the end of the seventeenth century, Françoise Prévost stands
on a peak of her own, for she was not only a star dancer for three decades
but also a choreographer and a teacher of international reputation. (See
the appendix at the end of this article.) That such an eminent, multifarious, and accomplished talent appeared so early in the history of professional female dancing is quite startling, but that it left historians of the
performing arts mostly indifferent is beyond comprehension. While full-
length biographies of Prévost's famous students, Marie Sallé and Marie-
Anne Cupis de Camargo, are available today,[1] nothing is to be found regarding their mentor.

Françoise Prévost is visually known to us through a lovely portrait
painted by Jean Raoux.[2] (See figure 5.1.) She is represented as a bacchante, dancing lightly to the pipes of a faun. In one hand she clutches
a cluster of grapes and in the other she holds a shepherdess's wand.
Her features are classical: dark hair, a well-shaped brow, a straight if
longish nose, a small and smiling mouth. Her slender yet rounded body

Figure 5.1. Portrait of Françoise Prévost as a bacchante (1723). Jean Raoux, 1677–1734. Reprinted by permission of the Musée des Beaux-Arts de Tours.

is suggestively revealed through layers of billowing gauze. Her bare legs are laced up to her calves with the ribbons of her Roman sandals.

There is no pretense at realism here, neither in the costume so unlike those bacchante costumes designed by the Bérains for the Paris Opera or in the attitude and gestures of the dancing figure, which are those

conventionally represented in all neoclassical paintings of the time. The portrait is clearly allegorical, perhaps at the request of the sitter herself, who owned it and may have supervised its execution. If this was so, she would have been satisfied, for her spirit, if not her dance, is masterfully present in her portrait. The roles of bacchantes and shepherdesses were plentiful in ballets of this period; Prévost excelled in them, as she did in any role that called for vivacity, lightness, grace, and acting ability. Press reviews, spectators' comments, and fellow dancers' testimonies seemed unanimous on this point: Prévost was a charismatic performer with a strong and subtle ballet technique matched only by a supreme sense of theater. The Parisian dancing master Pierre Rameau, in translation by John Essex, expressed it best when recalling the many facets of her talent: "I wish it in my Power to pay that just Tribute of Praise her Merit calls for. In one single Dance of hers are contained all the Rules we are able to give on our Art, and she puts them in Practice with such Grace, Justness, and Activity that she may be looked on as a Prodigy in this kind. She justly deserves to be regarded as *Terpsichore* the Muse, whom the Ancients made to preside over Dancing, and has all the advantages of *Proteus* in the Fable. She, at Pleasure, assumes all manner of shapes . . . to enchant the Greedy Eyes of those that look on her, and to gain the Applause of every Body which excites a noble Emulation among the other Women Dancers."[3]

Indeed, Prévost's gift of expression through dance had turned her into something of a legend in her lifetime. Long after her death, she was still remembered with respect and gratitude. Marie Sallé, who early shared her vision and would continue her work, laid claim to her lineage in a poem: "You have taught me which ornament suits a shepherdess's bosom, which gesture pleases, which step conveys the most meaning."[4] In 1760 even the caustic Noverre flatly asserted, "Before Prévost, no other female dancer is worth mentioning."[5]

The Mémoire

The search for Mademoiselle Prévost began with the discovery in the Arsenal Library in Paris of Manuscript 3137, titled "Mémoire pour l'Ambassadeur de Malte contre Mademoiselle Prévost. Factum." This "Mémoire" was known through various sources and through the correspondence of the time, for when it circulated in Paris in 1726, it raised many chuckles among the populace and some eyebrows in the upper spheres. The attorney Mathieu Marais, commenting on its publication to a friend, had declared, "'The Maltese Mémoire' was equally dishonorable for both parties."[6] What lay behind the legal battle between the ambassador to Malta and the Opera dancer? Spurned love, and a life annuity of 6,000 livres, which Prévost was claiming from the ambassador as a presumed debt, made at the time of their amours. In 1726, the unfortunate ambassador had seen himself replaced in the dancer's favors and keenly resented the callousness of her demands. Françoise Prévost, on the other hand, was armed with a legal document that could not be so easily dismissed. Since the ambassador could not be brought to court in view of his immunity, the affair was turned over to the public, as was often the custom in the eighteenth century when a man's honor was at stake.[7]

The ambassador's plea begins with these words: "Without examining whether it is pitiful or humorous for an ambassador to have to deal with a lawsuit of this nature, I feel compelled to clarify its origins. On the one hand will be seen the weakness of a man of honor and good faith, and on the other the scheming and crafty dealings of the theater woman, an Opera dancer." [8] In support of his case, the ambassador to Malta candidly proceeded to recall in lavish details eighteen years of his companionship with the dancer.

The ambassador's misfortunes, as quoted and summarized below from the "Mémoire," will be nevertheless condensed to retain the story's emotional vigor. Pauses will be taken between landmarks in order to date events, identify the protagonists, and document the authenticity of the disclosures in light of archival records.

Prévost's Early Life

Born in Paris in 1681 of a Spanish mother, Prévost had been a theater urchin. Her father was employed at the Opera as a "Piqueur" of actors.[9] In their "Histoire de l'Académie Royale de Musique," the Parfaict brothers stated that "she had appeared so early on stage that the public, without thinking, kept the habit of calling her 'la petite Prévost' until her retirement,"[10] at which time she was almost fifty years old. She may have studied dance under a Parisian master named Thibaud[11] —a piece of unexpected information found in Président Hénault's *Mémoires* in the chapter describing his education at the Jesuits: "I had learnt to dance from someone named Thibaud; he was asthmatic and looked more like a writing teacher than a dancing master. I only mention his name because he had taught 'la Prévost,' this daughter of the dance, proof enough that great talents have no need of masters."[12]

In October 1695 "La petite Prévost" is listed for the first time in the *Ballet des Saisons* with Mademoiselle Dangeville and the Sieurs Bouteville, Lestang, and Dumirail. Her name will not appear again until 1699 in Lully's opera *Atys*. Unfortunately for us, the 1690s are years when surviving ballet programs seldom list the dancers' names, and it is not possible to retrace Prévost's earliest career steps with absolute accuracy. She may have remained an apprentice or an understudy for several years, since new performers were usually tried out before being admitted officially in the Opera troupe. This was most likely Prévost's status in the late 1690s in view of her young age. From 1700 onward she was on fairly regular call and even occasionally featured in *entrées*. All the same, we are surprised to find her name on the 1704 payroll with one of the lowest annual salaries (400 livres), a wage usually reserved to choristers and third roles.[13] It will take her ten years to move up to the very top of the hierarchy, where she shared the lead with a new dashing and outstanding technician, Marie-Catherine Guyot. No fewer than five duets with this dancer, choreographed by Louis Pécour and recorded by Michel Gaudrau, have survived in the Feuillet notation system (see figure 5.2).

It was in those early years of her ascendency that Monsieur le Chevalier de Mesme, not yet ambassador, remembered noticing the dancer

---

Canarye dancée par Mlle. Provost et Mlle. Guiot au *Triomphe de lamour* (43–45).

Entrée de deux dancée par Mlle. Provost et Mlle. Guiot a l'opera d'yssée (51–56).

La Muszette a deux dancée par Mlle. Provost et Mlle. Guiot a l'opera de callirhoé (57–60).

Entrée de deux Bacchante dancée par Mlle. Provost et Mlle. Guiot a l'opera de Philomèle (61–63).

Entrée de deux femme dancée par Mlle. Provost et Mlle. Guiot au festevenitienne (64–66).

Source: Michel Gaudrau. *Nouveau Recueil de Dance de bal et celle de ballet contenant un très grand nombres des meillieures* Entrees de Ballet *de la composition de Mr. Pécour tant pour hommes que pour femmes qui ont été dancées a l'Opera ouvrage très utile aux Maitres et à toutes les personnes qui s'apliquent à la Dance.* Par Mr. Gaudrau Me. de Dance et de l'academie Royalle de Musique. A Paris: Chez le Sieur Gaudrau Ruede Seine aucoint de la rue ducolombier faubour St. Germain et Pierre Ribou Libraire au bout du pont neuf. Avec Privilege du Roy (ca. 1713).

Figure 5.2. Dances for Françoise Prévost recorded by Michel Gaudrau.

for the first time, confessing in the "Mémoire" to have found her "graceful and engaging." He went on to write:

The dancer, still young, already liked men who thought the way he did. She met the Chevalier and fell for him, but she lived with her parents and their living conditions at first disheartened the aspiring lover. He found the family in a high and obscure chamber barely furnished with a *Bergame* hanging[14] and four chairs upholstered in tapestry, the whole quite proper and clean nevertheless. The beloved object of the Chevalier's affection, who did not expect his visit was caught in her domestic state: this was not a néréide from Neptune's court, laden with all the sea bounty, this was not Flora, Zephyr's lover, adorned with colorful spring flowers, this was Fanchonnette,[15] dressed in striped calmande,[16] coiffed with a dirty nightcap trimmed with a rose-colored ribbon, grubbier still. Her face was unmasked, her neck and chest were bare, revealing a sallow complexion and prominent muscles. Fanchonnette stood thus, by a small fireplace, busy reviving ashes and a dying candle.

The Chevalier was startled, speechless, and found the scene embarrassing. The visit was abrupt, and after the customary civilities paid to the parents and the girl, he scuttled away, ashamed of his enterprise and resolved to avoid similar misadventures in the future.

This was to ignore the power of talent and the spell of the theater. A few days later he returned to the Opera and saw Fanchonnette metamorphosed into a shepherdess, dancing a pas de deux with the Sieur Balon,[17] and it was but charming coyness, seductive glances and a variety of postures constantly renewed and arresting. The public's ovation stirred the Chevalier's emotions anew. He went back to every performance and Fanchonnette became his obsession. . . . He loved her as a nymph, he adored her as a shepherdess, and exhausted through her the craving he had for novelty. He reproached himself for having missed his first chance and solicited another rendezvous, which met with a refusal. Fanchonnette, he learnt, had a lover who took immediate measures to secure his territory. This closed door was a cruel blow. The tormented Chevalier grew feverish, looked for expedients. His love was born in the middle of this confusion. He strove so well that he finally succeeded in obtaining a rendezvous in a dark alley of the Palais Royal.[18] The Chevalier's raptures of joy were not to be believed and defied all description. The bargain that was reached in the end was that he would take second place. He would be told when to visit and when to fill in when lover number one was absent, he would also pay the bills incurred at taverns and restaurants. This being settled, the lovers took immediate possession of each other that very night. Fanchonnette got drunk as well as her mother and was in high spirits. The infatuated young man found her eyes tender, her teeth beautiful, and her skin soft to the touch. He spent the night basking in the delights of his good fortune, and that night was followed by others, all equally passionate.

At the time, Fanchonnette was always impatiently waiting for the days when she was to perform at the Opera as if she was eager to keep alive the fantasies so dear to her lover. Fanchonnette "was dancing without pause" and the Chevalier grew more and more enamored.

Years passed by in this way, until fate finally disposed of lover number 1 and even of both parents. The Chevalier was at last free to take entire possession of his mistress. At this time, he also received large church benefits and was elevated to the dignity of Bailli and ambassador to Malta.[19] His concubine conceived considerable pride and requested to be (exclusively) addressed by her father's name, Demoiselle Prévost.[20] She requested a fully appointed apartment with cellar and kitchen, all manners of furniture, clothes for all seasons, not to mention a well-provided table. No sooner than her desires were known they were met. Her dressers filled up with china, her wardrobe with gowns, and the ambassador delighted in hiding all kinds of jewelry in her drawers. Their household soon grew very respectable. The two lovers took pleasure in entertaining equally well a most varied company: people of rank, gentlemen of the law or the army, hairdressers, dressmakers, chorus girls from the Opera, and the Demoiselle Prévost's former friends and relatives. They all spoke to her with respect, smothered her with care, and their conversation ran mostly on the dancer's charisma and talent.

The ambassador spent his life in this most delightful and peaceful manner. He blessed the day he had met this faithful mistress whom he adored and who showed him nothing but gratification and affection.

I have quoted the original text at great length because these keyhole vignettes of Françoise Prévost's domestic life are precious and introspection of this quality unheard of in a genre traditionally given to lampoons and satires. Of particular interest to us is Prévost's psychological portrait revealed in filigree through the description of her circumstances. At twenty-five, the dancer is still called Fanchonnette and lives with her parents despite the legal freedom she had acquired as a member of the Opera.[21] Looming large behind her stands her mother, who presides over the first rendezvous and with whom the Chevalier's preliminary transactions would have obviously taken place. We note that Prévost needs a few drinks before fulfilling her contract and that she was to remain faithful to her class, her old friends, and relatives during her social elevation. Above all, we retain that she "was always impatient to perform," that she "never stopped dancing," and even "danced more and more." Could Monsieur l'Ambassadeur have failed to see that his mistress's first and dominant passion was clearly the dance?

An Ascending Career

Indeed, Prévost's career was soaring at this point, and these years of peaceful companionship with the ambassador coincided exactly with her peak achievements. From 1704 to 1714 where we left the story, she appeared each year in four or five new Opera productions. The ethnic roles that often fell to her suited her southern physique and elusive sensual style. She was in turn Moorish, Greek, Egyptian, Spanish, Ethiopian, and would, on occasions, symbolically represent America (understand South America) and even Africa. The growing success met in these exotic roles, which requested that she be different, may have led her to imagine moods, define types, and search for specific indigenous traits. She had the good fortune to have rapidly found a collaborator willing to join her in this exploration. At the onset of her career she had met the *Violon du Roi* Jean-Féry Rebel, who was first hired in this capacity by the Opera between 1695 and 1700, then as its harpsichordist (ca. 1704), and finally as its conductor (1714). Musicologist Vladia Kunzmann suggested in her study on Rebel[22] that it was Prévost who inspired the musician to turn his attention to the composition of pieces suitable for the dance. With the dancer in mind, he composed *Caprice* in 1711, *Boutade* in 1712, *Les Caractères de la danse* in 1715, and *Terpsichore* in 1720. It was these little dance numbers, arranged in suites, that would bring him and Prévost fame and recognition.

As a musical form, the *Caprice* is described by Jean-Jacques Rousseau as "a sort of free piece . . . not bound to any particular subject and one which gives the composer full freedom of imagination and impetus."[23] Kunzmann describes the structure of Rebel's *Caprice* as "similar to that of the Chaconne and Passacaille" but "in duple time" and "containing the only marking of the pieces, *Gay*."[24] Interestingly, *chaconnes* and *passacailles* were part of the Spanish dance repertory and as such were considered theatrical *danses d'expression*.[25] As a dance form, the *Caprice* itself was defined as a free-form composition close to improvisation. Louis Bonin described "this blending of invention called *Caprice* in dancing as

> *Dance du Caprice* (solo). Music: Jean-Féry Rebel. 1712.
> *Les Horaces* in *Apollon et les Muses* (duet and collaboration with Claude Balon).
>   Music: Jean-Joseph Mouret. 1714.
> *Les Caractères de la Danse* (solo). Music: Jean-Féry Rebel. 1715.
> *Terpsichore* (solo). Music: Jean-Féry Rebel. 1720.
>
> *Note:* Françoise Prévost, as a *premier sujet*, had the privilege and option to compose all her *entrées* if she wished, and she also composed her pupils' whenever necessary.

Figure 5.3. Françoise Prévost's choreography.

nothing more than an alteration of that which one has learnt, such as one embellishes, expands, diminishes, takes from and adds to, and binds oneself to no fixed step but rather chooses what is most suitable, and in doing so, betrays no affectation, the desired embellishment appearing not tiresome or meaningless but clever."[26]

This flexibility of music and dance was particularly suited to Prévost's freer style, which mainly rested on instinct. She immediately turned Rebel's *Caprice* into a showpiece for her unique talent. In 1724 Jacques Bonnet testified that "one only has to see . . . the *Caprice* danced by Mademoiselle Prévost to conclude that theatrical dance cannot go further in its perfection."[27] Indeed, her personal way of investing steps with meaning would remain a reference point for female soloists throughout the eighteenth century.[28]

The rewards were quick to follow. In August 1711, Prévost was officially promoted to the rank of *premier sujet* with a salary raised to 1,200 livres. In this unpublished legal document the Opera administrator Pierre Guynemet further promised an annuity of 800 livres to be levied on the profits incurred by the Royal Academy of Music and to be paid in twelve even sums "from the moment the Dlle. Prévost is no longer able to dance at the Opera or give satisfaction to the Sieur Guynemet and/or to the public." She was nevertheless required to serve at least three more years.[29] A bright and secure future was in the offing. The dancer's destiny now rested in her own hands.

There is no record of Prévost having choreographed or danced the *Boutade,* but it is likely that the huge success met with by *Caprice* led her to follow up with a similar piece one year later. The *boutade* as defined by Rousseau was "an ancient form of playful little ballet which was or pretended to be impromptu"[30]—a definition endorsed by dance theoretician Michel de Pure who further noted that "skill and beauty of execution are all that are required in this informal and imaginative genre."[31] This miniature ballet of four solo *entrées* would have been the logical step leading up to Rebel's more extensive composition, *Les Caractères de la danse*, which gathered the best known dance types into a single suite destined to show off the versatility of Prévost's faceted talent. We do not know when the dancer presented this suite at the Opera for the first time since the official source of information, the *Mercure*, only began to spotlight performers in 1721. A fair guess is the year 1714, since the musical score went to print the year after, and the piece would have been shown during one of the galas that annually marked the beginning of the spring season, a new production, or a benefit performance. On these festive occasions, Opera fans would flock to see the newest *divertissements* sung and/or danced by their favorite *premiers sujets*.

With *Les Caractères de la danse* Rebel may not have thought beyond providing the *prima ballerina* with a worthy vehicle suitable for such light entertainment. He may have found inspiration in those delightful little ballroom suites of two or three contrasting dance movements that were so prized by connoisseurs and gifted court dancers alike. One by one, twelve fragments of the most popular dance types were strung like colorful beads to be finally clasped in the two halves of a rousing, if unexpected, sonata. Such a bravura piece was bound to set the dancer Prévost on fire. But the choreographer in her saw beyond the sheer display of technique, however compelling and brilliant. She sensed the dramatic impact that such a wide diversity of rhythms would provide if tied to one interpretative theme, and she came to center her composition on a subject of universal appeal, one which she knew only too well: love, in all its disguises. The dance movements of Rebel's suite were thus personified and made to express the whole gamut of love emotions from a young girl's first stirrings and commotion to the extravagances of an old fool, lost in his delusions. The dancer's metamorphoses, from female to male, young to old, melancholic to euphoric, were so masterfully and vividly carried out that the public was left spellbound and forever associated this piece with her. She was to perform it many times at the Opera, at private parties, and at court entertainments where important guests had requested it. In time, she entrusted this popular number to her students, the Mademoiselles Richalet, Camargo, and Sallé, who each added her personal touch. Indeed it soon became customary for aspiring ballerinas to make their debuts in that suite.[32]

After the unprecedented success met in *Les Caractères de la danse,* Françoise Prévost was universally seen as the muse of dance, a role that prompted Rebel to write a new piece for her, fittingly called *Terpsichore.* We understand from the dedication of his score to Mrs. Law—the wife of the Scottish financier John Law—that the lady had commissioned the piece out of deep admiration for the dancer and had in mind a composition similar to *Les Caractères de la danse.* Was Rebel's new piece less appealing?—Prévost's performance less convincing? We are left to wonder over the absence of comments on *Terpsichore* from either the press or individuals.

These busy and productive years brought Françoise Prévost such celebrity in France and abroad that she may be forgiven for continuing to "play at being Queen" at home—as her lover had ironically pointed out. This lover may have possibly felt that part of her success was due to him. At this point, it is imperative to return to "Monsieur l'Ambassadeur."

The Ambassador

Jean-Jacques de Mesmes was the third son of an important magistrate who had held the highest government functions, among which were that of state counselor and president of the Parliament. These functions were now filled by his eldest son, Jean-Antoine III, who was further elected to the supreme position of *premier président* in 1712. The family was typical of well-to-do households of the Ancien Régime: the second son, Henri, was a rich abbot, one daughter had married a marquis (de Fontenilles), the other had taken vows in a convent. The youngest son, our Jean-Jacques, born in 1674, was nothing much for a long time.

This is how the historiographer Saint-Simon remembers him in 1714: "He was a man of poor intellect and appearance, curiously dissolute, a spendthrift, altogether a rather obscure character who was in many ways a disgrace to his position which he almost lost on several occasions."[33] Such was the man Françoise Prévost professed to love and accepted as her protector.

Jean-Jacques de Mesmes was nominated ambassador to Malta in 1714 at the request, not to say orders, of Louis XIV. Without entering deeply into the political reasons behind this appointment, it must be remembered that the de Mesmes were major pawns on the chessboard of

Louis's succession, which favored the duc du Maine, an illegitimate son by Madame de Montespan, over the rightful heir, the duc d'Orleans. It was imperative to obtain the Parliament's approval in case of legal dispute, hence Louis's eagerness to dispense honors on the de Mesmes so as "to please Monsieur le Premier Président."[34] By the same token, the duc du Maine and his wife, Louise de Bourbon Condé, had every interest in opening wide the roads of privileged friendship that led triumphantly to Sceaux. Since 1703 they had established residence in the former and magnificent castle belonging to Colbert outside Paris. In an attempt to revive Versailles's former luster, the enterprising and ambitious duchesse du Maine was holding at Sceaux a court that all but replaced that of the dying king. Her renowned concerts and theatricals, in which she often performed, brilliantly met the challenge. They set the tone by encouraging novelty and embraced the carefree spirit of a transitional age soon to be called the *Régence*. An invitation to the *Grandes Nuits de Sceaux*, where all European intelligentsia was present and the most prestigious performers were showcased, was for many grandees a longed-for dream. Not so for the Demoiselle Prévost who, in the privileged wake of the de Mesmes and as a celebrated star in her own right, found her rightful place at Sceaux, that is to say, spotlighted and center stage. It is at Sceaux that she was to leave her indelible mark on the history of Western dance.

The play chosen in 1714 to mark the fourteenth year of the duchesse du Maine's *divertissements* was Pierre Corneille's *Horace*, with its customary *intermèdes dansés*. In the second of these interludes Apollo presented the duchesse with a *danse caractérisée* performed by Camille and Horace armed with a dagger.[35] At the end of act 4, when young Horace kills Camille, Françoise Prévost and her partner Claude Balon, who were cast in the scene, imagined a tableau staged as a pantomine to music by resident composer Jean-Joseph Mouret, and they so sincerely entered the pathos and grandeur of the action that they shed real tears during the performance, soon to be joined by the spectators. This unforeseen popular success would reorient dance in the coming decades toward that novel concept: the *danse d'action*. Marie Sallé was first to embrace this departure from tradition,[36] which the Opera only accepted thirty years later when Jean-Georges Noverre, claiming the genre as his own, staged his *pantomines héroiques* in full-scale productions.[37] The seed had been planted when a daring Prévost, trusting in her intuition, had proved to a receptive public that dramatic theater could find a powerful expression in the dance.

Much of her inspiration could have been drawn from the emotional roller coaster she was living at home, where a major domestic crisis had erupted.

The ambassador had been called away on duty to Versailles for a few days. Prévost had been fretting over his absence, making him promise to write every day and to acquaint her with the moment of his return. According to the ambassador's account, he had complied with the first request but failed to heed the second: "a surprise visit to a mistress one longs to see is so blissful!" He chose the middle of the night for his enterprise, but the surprise turned sour. The beloved one was found in bed with an Opera colleague.

She was quick at regaining composure and presence of mind. While the colleague vanished clutching his clothes, she pleaded her cause with astonishing aplomb:

> For years now, she had been uneasy about her state of concubine. In a recent dream, her Spanish mother had returned from the grave to reproach her with this sinful liaison. "How can you be involved with a man who cannot be your husband," the mother had said. "What will happen to you if he decides to leave you? Do you have any property?— enough money to sustain you in your present condition? It makes no sense to be so exclusively devoted to this man and to be so determined in loving none but him." Torn with guilt, she had yielded to a marriage of convenience with the man he had just seen. . . . She was relieved that the truth was known since she could now bring her marriage into the open.

Imagine poor Jean-Jacques's reaction at this disclosure. "He was soon in tears, on his knees, begging for this marriage to be severed at once. He would make up for his wrongdoings by immediately setting up a life annuity of 6,000 livres that would financially secure her future."

The crisis was averted, since the Opera actor had not totally finalized the marriage. Life soon returned to normal and the ambassador sighed a deep sigh of relief.

The second domestic affair, which came three years later, had far more lasting consequences. As the ambassador recalled, much of his life was now taken up by his functions so that his mistress "was no longer his unique passion."

She was getting older and prone to replace her former long rides in the park for card games held in the kinder dusk of her drawing room. She now spent much time studying her face for blemishes, which no amount of white, rouge, or patches could conceal. Her male admirers seemed oblivious of these changes for they were educated men, keen on talent, fond of fantasy, and with an imagination easily fired by the dancer's soft abandon in a sarabande or her saucy perkiness in a tambourin. They never stopped seeing the performer in her, even while playing cards. "This nymph is mine," they thought, "she draws all the hearts to her but only cares for mine." The ambassador tolerated these admirers but took umbrage at the costly presents of diamonds and snuffboxes that did not come from him. He finally banned from his mistress's home some of these embarrassing benefactors. Coercion called for defiance: the mistress ran away to the country with one of these lovers.

On discovering the empty nest, the ambassador felt like Orlando Furioso after the flight of Médor and Angélique.[38] His anger knew no bounds. Nothing was spared in the premises, which were torn to pieces: tapestries, mirrors, paintings, and the mistress's own portrait were knocked over. But Opera heroines seldom have to deal with the harsher realities of a dancer's career. The quietness of country life has its limited charm and money ran out. Angélique began to miss certain commodities that only Orlando could provide. She resolved to return to him, a penitent, and was once more reinstated on the solemn promise that she would never again attempt to see Médor. She had promised, and selflessly deciding to match Orlando's generosity by a sacrifice of equal magnitude, she had become pregnant. A "little Auguste" was prematurely born seven months later and presented to an ecstatic father. Domestic bliss was complete; the past was forgotten. A country house was bought for 'little Auguste' in Pantin and another one for the mother with views over the Palais-Royal gardens. The most luxurious furnishing made its daily appearance there: paintings, bronzes, japanware and furniture for all seasons. One by one the old friends began to reappear and so did the presents: a Persian hanging, the bacchante painting, Chinese flowerpots, clocks, and harpsichords. Every trinket found its place, from medals to jars of cherries preserved in brandy.

Let us pause a moment to state the true position. In this episode, a major event takes place: the birth of Prévost's illegitimate daughter confirmed by a certificate found in family papers, which will be examined later. On the first of January 1718, Anne-Auguste was declared of "unknown parents" and baptized in Saint-Roch church without a family name.[39] Prévost was thirty-seven years old at the time and the ambassador forty-four. Seven more years were to elapse before the outburst of yet another storm.

Professional Apex

We have arrived at 1726, a major date that signals the end of an era in Françoise Prévost's life. Professionally, she is at the apex of her power and the undisputed star of the Paris Opera. In the growing absence of an aging and sick Pécour, it can be guessed that she took on her share of the directorship assumed by senior *premier danseur* Michel Blondy. As a performer, she has no rival. The second *première danseuse*, Marie-Catherine Guyot, "had been forced to retire" in 1722, "due to her weight, which prevented her from performing with the same agility."[40] Nevertheless, Prévost's triumphs were behind her. She now made cameo appearances at the end of ballets or at fund-raising galas, which she contrived to spice up with fresh talents picked in her seraglio. Ahead of her were four years before retirement, enough time to implement a change of guard that would ensure her legacy. On 29 April she had once more performed her signature piece *Les Caractères de la danse* alongside the cluster of stars who were featured at the reopening of the theater. On 5 May she proudly "unveiled" her prized student, Mademoiselle Camargo, "a dancer from the Brussels Opera who had not been previously seen here" but whom she had coached since childhood. She had entrusted her with the now famous suite by Rebel, which the zealous protégée had "danced with all the liveliness and intelligence that could possibly be expected from a young person of fifteen or sixteen years old. Her *cabrioles* and *entrechats* were effortless and although she has still many perfections to acquire before she can venture comparison with her illustrious teacher, she is considered one of the most brilliant dancers to be seen on account of her strength, musicality and airborn quality."[41] This encouraging success prompted the teacher to reschedule the dancer in the same challenging piece two years in a row. Unwittingly, she had opened Pandora's box. In November 1728, the great actress Adrienne Lecouvreur reported to a friend: "Yesterday they played *Roland* by Quinault and Lulli. Although Mademoiselle Prévost surpassed herself, she obtained meagre applause in comparison with a new dancer named Camargo whom the public idolizes and whose great merit is her youth and vigor. You may not have seen her. Mademoiselle Prévost at first protected her but (premier danseur) Blondi [Blondy] has fallen in love with her and the lady is piqued. She seemed jealous and unhappy at the applause Camargo received from the public. . . . The clapping gets so extreme that Prévost will be foolish if she does not decide to retire."[42]

This was indeed unexpected, but to imagine that the senior Opera star would stand to be upstaged by a novice thirty years her junior, whom she had just brought out of the corps, was both laughable and preposterous! This was to forget that she reigned supreme over *Les filles du Magasin*.[43] In record time a tearful Camargo was summoned to rejoin the ranks and to look elsewhere for the composition and rehearsals of her *entrées*.[44] Fortunately for Prévost, there was yet another trump card in her hand. In April 1727, a beaming young Sallé was returning home after two glorious years spent in London at the Lincoln's Inn Fields Theater. Her last benefit performance had once more featured Rebel's *Les Caractères de la danse*.[45] On 14 September, and most likely with a push from Prévost, Sallé made her debut at the Paris Opera in the heroic ballet, *Les Amours des Dieux*. The *Mercure* reported: "The Dlle. Sallé, a young and greatly acclaimed dancer from the English court, danced in the *Fête* with the Sieur Dumoulin in replacement of Mademoiselle Prévost who was indisposed but will soon be back. The public liked her very much."[46] In the following revival of *Roland*, both Prévost and young Sallé were featured in their first duet. Was it complete coincidence that the closing number of the *première danseuse*'s farewell performance, in February 1730, would be a last pas de deux with her beloved and former student? In this formal public enthronement of Marie Sallé, Françoise Prévost had not only designated her successor but also reiterated her unconditional support to the reforms that the young dancer was about to propose.

Private Roller Coaster

On the private front, 1726 was equally decisive. Prévost, the "Mémoire" asserted, "was less and less careful at hiding her affairs" and was again caught in the act during one of the ambassador's untimely visits. To make matters worse, she was found dallying with Médor whom she had sworn never to see again some eight years earlier. This time, the weary ambassador beat a retreat and consented to surrender. He would leave, taking with him his property and his daughter. Once more Prévost

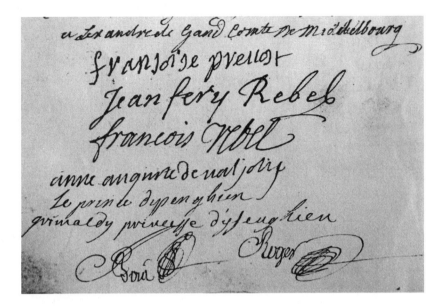

Figure 5.4. Signatures of Françoise Prévost, Alexandre de Gand, Jean-Féry Rebel, François Rebel, and Anne-Auguste de Valjoly on marriage document (1733).

moved up the line with this declaration: "I cannot satisfy you on the last two points. You are here in my house; I am here the sole mistress. Everything you see is mine. As an Opera dancer I depend on no one. As for taking Anne-Auguste away from me, this won't be either, for the child is not yours. Remember that I was seven months pregnant when she was born—seven months pregnant by you and nine months by this man. *He* is the real father."

Jean-Jacques de Mesmes was thunderstruck. "Enough has been said," he replied. "I am confounded by such horror." This was the end of the affair and I am sparing you the vituperations that followed his exit; they ended with the ambassador's deep regret at not having left the Demoiselle Prévost when she was Fanchonnette, in the chamber with the *Bergame* hanging.

The time has come to bring out the legal papers found in Parisian archives and to identify the faithful Médor found twice at the heart of the story. On 14 February 1726, Saint Valentine's Day, the Demoiselle Prévost and Alexander Maximilien Balthazar de Gand, Count of Middelbourg, a brigadier in the kings' armies, colonel in his marine and governor of Bouchain, were legally recognizing their daughter, the eight-year-old Anne-Auguste de Valjoly, named after a land in Hainaud, a settlement present from the count.[47] What happened to Prévost's liaison with the count may be some day found in another "Mémoire." What happened to Anne-Auguste de Valjoly is a bittersweet story typical of the times. In July 1733, in the presence of her parents, she was married to no less than François Rebel, Jean-Féry's son, who would achieve enormous fame a decade later as music director of the Paris Opera. (See figure 5.4.) The Count of Middelbourg gave his daughter a huge dowry of 30,000 livres. Prévost gave her a 2,000-livre annuity with the promise of 10,000 livres taken on her succession. François Rebel gave his fifteen-year-old bride a further 1,200-livre annual income. The young couple was to receive larger donations in the following years.[48] This marriage sealed the warm, lasting, and unique relationship between Françoise Prévost and Jean-Féry Rebel.

Epilogue

An appendix to the Factum included Françoise Prévost's reply to the ambassador: short, dignified, and not devoid of humor. She remained focused on her financial claim. The sum of 6,000 livres, she explained, was not a generous donation from the ambassador, but a debt that he had contracted from her when faced with the great expenses occasioned by his embassy appointment. She would not comment on the rest of the "Mémoire," knowing that the ambassador was angry, and that an angry man's words are not often judicious. To begin with, how could *Monsieur l'ambassadeur* have fallen in love with the kind of woman he describes? How could he have settled anything on such a woman? The public, she felt sure, would not be duped, for the story makes no sense. Françoise Prévost spoke the truth, as two legal documents attest. In a handwritten note co-signed by the dancer's lawyer, Jean-Jacques de Mesmes clearly stated having borrowed up to 60,000 livres from his companion—a considerable sum, which he confessed he was unable to repay. On 22 November 1725 a settlement was reached by which Prévost accepted a 6,000-livre annuity for the rest of her life.[49] So much for the "man of honor and good faith."

As for the Count of Middelbourg, barely one month after his daughter's wedding, he himself married Mademoiselle de la Rochefoucault, also fifteen, and "as beautiful as the light of day ... but her husband is about to return to his regiment, and tears will soon follow laughter."[50] The Count had settled down.

On 15 May 1737 Françoise Prévost's daughter suddenly died, leaving two small children, a two-year-old son, Alexandre Camille, and an eight-month-old daughter, Louise Henriette. She was not yet twenty. These unhappy and painful circumstances led Prévost to rethink her financial future and that of her grandchildren. On 6 March and 20 April 1738 she transferred to her grandchildren the part of her succession promised in her daughter's dowry. When she made her will on 12 March 1740 no further mention of them was necessary.[51] The lawyer's clerk who took down her deposition described her as an "invalid but sound of mind, memory and judgment" and found her "sitting in her armchair in a bedroom overlooking gardens." Françoise Prévost declared having been born in Paris and wanting to leave her estate to "the only relative she had in France," her first cousin, Jeanne Prévost, daughter of a bookbinder on Rue Saint Jacques. She further mentioned one brother who had settled in Spain with his children after having served in the Spanish king's army. It seemed that he was not eligible to his sister's succession, possibly on account of his foreign residency. The dancer had retired from the Opera in 1730 with a 1,000-livre pension, as befitted her position of *premier sujet*. The *Mercure,* which had *regretfully* related the event, stated, "the public would not easily forget a performer known for the grace and lightness of her dancing, who had received so much applause and given the public so much pleasure."[52] Indeed, to be forgotten had not been an option, and for the time being, her legacy seemed in good hands.

Françoise Prévost died on 30 September 1741, at age sixty, a bare few months after Jean-Jacques de Mesmes.[53] She left the best of her wardrobe to her friend Geneviève Giroux, who shared her house on Rue Cassette, and some money to her female cook and her male domestic servant. She also donated her precious damask hangings to Les Carmes Déchaussés, the church next door, in whose Saint Theresa chapel she requested to be buried. She gave one of her portraits, painted by Raoux, to her lawyer Roger. A broad inventory of her belongings was made in the following days when seals were affixed to the premises. A more complete inventory was made in October 1741. Both indicated a comfortable if not rich household.[54]

The story that has been told may have a familiar ring to dance specialists of the eighteenth century. Substitute the name of Prévost for that

of Desmâtins, Dufort, Ménés, Camargo, Guimard, and many others
who did not rise to such professional fame, and the difference will be of
degree, not substance. Many of these performers were acknowledged
courtesans who used their celebrity status to further their lot as women
artists. In this they were encouraged by the Opera privileges, which
emancipated them from the custody of family and spouses and protected them from police harassment, deportation, or imprisonment. In
matters of justice, they were under royal protection. Indeed, the status
of concubine was so well accepted at the Opera that a register of female
dancers listed their names with that of their protectors.[55] It was generally thought that any self-respecting female Opera performer must have
at least three lovers: one for prestige, one for money, and one for love —
often a colleague whom they could ultimately marry. For those who did
not fit the pattern — Mademoiselles Subligny and Sallé come to mind —
they were called "prudes," or "Vestales," and "the critics were per-
plexed": could they perhaps have a leaning toward their own sex?[56]

This being said, did these theater women have a choice in a patriarchal society that barred them from official positions?[57] The recruit-
ment and management of performers at the Royal Academy of Music
(l'Opéra) give a partial answer. The *Opera Statutes* approved by Louis
XIV in 1713 stipulated that "actors, actresses, dancers and members of
the Orchestra must have demonstrated their performing skill and received public approbation before being eligible for admission to the
Opera."[58] In pragmatic terms, this rule translated itself into "backstairs
influence." It was tacitly understood that a distinguished sponsor should
open the stage door for you. When relating their *encataloging*[59] at the
Opera, female dancers began their story by naming their patron, usually a titled man (sometimes a woman) or a known professional working
there. Invariably, they proceeded to recall the favors that were exacted
from them before the presentation. Take the example of Michel Blondy's
illegitimate daughter, known as Mademoiselle Dazincourt, who was an
apprentice seamstress: "I often looked at myself in the mirror and felt
that, with my figure, I could one day better my fortune, so that the idea
of entering the Opera came to me as a place where this could be done
more easily and faster. I talked to [famous Opera dancer] M. Javillier
who liked me very much and agreed to give me daily lessons and to pay
my pension. I gave him such proofs of gratitude that I became pregnant
and gave birth to a boy. M. Javillier did not have the means to support
me once I entered the Opera and he cleared the way for the duc de
Bouteville."[60]

Added to the initial difficulty of being admitted was the performers' insecure position once they were. A privately owned manuscript[61] described the daily life of female Opera singers at the turn of the eighteenth century and stressed the fragility of these official engagements: "Their [these women's] fate depends on the one man who reigns as an absolute monarch over the Opera [the Director],[62] one who decides on whims their wages, whether low or high, and who stands above control or supervision. They are devoted to him like slaves in their constant fear of losing their position. . . . They have no certification [*brevet*] and no contract and can be dismissed without compensation for the slightest reason."

These comments have a ring of truth and point to abuses that can more easily develop within a privately owned institution constantly battling for its financial survival. Salaries could be renegotiated with each change of directorship. Dancers were paid less than singers and female dancers less than their male counterparts. Yet to live up to the Opera's prestigious reputation, expenses could be considerable. The writer quoted above observed that "some women receive 400 livres, some 500 livres, and the very few at the top 1,000 livres, but what are these [sums] compared to what they must spend in decent clothes, linen, ribbons, accessories, shawls, trinkets, banquets, games, receptions, illnesses, medication, and rents in one of the most expensive districts of Paris."[63]

Many dancers rarely looked beyond the stage for their well-being and tended to be improvident. By the same token, responsible institutions were reluctant to step into such private territory. The Paris Opera was in this respect ahead of its time. A clause in the *Statutes* provided all dancers who had completed fifteen years minimum of "continuous services" with a pension amounting to half their latest salaries. The *premiers sujets* automatically received 1,000 livres.[64] Far from all dancers fulfilled these conditions. Then, as now, they faced accidents, disability, illnesses, and pregnancies. Compensation was not provided for those who were forced to leave.

Common sense dictated making good use of the prime exposure offered by a prestigious stage while it lasted. For a female dancer of humble origins who had nothing to lose, the road to bettering her present, and possibly her future, passed of necessity through much backstage and dubious bargaining.

That Françoise Prévost was such a woman there is no doubt. She steered her course in this unfavorable context with intelligence, energy, and conviction, and we sense that she enjoyed the journey. But let us muse for a moment. Prévost was amply qualified to replace Guillaume Louis Pécour at the head of the Opera. What if she had succeeded him in 1729? Would the course of dance history be utterly modified? Would her work, like Pécour's, have been saved, allowing for study and comparison? Would Marie Sallé have left the Opera so many times, done her pioneering work abroad, retired so early?

But Françoise Prévost's dances were to remain buried in her legend, where they exude a mysterious perfume that continues to captivate choreographers across continents and centuries. This was her legacy.

APPENDIX: FRANÇOISE PRÉVOST'S ROLES AND APPEARANCES

All performances were given at the Paris Opera, unless otherwise indicated.

1695   **Ballet des Saisons**. Music: Louis Lully and Collasse.
        Dancer with Mlle. Dangeville, the Sieurs Bouteville, Lestang and Dumirail.
1699   **Atys**. Trag. Op. Revival. Music: J. B. Lully.
        Ruisseaux [brooks, streams]: Sieurs De Ruel and Claude, and la Petite Prévost.
1700   **Ballet des Saisons**. Revival. Music: Louis Lully/Collasse.
        3ème entrée: Céphise.
        Ballet: Une petite Vendangeuse.
1701   **Aréthuse**. Ballet. Music: Campra.
        Une Petite Jardinière: La petite Prévost.
        Mlle. Prévost was not listed in the major productions of *Amadis de Grèce* and *Scylla*.
1702   **Médus Roi des Mèdes**. Trag. Op. Music: Bouvard.
        Ballet: Berger(e). La Petite Prévost and le Petit Grandval.
        Omphale. Trag. Op. Music: Destouches. A Trianon, devant le Roi.
        Mlle. Prévost was not in the November 1701 performance but was in the February 1702 revival where a third act was added.
        Acte 3. Grecs: La petite Prévost (duet).
        Fragments de M. de Lully. Ballet. Music: Campra.
        Dans Cariselli. (Divertissement Comique). Music: J. B. Lully.
        Arlequine. Duet with Arlequin Dupré.
        Mlle. Prévost was not listed in the major productions of *Phaéton, Acis et Galatée* and/or *Tancrède*.
1703   **Psyché**. Trag. Op. Revival. Music: J. B. Lully.
        Acte 3: Suite de la Jeunesse.
        Acte 4: Suite de Bacchus.

Les Muses. Ballet. Music: Campra.
Acte 2: Grecque.
Ballet: Une petite fille.
Le Carnaval et la Folie. Ballet. Music: Destouches.
A Fontainebleau devant le Roi.
La danse. Duet with Claude Balon.

1704   **Didon.** Trag. Op. Revival. Music: Desmarets.
Acte 5: Nymphe.
Iphigénie en Tauride. Trag. Op. Music: Desmarets.
Acte 3: Une Néréide (solo).
Acte 4: Prétresse.
Acte 5: Grecque.
Isis. Trag. Op. Revival. Music: J. B. Lully.
Acte 5. Egyptienne.
Ballet: Néréide.
Télémaque. Trag. Op. Music: Campra.
Suite de la Félicité.
Acte 2: Fête Marine.
Acte 5: Bergère.

1705   **Alcine.** Trag. Op. Music: Campra.
Acte 2: Néréide.
Roland. Trag. Op. Revival. Music: J. B. Lully.
Ballet: Une Fée.
Acte 3: Peuple.
Acte 4: Paysanne.
La Vénitienne. Comédie-Ballet. Music: La Barre.
Acte 1: Une Barquerolle.
Acte 3: Une Arlequine.
Le Triomphe de l'amour. Ballet. Revival. Music: J. B. Lully.
11 September 1705: Néréide. Grecque.
26 November 1705: Dryades. Duet with Mlle. Guyot. Orythie (solo).
2ème Divertissement: Les Songes. Grecque.
3ème Divertissement: Suivante de Flore.
Philomèle. Trag. Op. Music: La Coste.
Ballet: Bergère.
Acte 1: Athénienne.
Acte 3: Courtisans de Térée.
Acte 4: Bacchantes. Duet with Mlle. Guyot. (See figure 5.2.)
Acte 5: Matelotte.
(Same roles in the 1709 and 1727 revivals.)
Béllérophon. Trag. Op. Revival. Music: J. B. Lully.

Ballet: Bacchantes. Duet with Mlle. Guyot.

Acte 4: Prétresse.

1706   *Alcione*. Trag. Op. Music: Marin Marais.

Acte 3: Matelotte.

Acte 5: Une néréide (solo). Same role in the 1719 revival.

Europe Galante. Ballet. Op. Revival. Music: Campra.

4ème Entrée: More and Moresse. Duet with Claude Balon.

5ème Entrée: Sultane.

Cassandre. Trag. Op. Music: Bouvard and Bertin.

Ballet: Bergère (solo).

Acte 5: Grecque.

Les Feste de l'Amour et de Bacchus. Pastorale. Revival.

Music: J. B. Lully, to which was added: *Le Professeur et la Folie*.
   (Divertissement from *Carnaval et la Folie*, act 2.)

La Danse. Duet with Claude Balon.

Polixène et Pirrhus. Trag. Op. Music: Colasse.

Acte 2: Gràce.

Acte 3: Suite de Junon.

Acte 4: Amants heureux.

Acte 5: Paysanne. Duet with Mlle. Guyot.

Alceste. Trag. Op. Revival. Music: J. B. Lully.

Ballet: Habitants de la Seine.

Acte 5: Paysanne.

1707   *Amadis de Gaule*. Trag. Op. Revival. Music: J. B. Lully.

Acte 5: Une Héroine (solo).

Bradamante. Trag. Op. Music: La Coste.

Acte 1: Amants enchantés (solo).

Acte 4: Une Marseillaise (solo).

Acte 5: Génies.

Ballet des Saisons. Revival. Music: Louis Lully and Colasse.

3ème Entrée: Vendangeurs. Duet with Claude Balon.

In 1712 revival: La fille in *Fête du Village*. In 1723 revival: Suite de Flore
   (solo).

Tancrède. Trag. Op. Revival. Music: Campra.

Ballet: Suivantes de la Paix.

Acte 2: Sarrazine.

Acte 3: Nymphes.

In the 1717 Revival. Acte 2: Amazones. Duet with Mlle. Guyot.

Acte 3: Nymphe (solo).

In 1729 Revival: Un Plaisir (solo).

Thésée. Trag. Op. Revival. Music: J. B. Lully.

Suite de Cérés.

Acte 1: Prétresse. Acte 2: Grecque. Duet with Mlle. Guyot.
Acte 4: Bergèr(e). Duet with Claude Balon (alluded to in "Mémoire").
Acte 4 : Bergèr(e). Duet with D. Dumoulin in 1720 revival.

1708 *Hippodamie.* Trag. Op. Music: Campra.
Ballet: Bergère (solo).
Acte 1: Amantes. Duet with Mlle. Guyot.
Acte 2: Néréides. Prétresses.
Thétis et Pélée. Trag. Op. Revival. Music: Colasse.
Acte 1: Néréides.
Acte 2: Afrique (solo).
Same parts in the 1712 Revival.
Amérique instead of Afrique; Acte 1: Néréide (solo) in 1723 revival.
Les Fragments de M. de Lully. Revival. Music: Campra.
Bergère.
Ballet: Matelotte. Duet with Claude Balon.
2ème Entrée: Une Bergère (solo).
Same parts in the 1711 revival.
Masque (solo). Le Bal interrompu. 1717 revival.
Issé. Pastorale Héroique. Revival. Music: J. B. Lully.
Ballet: Une Hespéride (solo).
Acte 1: Chasseuses. Duet with Mlle. Guyot.
Atys. Trag. Op. Revival. Music: J. B. Lully.
Acte 2: Africaines. Duet with Mlle. Guyot.
Acte 3: Songes agréables.
Acte 4: Nymphe des eaux (solo).
Same roles in 1709 revival.

1709 *Sémélé.* Trag. Op. Music: Marais.
Ballet: Aegiparis. Duet with Claude Balon.
Bacchante (solo).
Acte 4 du Ballet: Bergère (solo).
Acte 5: Thébains with the whole cast.
Méléagre. Trag. Op. Music: Baptistin.
1ère Entrée du Ballet: L'Italie (solo).
Acte 3: Bergère (solo).
Hésionne. Trag. Op. Revival. Music: Campra.
Acte 2 du Ballet: Gràce.
Acte 3: Héroine.
Philomèle. Trag. Op. Revival. Music: La Coste. See 1705.
Atys. Revival. See 1708.

1710 *Phaéton.* Trag. Op. Revival. Music: J. B. Lully.
Acte 2: Ethiopienne (solo).
Diomède. Trag. Op. Revival. Music: Bertin.

Acte 1: Une Grecque (solo).

Acte 3: Berger(e). Duet with D. Dumoulin.

Les Fêtes vénitiennes. Ballet. Music: Campra.

1ère Entrée: Gondolièr(e). Duet with Claude Balon.

3ème Entrée: Espagnolette (solo).

8 Juillet 1710. Revival. Matelot(te). Duet with Claude Balon.

8 Aout 1710. Revival. Matelot(te). Duet with Claude Balon.

5 September 1710. Bohémien(ne). Duet with Claude Balon.

Persée. Trag. Op. Revival. Music: J. B. Lully.

Suivantes de Persée (solo).

1711   ***Manto la Fée.*** Trag. Op. Music: Baptistin.

Acte 2 du Ballet: Un Faune (solo).

Iphigénie en Tauride. Trag. Op. Music: Desmaret.

Acte 2 du Ballet: Une Nymphe (solo).

Cadmus et Hermione. Trag. Op. Music: J. B. Lully.

Acte 5 du Ballet: Suite de Comus (solo).

Amadis de Grece. Trag. Music: Destouches.

Acte 1 du Ballet: Bergères. Duet with Mlle. Guyot.

Acte 4: Matelotte (solo).

In the 1714 revival, Mlle. Prévost danced these two roles as a duet with
    D. Dumoulin.

Nouveaux Fragments de M. de Lully.

2ème Entrée du *Carnaval et la Folie*. Une Matelotte (solo).

1712   ***Idoménée.*** Trag. Op. Music: Campra.

Acte 3 du Ballet: Matelotte (solo).

Acte 4: Duet with Mlle. Guyot.

Creuse l'Athénienne. Trag. Op. Music: La Coste

Ballet: Suivants de la Fable et de l'Histoire (solo).

Acte 2: Athénienne (solo).

Acte 3: Bergères. Duet with Mlle. Guyot.

Thétis et Pélèe. Trag. Op. Revival. Music: Colasse.

Acte 2 du Ballet: L'Afrique (solo).

Ballet des Saisons. Revival. See 1707.

Ballet: Fête du Village. La Fille.

Les Amours de Mars et Vénus. Ballet. Music: Campra.

Divertissement: Moresse (solo).

Achille et Polixène. Trag. Op. Revival. Music: J. B. Lully.

Acte 1 du Ballet: Gràces.

Acte 3: Pastorelle (solo).

Les Fêtes vénitiennes. Revival. Music: Campra.

Chef des Bohémiens. Duet with D. Dumoulin.

Bohémienne (solo).

2ème Entrée du Ballet: Espagnolettes. Duet with Mlle. Guyot.

Callirohé. Trag. Op. Music: Destouches.

Acte 3 du Ballet: Faune et Dryade. Duet with D. Dumoulin.

Acte 4: Bergères. Duet with Mlle. Guyot.

1713   **Les Fêtes vénitiennes.** See 1712.

Médée et Jason. Trag Op. Music: Salomon.

Acte 3 du Ballet: Amants Contents (solo).

Acte 4: Fête Marine (solo).

Psyché. Ballet. Revival. Music: J. B. Lully.

Acte 3 du Ballet. La Jeunesse (solo).

Les Amours Déguisés. Ballet. Music: Bourgeois.

Une Bergère (solo).

In 1714 Revival: Lemniennes. Duet with Mlle. Guyot.

Téléphe. Trag. Op. Music: Campra.

Acte 1: Bergères. Duet with Mlle. Guyot.

Armide. Trag. Op. Revival. Music: J. B. Lully.

Acte 4 du Ballet: Duet with D. Dumoulin.

Acte 5: Amante Fortunée (solo).

1714   **Les Fêtes de Thalie.** Ballet. Music: Mouret.

Noces du Village: Marié et Mariée. Duet with D. Dumoulin.

Télémaque. Trag. Op. Music: Destouches.

Acte 4: Bergère. Duet with Mlle. Guyot.

Arion. Trag. Op. Music: Matho.

Acte 1: Bergère. Duet with Mlle. Guyot.

Acte 4: Une Néréide (solo).

Armide. Revival. See 1713.

Apollon et les Muses. Music: Mouret.

Duet with Claude Ballon as Camille and Horace.

Les grandes nuits de Sceaux (14ème nuit).

1715   **Proserpine.** Trag. Op. Revival. Music: J. B. Lully.

Acte 4 du Ballet: Ombre Heureuse (solo).

Les Plaisirs de la Paix. Ballet. Music: Bourgeois.

Fête du Village: Bergère. Duet with D. Dumoulin.

Zéphir et Flore. Op. Revival. Music: Louis and Jean-Louis Lully.

Masque and Sultane (solos).

Théonoé. Trag. Op. Music: Salomon.

Acte 2 du Ballet: Prétresse d'Apollon (solo).

Les Fêtes de Thalie. Revival. See 1714.

1716   **Alceste.** Trag. Op. Revival. Music: J. B. Lully.

Acte 1 du Ballet: Matelotte. Duet with Guillaume Louis Pécour.

Ajax. Trag. Op. Music: Bertin.
Ballet: Suite de Pallas. Duet with D. Dumoulin.
Acte 5: Matelotte (solo).
Les Fêtes de l'été. Ballet. Music: Monteclair.
Ballet: Marinière.
First performance in June and second performance in September 1716.
Hypermestre. Trag. Op. Music: Gervais.
Acte 3: Bergères. Duet with Mlle. Guyot.
Acte 2: Matelotte (solo).
Same cast in 1717.
Roland. Trag. Op. Revival. Music: J. B. Lully.
Acte 3: Peuple de Cathay (solo).
Acte 4: Noces du Village. La Mariée (solo).

1717   ***Ariadne.*** Trag. Op. Music: Mouret.
Bergères dansantes. Duet with Mlle. Guyot.
Acte 2 du Ballet: Crétoise (solo).
Isis. Trag. Op. Revival. Music: J. B. Lully.
Ballet. Néréide (solo).
Hypermestre. See 1716.
Tancrède. Trag. Op. Revival. Music: Campra.
Acte 2: Amazones. Duet with Mlle. Guyot.
Acte 3: Nymphes et Bergères (solo).
Vénus et Adonis. Trag. Op. Revival. Music: Desmaret.
Acte 3: Grâce (solo).
Note: Françoise Prévost was pregnant for most of 1717 and obviously
did not dance all these roles. The only suggestion for a replacement
was in January 1718, the month her child was born.

1718   ***Béllérophon.*** Trag. Op. Music: J. B. Lully.
January 1718. Acte 3: Prétresse. Mlle. Prévost or La Ferriere.
Acte 4: Duet with D. Dumoulin.
April 1718. Prétresse (solo).
Le Jugement de Paris. Pastorale Héroique. Music: Bertin.
Acte 1: Bergères. Duet with Mlle. Guyot.
Sémiramis. Trag. Op. Music: Destouches.
Acte 1: Babylonienne (solo).
Acte 2: Peuples élémentaires. Duet with Mlle. Guyot.
Ballet des Ages. Opera-Ballet. Music: Campra.
La fille du Seigneur.

1719   ***Les Plaisirs de la Campagne.*** Ballet. Music: Bertin.
Bergère (solo).
Issé. Pastorale Héroique. Revival. Music: Destouches.
Acte 2: Bergère (solo).

Acte 3: Une Dryade (solo).
Same roles in 1721 production.
Alcione. Trag. Op. Revival. Music: De la Motte.
Acte 3: Matelotte (solo).
Iphigénie en Tauride. Trag. Op. Revival. Music: Demarets.
Acte 1: Scythes. Duet with D. Dumoulin.
Acte 2: Nymphe (solo).
Le Carnaval et la Folie. Comédie-Ballet.
Acte 3: La Danse: Duet with D. Dumoulin.

1720   ***Polydore.*** Trag. Op. Music: Baptistin.
Acte 2: Matelotte (solo).
Acte 3: Thraciennes. Duet with Mlle. Guyot.
Les Amours de Protée. Ballet. Music: Gervais.
Acte 1. Une Néréide (solo).
Acte 2. Bergèr(e). Duet with D. Dumoulin.
Scylla. Trag. Op. Revival. Music: Théobalde.
Acte 1. Suite de Minos (solo).
Thésée. Trag. Op. Music: J. B. Lully.
Acte 4. Bergèr(e). Duet with D. Dumoulin.
L'Inconnu. 1er ballet dansé par le Roi aux Tuilleries. Music Delalande.
Chorégraphe: Claude Balon, Maitre à danser de Sa Majesté.
2ème Entrée: Bergère. Passepied and Muzette (solo).
5ème Entrée: Suite des Noces du Village. Mariée and Marié. Duet
    with Claude Balon.
Les Folies de Gardenio. Pièce Héroique, 2ème ballet dansé par le
    Roi aux Tuilleries. Music: Delalande. Chorégraphe: Claude Balon.
1ère Entrée: Les Plaisirs. Duet with D. Dumoulin.
Quadrille des Indiens: Mlles. Guyot, Ménes, Prévost, M. Dupré.
Entrée des Matelots. Duet with Claude Balon.

1721   ***Endymion ou l'Amour Vengé.***
Issé. Pastorale Héroique. Revival. Music: de La Motte. See 1719.
Omphale. Trag. Op. Revival. Music: de la Mothe.
Acte 2: (solo) no mention of specific role.
Acte 3: Grecque (solo).
Phaéton. Trag. Op. Revival. Music: J. B. Lully.
Acte 2: Indienne (solo).
Les Élements. 3ème Ballet dansé par le Roi aux Tuilleries.
Chorégraphe: Claude Balon.
Music: Delalande and Destouche.
2ème Entrée: Néréide (solo).
4ème Entrée: l'Amérique (solo).
In the 1725 revival. Zéphir (solo). La Terre (solo).

1722   ***Renaud ou la fuite d'Armide.*** Trag. Op. Music: Desmaret.
Acte 1: Bergèr(e). Duet with D. Dumoulin.
Acte 3: Matelotte (solo).
Ballet des Saisons. Ballet. Revival. Music: Colasse.
Suite de Flore (solo).
Persée. Trag. Op. Revival. Music: J. B. Lully.
Acte 4: Peuple (solo).
This Opera was again given on 13 November as a benefit for the performers. "La Dlle. Prévost danced a Muzette which Campra had added in 1718 to the *Ballet des Ages.*"
At Reims, festivities given at Louis XV's coronation: A little ballet with a *tambourin basque* led by Mlle. Prévost and Sieur Dumoulin as Shepherd and Shepherdess.
Ballet des 24 heures. Ambigu comique représenté devant Sa Majesté à Chantilly le 2 Novembre 1722.
Part 1, 2ème entrée: Thalie.
Part 4: Une dame de Cour.

1723   ***Thétis et Pélée.*** Trag. Op. Revival. Music: Colasse.
Acte 1: Néréide. Suite de Neptune (solo).
Acte 2: Amérique (solo).
Pirithous. Trag. Op. Music: Jean-Joseph Mouret.
Acte 2: Esprits transformés en songes inquiets (solo).
Fête du Village. Duet with D. Dumoulin within a cast of twelve.
Philomèle. Trag. Op. Music: de la Coste.
Acte 4: Bacchante (solo).
Les Fêtes Grecques et Romaines. Ballet. Music: Colin de Blamont.
Terpsichore (solo).
Berger(e). Duet with D. Dumoulin.

1724   ***Amadis de Grèce.*** Trag. Op. Revival. Music: Destouches.
Acte 1 du ballet: Berger(e). Duet with D. Dumoulin.
Acte 4: Matelotte (solo).
Ballet des Ages. Revival. Music: Campra.
Masques. Duet with Mlle. Richalet.
Fille du Seigneur (solo).
Armide. Trag. Op. Revival. Music: J. B. Lully.
Acte 2: Démon transformé (solo).
Acte 4: Berger(e). Duet with D. Dumoulin.

1725   ***La Reine de Péris.*** Comédie Persanne. Music: Aubert.
Acte 1: Fête Marine (solo).
Acte 4: L'Inconstance (solo).
Les Eléments. Ballet. Music: Lalande and Destouches. Chorégraphe: Claude Balon.

1ème Entrée: l'Air (solo).

4ème Entrée: La Terre. Suite de Pomone (solo).

Les Fêtes de l'Eté. Ballet. Revival. Music: Monteclair.

Marinière: Duet with Mlle. Ménes.

Télégone. Trag. Op. Music: de La Coste.

Acte 1: Matelott (solo).

Acte 2: Démons transformés en Plaisirs (solo).

Acte 5: Bergère (solo).

1726 ***Les Stratagèmes del'Amour.*** Ballet. Music: Destouches.

1er Divertissement: Troyenne (solo).

2ème Entrée: Abdérides en fureur. Duet with D. Dumoulin.

3ème Entrée: La Feste de Philotel. Duet with D. Dumoulin.

Ajax. Trag. Op. Revival. Music: Bertin.

Acte 4 du Ballet: Une Prétresse de l'Amour (solo).

Pyrasme et Thisbé. Trag. Music: Rebel fils and Francoeur.

Acte 2: Egyptien(ne). Duet with D. Dumoulin.

Acte 3: Berger(e). Duet with D. Dumoulin.

Ballet sans Titre. Music: Campra.

2ème Divertissement: La Comédie. Berger(e). Duet with D. Dumoulin.

1727 ***Médée et Jason.*** Trag. Op. Revival. Music: Salomon.

Acte 3: Amants Heureux (solo).

Proserpine. Trag. Op. Revival. Music: J. B. Lully.

22 January 1727. Acte 4: Ombre heureuse (solo).

22 April 1727. Mlle. Prévost danced a muzette and Mlle. Camargo, *Les Caractères de la Danse.*

Les Amours des Dieux. Ballet Héroique. Music: Mouret.

Berger(e). Duet with D. Dumoulin.

Roland. Trag. Op. Revival. Music: J. B. Lully.

Acte 4: Les Noces du Village. La Mariée (solo).

Acte 5: Suite de Logistille. Duet with Mlle. Sallé.

Mlle. Prévost is not in the July revival of *Le Jugement de Paris.*

1728 ***Orion.*** Trag. Op. Music: de La Coste.

Acte 2 du Ballet: Nymphe de Diane (solo).

Béllérophon. Trag. Op. Revival. Music: J. B. Lully.

Acte 3: Une Prétresse (solo).

Les Amours de Protée. Ballet. Revival. Music: Gervais.

Acte 1: Une Néréide (solo).

Acte 2: Berger(e). Duet with D. Dumoulin.

Mlle. Prévost is not scheduled in the 7 September performance.

Hypermestre. Trag. Op. Revival. Music: Gervais.

Acte 3: Bergères. Duet with Mlle. Sallé.

La Princesse d'Elide. Ballet Héroique. Music: Villeneuve.
Acte 1 du Ballet: Bergères. Duet with Mlle. Sallé.
Tarcis et Zélie. Trag. Op. Music: Rebel Fils and Francoeur.
Acte 3: Suite de la Sybille Delphique (solo).
Acte 4: Bergers Héroiques. Duet with D. Dumoulin.
Alceste. Trag. Op. Revival. Music: J. B. Lully.
Prologue: Nymphe (solo).

1729   *Tancrède.* Trag. Op. Revival. Music: Campra.
Second performance: 3 March.
Acte 3: Plaisir et Nymphe (solo).
Le Parnasse. Ballet. Music: arranged by Blamont and Pellegrin.
This ballet was given in the marble court of the Versailles castle in
the presence of the king and to celebrate the birth of the crown
prince.
Ballet: Duet from *Béllérophon* danced with Sieur Laval.
Thésée. Trag. Op. Revival. Music: J. B. Lully.
Acte 2: Vieux et Vieille. Duet with D. Dumoulin.
Mlle. Prévost did not appear in the revival of *Cariselli* (28 February
and 28 March), in *Les Amours des Déesses* (9 Aout), or in *Hésionne* (13
September).

1730   *Télémaque.* Trag. Op. Revival. Music: Destouches.
23 February 1730.
Acte 3: Démons transformés en Nymphes et Plaisirs (solo).
Acte 4: Bergères. Duet with Mlle. Sallé.
Mlle. Prévost did not appear in *Pastorale Héroique, Amours de Mars et
Vénus, Pourceaugnac and Cariselli* (January 1730), *Alcyone* (9 May),
Carnaval et la Folie (13 July), or *Caprice d'Erato* (8 October). Her
roles were from now on shared between her three students,
Mlles. Sallé, Camargo, and Richalet, and a newcomer, Mlle.
Mariette.

Notes

Twenty-three years ago, at the Society of Dance History Scholars' Conference
at Goucher College, Baltimore (February 1984), I presented the first sketch of
Françoise Prévost's private life to an audience of historians. I gratefully thank
the Society of Dance History Scholars for giving me a second chance at spot-
lighting this exceptional artist.

1. Emile Dacier, *Une danseuse de l'Opera sous Louis XV, Mademoiselle Sallé, 1707–
1756* (Paris: Plon-Nourrit, 1909); Gabriel Letainturier-Fradin, *La Camargo, 1710–
1770* (n.d.; reprint, Geneva: Minkoff, 1973).

2. Jean Raoux (1677–1734), French painter, was best known for his mythologized female portraits of court women and Opera performers. Françoise Prévost's portrait as a bacchante, considered one of his best, was painted in 1723.

3. John Essex, *The Dancing Master or the art of dancing explained. Done from the French of Monsieur Rameau* (London: sold by him at his House, 1728), the French preface, xxvi.

4. Dacier, *Danseuse*, 106. The poem is attributed to Gentil-Bernard.

5. Jean Georges Noverre, *Lettres sur la Danse et les arts Imitateurs* (1760; reprint, Paris: Editions Lieutier, 1952), 287.

6. Mathieu Marais, *Journal et Mémoires*, vol. 3 (Paris: Firmin Didot, 1864), 397.

7. These texts were entrusted to the ghostwriter who expressed the injured party's viewpoint. The names put forward in this case were: Raymond (le Grec), M. de la Popelinière, Saint-Méry (Mathieu Marais, *Journal et Mémoires*, 3:402).

8. This information is given in "Mémoire pour M. le Bailly de Mesmes, ambassadeur de Malte contre la demoiselle Prévost, danseuse de l'Opéra. Factum," B. Arsenal, MS 3137. Reprinted in Jacques Claude de Bois-Jourdain, *Mélanges historiques, satiriques et anecdotiques de M. de B . . . Jourdain, écuyer de la Grande Écurie du Roi (Louis XV)*, vol. 2 (Paris: Chèvre et Chanson, 1807). Unless otherwise noted, all translations are my own.

9. A person who calls the roll and reports absentees. Was the "Sieur Prévost" also occasionally dancing? A "Sieur Prévost" is found in the 1691 revival of Lully's *Cadmus* and again in the *Ballet de Villeneuve St. George* in 1692. A "Jacques Prévost, dancing-master of the Royal Academy of Music," is also found as a marriage witness on 28 September 1693. See *Musiciens de Paris, 1535–1792* (Paris: Picard, 1965), 246. Was this perhaps the same person?

10. Claude Parfaict and François Parfaict, "Histoire de l'Académie Royale de Musique," Bibliothèque nationale, Paris, MS nouv. acq. fr. 6532.

11. A "Sieur Thybaud" is also listed in the cast of the *Ballet de Villeneuve St. George* in 1692 alongside the "Sieur Prévost" mentioned above—a puzzling coincidence that needs to be investigated further.

12. *Mémoires du Président Hénault* (reprint, Geneva: Slatkine, 1971).

13. Jérome de la Gorce, "L'Académie Royale de Musique en 1704," *Revue de Musicologie* 65 (1979): 161–91.

14. Coarse type of hanging found in humble households.

15. Pet name for Françoise, of low class or peasant origin.

16. Thick material used in upholstery but also for dressing gowns.

17. This may date the event to 17 November 1707, *Thésée*, act 4, the only duet found in ballet programs listing Claude Balon and Françoise Prévost as shepherd and shepherdess.

18. This alley leading to the Opera House and their studios was famous for its gallant rendezvous.

19. "Thursday, 31 January 1715, at Versailles: The 'Grand Maitre de Malte' named the Bailli de Mesmes his ambassador, as the king had requested. He is Monsieur le Premier President's brother to whom his Majesty is pleased to give satisfaction" (Philippe de Courcillon, *Journal du Marquis de Dangeau,* 19 vols. [Paris: Firmin Didot, 1854–60], 16:351).

20. Demoiselle or Damoiselle was a title of respectability in upper bourgeois circles and was also used for married women.

21. The Opera *privileges* freed female performers from parental and conjugal custody.

22. Vladia Kunzmann, "Jean-Féry Rebel, 1666–1747, and His Instrumental Music" (Ph.D. diss., Columbia University, 1993), 16–17, 61.

23. Jean-Jacques Rousseau, "caprice," quoted in Kunzmann's "Jean-Féry Rebel," 155, note 66.

24. See Kunzmann, "Jean-Féry Rebel," 156.

25. Jacques Bonnet, *Histoire Générale de la Danse* (Paris: d'Houry, 1724), 62.

26. Louis Bonin, *Die neuste art zur galanten und theatralischen Tantz-Kunst* (Frankfurt: C. Lockner, 1711), 182. The quote is translated by Edmund Fairfax in his *Styles of Eighteenth-Century Ballet* (Scarecrow Press, 2003).

27. Bonnet, *Histoire Générale de la Danse,* 69.

28. In April 1716 *The London Stage* advertised for the Drury Lane Theater, "an entertainment of mimic dancing by Harlequin called *Caprice,* in imitation of Mademoiselle Prévost, the famous dancer of the Paris Opera," and the *Mercure de France* reported in 1744 "the expert rendition full of lightness of *Les Caractères de la Dance,* as well as Rebel's famous *Caprice,* by French-born Mademoiselle André, working at the Polish Court." In 1749 it will once more recall the performance of the *Caprice* by Mademoiselle Puvigné on the occasion of a Royal Academy of Music fund-raising for its dancers.

29. Archives nationales, Paris (hereafter cited as Arch. nat.), minutier central (m.c.), LXVI-329, 30 August 1711, "Création de pension sur l'Opéra à Françoise Prévost." Prévost lived at Rue Nicaise, Parish Saint-Germainl'Auxerrois.

30. Rousseau, *Dictionnaire de Musique,* 58, quoted in Kunzmann's "Jean-Féry Rebel," 174.

31. Michel de Pure, *Idée des Spectacles anciens et nouveaux* (1668; reprint, Geneva: Minkoff, 1985), "De la Boutade," section 18, 304.

32. *Mercure de France,* May 1732, 992–93: "Mademoiselle Roland . . . made her debuts with her father at the Italian Theater and danced *Les Caractères de la Danse* at the end of the spectacle." Also, *Les Petits Caractères* was performed under this title on 9 October 1755: "They were Rebel's *Les Caractères de la Danse,* performed by a young dancer called Mademoiselle Guimard, a student of Hiacinte Du But, dancer at the Opera." (Parfaict and Parfaict, *Dictionnaire des théâtres de Paris,* 7 vols. [1756; reprint, Geneva: Slatkin, 1967], 2:486). Mademoiselle

Lany, Mademoiselle Puvigné, Mademoiselle Dallemant, and Mademoiselle Cochois were all reported by the *Mercure de France* to have made their stage debuts in *Les Caractères de la Danse*. See Pierre Aubry and Emile Dacier, *Les Caractères de la danse* (Paris: Honoré Champion, 1905), 24.

33. Louis de Rouvroy (duc de Saint-Simon), *Mémoires de Saint-Simon* (Paris: Hachette, 1910), 119.

34. de Courcillon, *Journal du Marquis Dangeau*, 15:351.

35. Adolphe Jullien, *La Comédie à la Cour* (1885; reprint, Geneva: Slatkine, 1971), 119.

36. Marie Sallé created her ballet-pantomime *Pygmalion* in London in 1734.

37. Noverre created his first ballet-pantomime, *Les Fêtes Chinoises*, at Marseilles in 1751, but most of his work was also produced abroad.

38. Ariosto's *Orlando Furioso* featured the beautiful Angélique, Queen of Cathay in Asia, who was brought to France by a knight, Roland, but fell in love and fled with a young Saracen, Médor, driving Roland to madness. The story was turned into an opera by Jean-Baptiste Lully in 1685. Françoise Prévost danced in all the revivals from 1705 to 1727.

39. Arch. nat., m.c., XCII-446, 14 February 1726, "Reconnaissance." Prévost lived at rue des Bons Enfants, Parish St. Eustache, in the house described in the "Mémoire."

40. Parfaict and Parfaict, *Dictionnaire des théâtres de Paris*, 3:55.

41. *Mercure de France*, 5 May 1726.

42. Adrienne Le Couvreur, *Lettres* (Paris: Plon, 1892), 156.

43. *Le Magazin* was the Opera annex built in 1712. The building housed the Opera administration, its costume shop, decors, machines, and rehearsal studios.

44. *Nécrologe des hommes célèbres de France* (Paris: Despres, 1771), 109.

45. Dacier, *Danseuse*, 28. See also Sarah McCleave's article in the current volume, "Marie Sallé, a Wise Professional Woman of Influence."

46. *Mercure de France*, September 1727, 2083, quoted in Dacier, *Danseuse*, 44.

47. Arch. nat., m.c., XCII-446, 14 February 1726, "Reconnaissance."

48. Arch. nat., m.c., XCII-475, 23 July 1733, "Mariage."

49. Arch. nat., m.c., XCII-445, 22 November 1725, "Depot."

50. Marais, *Journal et Mémoires*, vol. 3, letter 26, 1 August 1733.

51. Anne de Valjoly-Rebel died on 15 May 1737. An inventory of her belongings was made on 19 June 1737 (Arch. nat., m.c., XCII-490, "Inventaire"). Her two small children were given a tutor who would ultimately renounce, on their behalf, the portion of Françoise Prévost's estate that would have gone to their deceased mother (Arch. nat., m.c., XCII-511, 18 September 1741, "Reconciliation"). Anne de Valjoly-Rebel's son, Alexandre Camille, died on 2 April 1742 (Arch. nat., m.c., XCII, 600). The author is grateful to musicologist Catherine Cessac, of the Centre de Musique Baroque de Versailles, for providing information on Alexandre Camille's death. Information on Prévost's financial

arrangements is in Arch. nat., m.c., XCII-494, 6 March 1738, "Quittance," and 20 April 1738. Information on Prévost's will is from Arch. nat., m.c., XCVIII-472, 12 March 1740, "Testament."

52. *Mercure de France,* 30 September 1730, 146.

53. Jean-Jacques de Mesmes died on 2 February 1741, aged sixty-seven.

54. Arch. nat., Y. 13228, 13 September 1741, "Scéllés," and m.c., XCVIII-477, 4 October 1741, "Inventaire."

55. "Demoiselles de la danse 1730-40," Archives 18 [20 Opera].

56. Quoted in Dacier's *Danseuse,* 189-92.

57. One exception comes to mind: Louise Couperin, François Couperin's daughter, who was "the successor of her father in charge of the harpsichord in the king's chamber, which, except in this instance, was never known to have been conferred on any but men." See Ursula M. Rempel, "Women in Music: Ornament of the Profession?" in *French Women and the Age of Enlightenment* (Bloomington: Indiana University Press, 1984), 172.

58. "Règlement au sujet de l'Opéra," article 18, 19 November 1714, quoted in Jacques-Bernard Durey de Noinville, *Histoire du théâtre de l'Académie royale de musique en France* (1757; reprint, Geneva: Minkoff, 1972).

59. Official registration.

60. "Histoire de la demoiselle d'Azincourt, danseuse de l'Opera écrite par elle-même, 1743," Bibliothèque nationale, Paris, MS fr. 12646. This dancer died in October 1743, age 23, from venereal disease. Michel Blondy, ca. 1673-1739, *premier danseur,* succeeded Guillaume Louis Pécour at the Opera in 1729.

61. "Description de la vie et moeurs, de l'exercice et l'état des filles de l'Opéra," anonymous manuscript attributed to the abbé de Vassetz, ca. 1694, presented and annotated by Jérôme de La Gorce in Louis Ladvocat, *Lettres sur l'Opéra à l'abbé Dubos* (Paris: Cicero, 1993).

62. The administrator who had bought the Opera privileges and therefore ran the institution as he pleased.

63. The Palais Royal, where the Opera stood.

64. "Règlement au sujet de l'Opéra," articles 40 and 42, 19 November 1714.

Additional Sources Consulted

Delaunay, Rose, Baronne de Staal. *Mémoires,* with an introduction by F. Funk-Brentano. Paris: Arthème Fayard, n.d.

Dubos, Jean-Baptiste. *Réflexions critiques sur la poésie et sur la peinture.* Paris: Jean Mariette, 1719.

Durey de Noinville, Jacques-Bernard. *Histoire du théâtre de l'Académie Royale de Musique depuis son établissement jusqu'à présent.* Paris, 1753. Reprint, Genève: Minkoff, 1972.

Du Tralage, Jean Nicolas. *Notes et documents sur l'histoire des théâtres de Paris, 1696.* Paris: Librairie des Bibliophiles, 1880.

Gourdin, Jean-Luc. *La Duchesse du Maine.* Paris: Pygmalion, 1999.

Ladvocat, Louis. *Lettres sur l'Opera à l'abbé Dubos.* Presented and annotated by Jerome de la Gorce. Paris: Cicero, 1993.

La Vallière, Louis-César de la Beaume-le-Blanc. *Ballets, Opera et autres ouvrages lyriques par ordre chronologique.* Paris: J. Baptiste Bauche, 1760.

Suite des Divertissements de Sceaux contenant la description des nuits qui s'y sont données et des comédies qui s'y sont jouées. Paris: Chez Etienne Gaveau, 1725.

Trévoux, A. *Les Divertissements de Sceaux.* Paris: Chez Etienne Gaveau Rue Saint-Jacques, 1712.

Viollier Renée. *Jean Joseph Mouret, le musicien des gràces.* Paris: Floury, 1950.

6

Marie Sallé, a Wise Professional Woman of Influence

SARAH MCCLEAVE

Marie Sallé (1707–56) was clearly a prominent figure in early eighteenth-century dance who continues to hold an interest for scholars and performers today. Yet how much do we actually know about her influence on others as a performer? And how can we measure her impact as a choreographer when no detailed information about any of her works is known to survive?

This article will consider Sallé's influence as a performer, choreographer, and teacher by examining theatrical calendars, records, and the writings of her contemporaries. This most obvious means of measuring her influence, a study of theatrical dictionaries, diaries, and letters of the time, is fraught with complications. A preoccupation with Sallé's imagined conduct and her public image colors many of these accounts, so understanding the motivations behind this fascination becomes central to our understanding of her potential contribution to her milieu as her changing image is closely linked to developments in her career.

Key Events in Sallé's Career

Marie Sallé was born somewhere in France in 1707. Her family background was not auspicious, as most of her relatives were fairground performers. Her first public performances were at London's Lincoln's Inn Fields during the 1716–17 theatrical season. For her first performance with her brother Francis at this theater, the children were advertised (in the *Daily Courant* for 18 October 1716) as "Scholars of M. Ballon, lately arriv'd from the Opera at Paris." Presumably this was a reference to Claude Balon (1671–1744), a prominent performer and choreographer from the Paris Opera, who participated in a dance and mime scene from Pierre Corneille's *Les Horaces* for the duchesse du Maine's court at Sceaux in 1714. His partner in this production, Françoise Prévost (ca. 1681–1741), is also assumed to have been one of Sallé's teachers. Both women were acclaimed mimic artists. Sallé's biographer, Emile Dacier, discusses sources referring to an early appearance of the dancer at the Opera that suggest she may have been a pupil of Michel Blondy (ca. 1673–1739) rather than Prévost.[1] Sallé spent many of her teenage years in the early 1720s as an itinerant fairground performer in France. At twenty, she became a performer at the Paris Opera after two further seasons at Lincoln's Inn Fields (1725–27). She was quickly elevated to solo status and managed to negotiate a successful career on both sides of the Channel. Her season at Lincoln's Inn Fields in 1730–31 was followed by a year at the Opera and a further period as a freelance performer in Paris. Her London season of 1733–34 at Covent Garden saw her two pantomimes—*Pigmalion* and *Bacchus and Ariadne*—staged in the spring of 1734. She collaborated with the composer George Friedrich Handel (1685–1759) during his 1734–35 London opera season. Upon returning to Paris in July of 1735, she choreographed and danced in scenes for Jean-Philippe Rameau's (1683–1764) *opéra-ballets*. Although she retired from the public stage in 1741, she continued to dance at court and became a coach at the Opéra-Comique in 1743. It is probable that she returned to London in 1746 for an intended collaboration with Handel that did not bear fruit.[2]

Theatrical Hierarchies

Sallé's achievements were incredible given her background and gender. In both Paris and London, men held the influential artistic positions at court and in the repertory theaters. In the latter environment, men were also the entrepreneurs. French governmental structures treated the arts as a state concern; the Opera had a very centralized management structure and was not open to reform. Developments in theatrical dance were determined by the state-appointed Académie Royale de Danse, an all-male group that was notoriously unreceptive to change. In this world, men were the *creators*—of dance choreographies, dance music, and writings on dance. Women were permitted to interpret the creations of men. Although female dancers had some creative and entrepreneurial scope in the popular theaters, Sallé spent the central portion of her career seeking recognition in the more prestigious venues—she most probably was the first female dancer to stage her own creations in the opera houses of London and Paris. The various labels applied to Sallé, from vestal virgin to "jilt," suggest her male contemporaries' need to control her by creating and championing images that were not always grounded in reality. As we will see, Christine Battersby's theory that male writers consciously excluded women from their definitions of creative genius would seem an apt explanation for the negative press she received during a particularly fruitful time in her creative career.[3]

Sallé's Public Image

In her early years Sallé was praised by her contemporaries for her virtue. A poetic tribute by Louis de Boissy, written in 1730, is typical:

> For a decent and noble air,
> A light and elegant dance style,
> For a decent and noble air,
> [Sallé] is a charming example.
> A prodigy of our age,
> She is both pretty and sage:
> Applaud her well!
> Virtue, herself,
> Dances at the Opera.[4]

Figure 6.1. Sallé as Diana, virgin goddess of the hunt (1732). Nicolas Lancret, 1690–1743. Reprinted by permission of Professor Donald Burrows.

Here Sallé is personified as Virtue, applauded for her wisdom. Her virginal image was so entrenched that it earned her the sobriquet "La Vestale." In Roman times, the vestal virgins were the only females exempt from male guardianship—perhaps this label was also a comment on her independence. Indeed, at this stage of her career, her perceived virtue is seen as the explanation for her continual rejection of male suitors.

Sallé's identification with this identity was exemplified in Nicolas Lancret's 1732 portrait of the dancer as Diana, virgin goddess of the hunt (see figure 6.1). This image inspired verses by Voltaire and Pierre-Joseph Bernard lauding her virtue and her modesty.[5] Her role as a Rose in an encounter with Zéphire and Borée in Rameau's *Les Indes galantes* (1735) was arguably a further cultivation of this image. Although the story of a conflict between the west and north winds was popular in the eighteenth century, all other versions featured the lewd mythological character Flora as the female protagonist.[6] The rose was a flower that had particular associations for the French: since the twelfth century, the inhabitants of Salency in Picardie awarded their most virtuous girl a crown of roses during their annual Fête de la Rose.[7]

Contemporaries viewed Sallé as a highly sensual woman. Her dancing was termed "ravishing"; she was the "goddess of the Graces and of Voluptuousness" when she danced in Rameau's *Dardanus* in November of 1739.[8] Her performance in a new ballet in May 1737 was described as full of "lascivious grace, by which the young men will be charmed."[9] An undated chanson referred to Sallé's "voluptuous" movements— her arms are "amiable seducers" that charm and move her spectators.[10] These sensual references were made throughout her career. Jean-Georges Noverre (1727–1810) referred to the "nobility and harmonious simplicity of the tender, voluptuous, but always modest movements of that pleasant *danseuse*";[11] these measured observations by a colleague suggest that Sallé's sensuality was harnessed to serve her art.

Sexual Scandals

The relentless gossip about her private life complicates our understanding of this dancer's reception by her contemporaries. The critics and her public apparently needed to reconcile Sallé's virtuous conduct with her sensual style of dance. This conflict created a particular tension for male spectators: the barrister Mathieu Marais commented with relief in the summer of 1735 when he perceived that her dancing had become somewhat less voluptuous.[12]

It is significant to note that several rumors of heterosexual liaisons made earlier in her career involved alleged marriages or proposals of marriage.[13] This type of gossip contrasted sharply with the scandals attributed to her colleagues.[14] By the mid-1730s Sallé, aged nearly thirty, had no firm record of a heterosexual attachment. Her pure reputation, however, began to unravel: upon her return to Paris in July 1735, a rumor started that she was having a passionate affair with Manon (Marie) Grognet (fl. 1724–47?), a French dancer who had just completed a season in London. The assumption that an affair took place seems to have been based on the fact that the two women traveled from London together and also on the purported existence of a love letter that the anonymous correspondent had not actually seen. From 1736, Sallé's French contemporaries chose to explain her chastity as a symptom of .

perverse sexual predilections, on the basis of much rumor and no known solid evidence. Voltaire, who had previously been a champion of Sallé's virtue, condemned this aspect of her character as inappropriate and implausible for one in her line of work. He referred his friend, Nicolas-Claude Thieriot, to a "perfect epigramme" by a disgruntled admirer of the dancer, the writer Pierre-Joseph Bernard:

> About Sallé, the critic is perplexed
> One says that she has made many people happy;
> Another that she does not like her own sex;
> A third claims she does not like either sex.
> It is wrong for each of them to defame her;
> For myself, I am certain of her virtue:
> Resnel proves that she is no lesbian,
> Grognet that she is no prostitute.

This epigram appeared in many manuscript and printed versions. Although the details of the slander sometimes differed, it is always Sallé's sexual conduct that was being attacked.

This marked change in public perception was also expressed in a tale published in London's *Universal Spectator and Weekly Journal* on 29 January 1737. A young English gentleman (identified in the Parisian manuscript gazettes, the source of this story, as Lord Cadogan) was praised for having seduced Sallé. Hearing of her "uncommon Coldness and Indifference to the Male Sex," he dressed as a woman, gained her favor, and "was permitted to take Part of her Bed." The reporter, suggesting that Sallé was "perfectly well reconciled to the Cheat," assumed the encounter would alter her sexual preferences.[15] This improbable account was the longest press notice ever afforded to her by any English newspaper. Battersby argues that creative female artists were often deemed unfeminine by their critics; it is probably no coincidence that this new perception of Sallé emerged as she was making considerable achievements as a creator.[16]

Costume Reforms

Sallé's changing image arguably influenced the reception of her costume reforms. As we know, she was performing at a time when dancers' costumes were not realistic. Her appearance in figure 6.1, although not depicting an actual stage performance, is an accurate reflection of standard dress, which would have been modified by appropriate props and masks to depict particular characters. Noverre's passion for costume reform may well have stemmed from his association with her—his rejection of the dancer's mask could have been motivated by her "noble, expressive and spiritual countenance," which inspired particular comment in his *Letters*.[17] In her performance as Galatea in *Pigmalion* (London, 1734) Sallé "dared to appear in this *entrée* without a pannier, without a skirt, with her hair all disheveled and no ornament on her head; dressed neither in a corset nor a petticoat, but in a simple muslin robe arranged as a close-fitting drapery, in the manner of a Greek statue."[18]

It is symptomatic of the difficulties that she faced that one of her boldest attempts at costume reform—an appearance as a scantily clad Cupid in Handel's *Alcina* (1735)—was poorly received for an apparently frivolous reason. The Abbé Prévost wrote that Sallé, performing as Cupid, "took it upon herself to dance . . . in male attire. This, it is said, suits her very ill and was apparently the cause of her disgrace."[19] The theatrical entrepreneur Benjamin Victor (d. 1778) advised actresses of the certain risks attached to donning breeches, noting that "there is something required *so much beyond the Delicacy of your Sex*, to arrive at the Point of Perfection, that, if you hit it, you may be condemned as a Woman, and if you do not, you are injured as an Actress."[20] Sallé had already stretched the boundaries of her art and the male-oriented theatrical structure of the time with her individual performance style, her reforms to costuming, and her innovative pantomimes. Perhaps this trousers role was a symbolic irritation for those who wished that she were a little less enterprising?

Career Management

Sallé had repeatedly demonstrated a certain independent streak in her professional life, which was filled with fraught encounters with management.[21] This tendency combined with the difficulties she encountered in the press during the late 1730s suggests she must have had considerable abilities besides her talent in order to be offered atypical creative opportunities: her professionalism and cultivation of an attractive image seem to have garnered sufficient support from persons of influence to overcome any obstacles. She rose from very humble origins to associate herself with men of letters such as Voltaire, while attracting powerful patrons in London such as Charles Lennox, the second Duke of Richmond. It has been argued that her contact with the latter led to her engagement at Handel's opera company during the 1734–35 season, for she expressed a clear desire to dance at the English opera in a letter to the duchess written in the summer of 1731.[22] The ambassador of France, Charles de Montesquieu, wrote a letter to Lady Mary Wortley Montagu encouraging her to attend the dancer's London benefit in the spring of 1731.[23] Occurring on 25 March, this was the first of her London benefits to take place by royal command. That same season, the writer Bernard le Bouvier de Fontenelle urged Montesquieu to recommend Sallé as a most suitable tutor for the English princesses, at a time when theatrical dancers were viewed as having exceedingly dubious morals.[24] Her diplomatic skills were the subject of a comedy written and staged at the Palais Royal in June 1841, some 85 years after her death.[25]

A marked change in her repertory occurred as Sallé's status, through acquiring influential and powerful connections, increased. Her first two London seasons were dominated by comic dances—her abilities in this style were recognized by John Rich, who assigned her prominent roles in the repertory pantomimes as early as 1725. During the 1733–34 season, she no longer danced in others' pantomimic works, staging two of her own creations instead. Her final London season was largely taken up with her performances in Handel's operas, while *Pigmalion* accounted for many of her additional appearances. The most notable change in her status at the Opera occurred after her London season with Handel, as she performed scenes of her own devising in Rameau's *Les Indes galantes* (1735) and *Les Fêtes d'Hébé* (1739), while also creating a memorable role as a rejected concubine in a 1736 revival of André Campra's *l'Europe galante*.[26]

Sallé retired in 1740 at the youthful age of thirty-three. Despite her short period of service at the Opera, Louis XV granted her a full pension in recognition of her extraordinary talent. She danced occasionally at court, also working behind the scenes as a teacher and choreographer at the Opéra-Comique. Her early retirement gave her the freedom to pursue new career opportunities while also having the effect of restoring her reputation. Having removed herself from the public gaze, she effectively disappeared from the letters and diaries of her contemporaries— the few references to her written after her retirement refrained from sexual speculation, alluding instead to her earlier virginal image.[27] Indeed, her death in 1756 was marked only by the duc du Luynes, who commented on her "consistent and singular sagacity."[28]

The discrepancy between Sallé's conduct and the scandals that sometimes circulated is notable. She appears to have had only one personal attachment of significance: a female companion, Rebecca Wick, lived with her during her final years, and Dacier assumed that Wick was the "amiable friend" to whom Sallé referred in a letter to Titon du Tillet.[29] The relationship was clearly significant (although there is no particular reason to assume that it must have had a sexual dimension), for Wick was to become her sole legatee, petitioning the Treasury for the outstanding sum owed on her friend's pension.[30] The dancer could have been considering Wick's dependency when she drew up her will.

Sallé's Influence as a Teacher and Colleague

Sallé could have exerted an influence on her peers in a number of ways. This study will consider dancers clearly identified as her pupils (usually named as such in the press), her regular dancing partners, and those whose repertory or careers demonstrated close parallels with hers. The first known public appearance of a pupil occurred on 6 April 1727, when Elizabeth Rogers (fl. 1727–40), aged nine, made her dancing debut at Lincoln's Inn Fields, performing a "Pastoral." Also active as an actress and a singer, Rogers was still billed as a student of Sallé's when she danced a sarabande and tamborine on 5 April 1731; she performed alongside her teacher as a Bridal Nymph in Covent Garden's production of *The Nuptial Masque* in the spring of 1734. Master Weeks (fl. 1732–40), also identified as Sallé's student, performed with Miss Rogers in "The Pastorella" at Lincoln's Inn Fields on 28 April 1732.[31]

Mademoiselle Le Fèvre was the first Parisian pupil to have distinguished herself, in a performance before the king and queen at the Chateau de Meudon in the autumn of 1736.[32] Sallé's most intensive period of influence as a teacher stemmed from her time at the Opéra-Comique. A change of management in the spring of 1743 excited considerable comment in the *Mercure*, which anticipated a definite improvement in this establishment's fortunes due to the new entrepreneur (elsewhere identified as Jean Monelle), a man of "good taste" who was making careful choices about repertory and personnel.[33] Sallé's pupils, including Jean-Georges Noverre, made an immediate impact on their audience, for the "intelligence and precision" of Mademoiselle Lany *cadette* (Charlotte) was noted when she performed a new version of *Les Caractères de la danse*,[34] while the seven-year-old Mademoiselle Puvignée performed an acclaimed solo *entrée* with "all possible grace and vivacity."[35] Charlotte Lany was not the only sibling from this famous dancing dynasty to perform at the Opéra-Comique that season, for her brother Jean-Barthélemy (1718–86) and elder sister Louise-Madéleine (1733–77) were also in the company—the latter receiving an anonymous poetic tribute that, by commenting on her lightness and grace, was reminiscent of the accolades that Sallé excited in her prime.[36]

The career of Mademoiselle Puvignée *cadette* (b. 1735) had several parallels with that of her teacher, for not only did she start her career in the *foires* but she also rose to prominence in the Opera—at an even younger age than had Sallé. Her particular role as the Rose in a *parodie* of *Les Indes galantes* at the Opéra-Comique in 1743 and her performance in Sallé's former role of Hébé in a 1754 revival of Rameau's *Castor et Pollux* strengthens the artistic bond between these women.[37] Vince suggests that Puvignée "inherited [Sallé's] expressive lyricism"; her receipt of the elder dancer's pension in 1756 was perhaps a tangible recognition of this artistic inheritance.[38]

Sallé appears to have exerted an influence on the repertory of many of her younger contemporaries. Miss Robinson's (fl. London 1723?–35) performance of "A New Dance . . . in which will be expressed all the different Movements in Dancing" on 14 April 1730 was presumably inspired by Sallé's earlier performances of *Les Caractères de la danse*.[39] The French dancer appears to have given the London public a taste for this entertainment, for it continued to feature in the repertory, with several performances by Mademoiselle Marie Chateauneuf (b. 1721) between 1734 and 1740. Chateauneuf's first two seasons in London were with troupes run by Sallé's uncles, Francisque and Simon Moylin.

The daughter of dancer François Michel, who made her stage debut at the Saint Laurent Fair in 1739, performed *Les Caractères de la danse* at Covent Garden on 16 April 1746. The French dancer Anne Auretti (fl. 1742–54) performed dances variously titled *Les Caractères de la danse* or *Les Caprices de la danse* at Drury Lane between 1746 and 1748. She was joined by her sister Janneton, Philip Cooke the younger (fl. 1739–55), and others in a group performance of this work on 10 January 1749. Cooke obtained a position at the Paris Opera in 1740 and thus would have seen Sallé perform during her final season there. He could have drawn on this experience during his performance as the sculptor in a London production of *Pigmalion* (1746).

Winter claims that Catherine Roland (1714?–88) was also Sallé's student.[40] The Venetian-born Roland made her debut at the Théâtre Italien on 1 May 1732 with an "intelligent and vivacious" performance of *Les Caractères de la danse*.[41] She was Galatea in that company's first production of *Pigmalion* on 28 June 1734. Roland became a notable performer in the London theaters, often dancing with her partner Michel Poitier during her first stint there, between 1734 and 1742. She must have had considerable ability as a performer, for she is compared as an equal to Sallé and Camargo in a poem published by the *Mercure* a few months after her debut.[42] Whether she studied formally with Sallé or not, her choice of roles suggests that the older woman served as an inspiration. Roland certainly would have had opportunity to see Sallé perform in a number of significant works, both in London and Paris. Manon Grognet, who is presumably the Mademoiselle Grognet identified as having made her debut in Sallé's father's troupe at the Foire Saint Laurent around 1725, would also have seen many of Sallé's more important creations.[43] Grognet was in London from 1733–35, leaving Francisque Moylin's Haymarket company temporarily to dance in Sallé's 1735 benefit. The women traveled back to Paris at the end of the season, where Grognet joined the Opéra-Comique.

Another dancer who made a remarkable debut with *Les Caractères de la danse* was Lolotte (Charlotte) Cammasse, who, aged ten, "captivated all spectators" with her performance on 14 April 1738 at the Comédie-Française, earning the public congratulations of Sallé herself.[44] It is not known if this was the act of a teacher praising her precocious pupil, but it is surely significant that both Cammasse and Sallé took the role of Terpsichore, a statue who comes to life, in different 1740 productions of *l'Oracle*—the younger dancer performing at the Théâtre-François on 22 March while the elder took over the role for a summer production at court, presumably after Cammasse had left for Poland. Had Sallé coached this prodigy, whose expressive abilities excited particular comment in the *Mercure?*[45] It is also reasonable to assume that Marianne Cochois (fl. 1734?–49?) was influenced by her more famous cousin. Winter claims that Cochois studied with *Le Grand* Dupré, particularly for the role of Terpsichore in a 1741 revival of Colin de Blamont's *Les Fêtes grecques et romaines*.[46] As Sallé performed the title role in Handel's *Terpsichore* (1734), which was modeled on that *opéra-ballet*, it seems probable that she also coached the younger dancer.

The sensation caused by Barbarina Campanini's (1721–99) Parisian debut in 1739 is assumed to have motivated Sallé's early retirement. As the elder dancer dealt with far more difficult obstacles during her career, this seems a rather trite explanation for her severed connections with the Opera—and we must not forget that Sallé's career continued beyond her "retirement." The two women frequently danced together as colleagues, and Barbarina assumed the role of Galatea in productions of *Pigmalion* in Berlin (1745) and London (1746). As their collegial relationship was not marked by any actual ruptures, Barbarina's later association with Covent Garden in a role created by Sallé suggests that the elder dancer may have acted as a mentor.[47]

A dancer so renowned for her grace and expressivity surely must have had some impact on the style of her regular dancing partners. Noverre felt that David Dumoulin (fl. 1705–51), Sallé's most frequent partner at the Paris Opera, was "always animated by a new sentiment, [expressing] every stage of tender affection with voluptuousness."[48] Sallé's elder brother Francis (who was always partnered with his sister during her London seasons until his death in 1732) became a very prominent performer in London's newly established pantomimes from 1725, receiving praise from the Parfaict brothers for his "characterization" of a Scotsman in a 1729 performance at the *foires*.[49] Malter *l'anglais*'s (fl. 1733–50) association with Sallé during the 1733–34 London season, when he partnered her in several *pas de deux* and played leading roles in her pantomimes, was possibly the highpoint of his artistic career. In 1740 his wife was advertised as having "lately arrived from the Opera in Paris,"[50] which suggests that Malter's apparent five-year absence from London afforded him the opportunity to see Sallé's *Ballet des Fleurs*. "La Rose Borée et Ziphirs," staged for his Drury Lane benefit on 9 April 1741, was presumably a tribute to his famous partner. Michael Lally (d. 1757?) worked closely with Sallé during her final London season. In the late 1730s, he was an active teacher, and it is plausible that he would have conveyed aspects of her style to his pupils.

Critical Recognition

Sallé's performances as Galatea in *Pigmalion* and Ariadne in *Bacchus and Ariadne* at Covent Garden in 1734 received an unprecedented amount of recognition, with a detailed review in Paris's leading journal and a lengthy laudatory poem being the most notable responses to her work.[51]

The anonymous correspondent for the *Mercure* made a tribute by comparing her with some contemporaneous actresses:

> Do not expect me to explain *Ariadne* to you as I have *Pigmalion:* this has beauties which are both more subtle and more difficult to describe. These beauties are feelings and portrayals of the deepest sorrow, despair, fury, and prostration. In a word, every action and emotion of a woman abandoned by the man she loves is shown, perfectly, by means of steps, attitudes, and gestures.
>
> You may rest assured, Monsieur, that Mademoiselle Sallé has now become the rival of Journal, Duclos, and Le Couvreur. The English retain fond memories of the famous Mrs. Oldfield . . . and they are saying that she is reincarnated in the person of Mademoiselle Sallé when she performs in *Ariadne*.[52]

Sallé was acknowledged as a significant creator by writer and critic Louis de Cahusac (1706–59), who had the following to say about her role as an odalisque in the June 1736 revival of André Campra's *l'Europe galante:*

> Mademoiselle Sallé, who had, always, a sound reason for whatever she did, had the skill to introduce a most ingenious episodic action into the passacaglia to *l'Europe galante.*
>
> In it we see her portraying a young odalisque or concubine. She is surrounded by her companions and rivals, and shows all the grace and passion one could expect from a young girl with designs upon her master's heart. Her dancing has all the pretty mannerisms which betray such a desire, a desire which we actually see forming and developing.
>
> Into her expression one can read a whole range of feelings. We see her hovering in turn between fear and hope. But when at last the moment arrives for the Sultan to make his choice and he awards the handkerchief to the favorite her face, looks and whole bearing take on a wholly different aspect. She hurls herself off the stage in utter despair, despair of the kind felt only by the most sensitive people, people who in the space of a second can be plunged into the deepest despondency.
>
> One must praise all the more this most artistic performance, full of feeling, because *it was entirely devised by the dancer. She has filled out and improved upon the framework laid down by the poet. In this she has far surpassed the talents of the ordinary performer, and shown herself to possess a rare creative talent.*[53]

As Battersby has noted, women's *creative* abilities were seldom, if ever, acknowledged by their peers.[54] Cahusac's recognition of Sallé suggests that her talent must have been truly exceptional to warrant such an unusual compliment.

Sallé's gifts were also noted by Ranieri Calzabigi (1714–95), the Italian writer and librettist who collaborated with the composer Christoph Willibald Gluck (1714–87) and the choreographer Gasparo Angiolini (1731–1803) in the so-called Viennese reform operas of the 1760s. These operas "[took] inspiration . . . from the large-scale tableaux and integral ballets of *tragédie lyrique*";[55] as Calzabigi was in Paris during the 1750s, it is plausible to assume that he might have met Sallé, and perhaps he even saw her perform, either privately or at any of her four documented performances at Fontainebleau in 1752–53. Sallé would have had a further link to Angiolini through his teacher Franz Hilverding (see discussion below). Calzabigi honored Sallé in his "Dissertation sur les ballets pantomimes des anciens" (Vienna, 1765). In a section where he lamented the confused theatrical aesthetics of his day, he mocked those who would equate "an able jumper with [Gaëtan] Vestris and a woman who can effect light *entrechats* with someone performing at the level of [Marie] Sallé."[56] While comparing tragic danced pantomime with other forms of theatrical tragedy, Calzabigi suggested that the "perfect dancer of tragic pantomimes would unite the two talents [of declamation and dance], being at once Vestris and Riboux, la Sallé and la Clairon."[57] Nicolas Riboux (1723–ca. 1773) and Clairon (1723–1803) were acclaimed tragic actors whom Calzabigi probably observed while in Paris. Sallé is the only dancer of her generation to be mentioned in the "Dissertation"—Vestris was born in 1729.

Influence of Sallé as a Choreographer

At least three of Sallé's creations seem to have inspired progeny: *Pigmalion*, the *Ballet des Fleurs*, and *Bacchus and Ariadne*. The response to *Pigmalion* (London, 14 January 1734) was both immediate and long lasting; although this pantomime can trace its roots to earlier operatic renditions of dances for statues,[58] Sallé's work seems to have been particularly influential, possibly germinating much later variants such as *Coppélia* (1870). Details about related eighteenth-century productions can be found in Marian Hannah Winter, Lincoln Kirstein,[59] Aloys Mooser, and Susan Leigh Foster.[60] Some of these are worth highlighting here because of particular connections to Sallé through the casting or choreographer.

The earliest tribute was Lélio Riccoboni's Paris *Pigmalion* of 28 June 1734, with Catherine Roland and himself in the leading roles. Riccoboni would have seen some of Sallé's earlier work; she had intended to work at his theater during a sabbatical from the Opera in 1733, but was prevented by a court order.[61] The Berlin production of 1745 was choreographed by Sallé's former Opéra-Comique colleague, Jean-Barthélemy Lany, and featured another ex-colleague, Barbarina Campanini, as the statue, with Noverre in a supporting role. The London 1746 production at Sallé's former theater, Covent Garden, also featured Campanini as Galatea.[62] The 1748 and 1751 productions of Rameau's ballet *Pigmalion* had many connections with Sallé, not least being her frequent collaborations with that composer in the late 1730s. Lany was the choreographer and took a role as a grotesque peasant; Galatea and two of the Graces were performed by Sallé's former pupils, Mademoiselle Puvignée and the two Mademoiselles Lany. A Paris revival of Riccoboni's *Pigmalion* dating from 26 March 1735 may have been seen by Franz Hilverding (1710–68), who could certainly have studied Sallé herself in some of her pantomimic scenes for Rameau's *opéra-ballets*.[63] Given the several opportunities he would have had to observe Sallé, and their shared interest in ballet reform, it is plausible to assume that Hilverding's *Pygmalion* (Vienna, 1756) was influenced by her work.

Evidence of connections between Sallé's *Bacchus and Ariadne* and other stage entertainments is more difficult to accumulate. In Paris, her work was preceded by two related *tragédies lyriques* and two ballets.[64] Extant cast lists published in the Parfaicts' *Dictionnaire* do not suggest strong parallels with Sallé's staging of the story and the ballets, for they lack her younger sister Phaedra, who was the catalyst for Theseus's abandonment of Ariadne. Later works on this theme may have had connections with Sallé. Marie-Françoise Christout remarks that actor, dancer, and choreographer Jean-Baptiste De Hesse (1705–79) departed from his preference for popular subjects when he choreographed *Ariane abandonée par Thésée, et secourue par Bacchus* for the Comédie-Italienne (25 February 1747).[65] The plausible suggestion in the *Biographical Dictionary of Actors* that he was the Monsieur Deshayes who briefly appeared with Francisque Moylin's London troupe in the spring of 1735 provides his first connection with Sallé, for he would have been able to observe her in the dream sequence from Handel's *Alcina* and in her own *Pigmalion*. Moreoever, Sallé and De Hesse were both active in Paris from the summer of 1735. *Ariadne* is the most direct link we have between him and Sallé, for establishing her influence on choreographers in the comic opera circuit is beyond the scope of the present article.[66] On the London stage, *Bacchus and*

Ariadne seems to have disappeared until 8 February 1781, when a pas de deux with that title was performed at Covent Garden featuring Robert Aldridge and Esther Besford. *Ariadne and Bacchus,* "a new, Grand, Heroic, Pastoral Ballet" staged at the King's Theatre on 28 November 1797 may have some connection with Sallé, for its choreographer, Sébastien Gallet (1750–1807), had studied with Noverre. The *London Stage* does not confirm a role for either Phaedra or Theseus until a revival at Drury Lane on 9 May 1798. Presumably this work bore some relationship to Gallet's ballet pantomime that had been staged at the Paris Opera in 1791.

The close connection between the descriptions of Sallé's *Ballet des Fleurs* and Gasparo Angiolini's *Zéphire et Flore* (Schönbrunn Castle, 1759) is featured in an article by Bruce Alan Brown, who also identifies other seventeenth- and eighteenth-century entertainments based on this story.[67] Although Angiolini (1731–1803) would not have known her work firsthand, he would have heard of it from his teacher, Hilverding. On 8 November 1774 Jean-Barthélemy Lany's *Le Baillet de Fleur (sic)* was staged at London's King's Theatre, with Lany taking the role of Zephyr. The Parisian-born Lany probably saw Sallé's ballet of that name in 1735. The exceptional reception of her *Fleurs* arguably established a niche in ballet for personified flowers who danced in a passionate and expressive manner, a tradition observed in Michel Fokine's *La Sceptre de la Rose* of 1911, with Vaslav Nijinsky (1889?–1950) in the title role.

Many of Rameau's works inspired *parodies* that were staged at the fairgrounds. *Les Indes galantes* gave rise to at least eight,[68] including one where a direct tribute to Sallé was offered: "And now we see we are in Persia — Oh! The beautiful scenery! the beautiful flower garden! See how the flowers are beaten upside down by a terrible wind, and set right side up by a gentle little breeze which caresses them, and above all, the Rose. This Rose is a curious product, made in France, perfected in England."[69]

The *parodie* with the closest connection to Sallé would be *l'Ambigu de la Folie, ou, Le Ballet des Dindons* (1743), which was staged at the Opéra-Comique during her tenure there as a dancing coach and occasional choreographer. Mademoiselle Puvignée took Sallé's role of the Rose while Noverre assumed the part of Borée.

The story line for Noverre's *Les Jalousies du sérail* (1758) suggests that he may have derived some inspiration from Sallé's passionate performance as a rejected concubine in *l'Europe galante*. Moreover, the ballets that he admired were connected with this dancer, many credited as being of her own creation. "I cannot shut my eyes to the point of admitting that dancing without action, without rules, without intelligence, and without interest forms a ballet, or a poem expressed in terms of dancing. To say that there are no ballets at the Opera would be a falsehood. The act of *Les Fleurs,* the act of Eglé in *Les Talents Lyriques,* the prologue to *Les Fêtes Grecques et Romaines,* the Turkish act in *l'Europe Galante,* one act among many from *Castor et Pollux,* and a quantity of others where dancing is, or can be, easily united to action, and without any extraordinary effort on the composer's part, truly offer me agreeable and very interesting ballets."[70] Sallé's work was arguably the inspiration for many of Noverre's reforms.[71]

Conclusion

This study has attempted to provide an overview of Sallé's contribution to the art of dance as a performer, teacher, and choreographer.[72] There are several obstacles to defining her influence in all spheres with precision, not least being her relative obscurity in the press in the 1740s. Her impact as a performer becomes clear when we consult descriptions of her dancing, but these seldom provide more than the merest hints as to how she appeared on stage. To claim to have determined absolutely her influence on colleagues and subsequent generations of dancers, we would have to assume that pertinent commentaries were absolutely consistent in remarking upon perceived stylistic influences between dancers. The consideration of Sallé's role as a teacher has explored confirmed associations as well as those where we can observe considerable similarities in the roles, repertory, and careers of dancers who worked in close proximity to her. A similar approach has been adopted in order to explore her influence as a choreographer, for detailed textual or notational sources are often lacking.[73]

Establishing Sallé as an early example of a truly professional theatrical artist was perhaps the most straightforward aspect of her career to document. From the 1730s we can see her planning and networking in order to achieve certain artistic goals. She could only succeed by taking extraordinary care over her reputation, for her male peers insisted on sculpting her public image much as Galatea was shaped by Pygmalion. Sallé appears to have eschewed heterosexual liaisons, a choice which makes perfect sense for an ambitious woman in her field who prized her independence; her contemporaries' allusions to her "wisdom" suggest that she made careful choices and acted with discretion. Sallé's professionalism facilitated the unprecedented creative opportunities that she, as a woman, enjoyed in the 1730s and 1740s.

NOTES

An earlier version of this research, "Romanticism and the New," was read at the conference of the North American Society for the Study of Romanticism in the summer of 1999. All translations are my own unless otherwise noted. I am grateful to Mrs. Stanley Vince for giving me a manuscript copy of her late husband's book and his notes. The School of Music, Queen's University Belfast, funded the final stages of research toward this chapter. Particular thanks to Professors Jan Smaczny and Judith Green for their support, and to my husband, Brian Holmes, for his forbearance.

1. Emile Dacier, *Une Danseuse de l'Opéra sous Louis XV: Mademoiselle Sallé 1701–1756* (Paris: Plon-Nourrit, 1909), 11, n.3. This author always provides full bibliographical details of his primary sources, many of which have been checked during my research. See also Régine Astier's article in the current volume, "Françoise Prévost: The Unauthorized Biography."

2. For a probable account of Sallé's 1746 plans, see David Charlton and Sarah Hibberd, "'My Father Was a Poor Parisian Musician': A Memoir (1756) concerning Rameau, Handel's Library and Sallé," *Journal of the Royal Musical Association* 128, no. 2 (2003): 161–99.

3. Christine Battersby, *Gender and Genius: Towards a Feminist Aesthetics* (London: The Women's Press, 1989), especially 23–34.

4. The original is reproduced in Dacier, *Danseuse*, 101. Both Dacier and Stanley Vince, "'With Entertainments of Dancing': A Life of Marie Sallé, Dancer at the Paris Opera in the Time of Louis XV" (London: typescript, ca. 1965), reproduce many of the poetic tributes and written references concerning this dancer (Vince in translation). Copies of Vince's "With Entertainments of Dancing" have been deposited in the British Library and the New York Public Library.

5. See Dacier, *Danseuse*, 82–87, for a discussion of this painting and a reproduction of the poems.

6. Sallé herself took the role of Flora in the London pantomime *The Rape of Proserpine* (1727) but disassociated herself from it during her final two London seasons.

7. See the program note to Noverre's *La Rosière de Salency*, as reproduced in vol. 3 of *Oeuvres de Noverre* (St. Petersburg: Jean Charles Schnoor, 1803–4), 191–214.

8. Dacier, *Danseuse*, 215–16.

9. Dacier, *Danseuse,* 195.

10. Dacier, *Danseuse,* 255, n.2.

11. Jean-Georges Noverre, *Letters on Dancing and Ballets* (St. Petersburg, 1803), trans. Cyril W. Beaumont (New York: Dance Horizons, 1966), 67.

12. Letter to President Bouhier, MS fr. 24414, fol. 466v, Bibliothèque nationale, Paris, reproduced in Dacier, *Danseuse,* 181.

13. See Dacier, *Danseuse,* 113–14, 120–21.

14. See Adolphe Jullien, *Amours d'Opéra au XVIIIe siècle* (Paris: H. Daragon, 1908), 35–39, for an account of an orgy involving Marie-Anne Cupis de Camargo (1710–70) and one of the directors of the Opera; see Dacier, *Danseuse,* 210, for a liaison between Barbarina Campanini and the Prince de Carignan.

15. See Dacier, *Danseuse,* 188–92, for more on these scandals, including the most complete version of the epigram, which is translated here with assistance from Shona Potts. Rumors concerning Sallé and Grognet persisted: a 1737 entry in the manuscript gazettes described the latter as "famous for her affair with Mademoiselle Sallé." Dacier plausibly suggests that the source of this rumor was a spurned suitor of Sallé's, Nicolas-Claude Thieriot.

16. Battersby, *Gender and Genius,* especially 39, 45, 99, 122.

17. Vol. 4 of Noverre, *Oeuvres,* Lettre 14, 77; see Letter 9, 78–98, in his *Letters,* trans. Beaumont, for Noverre's thoughts on masks.

18. *Mercure de France,* April 1734, 770–72.

19. English translation in Otto Erich Deutsch, *Handel: A Documentary Biography* (London: Adam and Charles Black, 1955), 390–91.

20. *The History of the Theatres of London and Dublin From the Year 1730 to the Present Time* (1761), as quoted in Kristina Straub, *Sexual Suspects: Eighteenth-Century Players and Sexual Ideology* (Princeton, NJ: Princeton University Press, 1992), 132 (my emphasis).

21. See Dacier, *Danseuse,* including 52–54, 59–60, 96–99, 107–14, 176–78, 217–19; also Sarah McCleave, "Dancing at the English Opera: Marie Sallé's Letter to the Duchess of Richmond," *Dance Research* 17, no. 1 (1999): 22–46.

22. For further on her English connections and the development of her London career in particular, see McCleave, "Dancing at the English Opera."

23. Reproduced in vol. 1 of *The Complete Letters of Lady Wortley Montagu,* ed. Robert Halsband (Oxford: Clarendon, 1966), 94; see also Vince, "With Entertainments of Dancing," 143.

24. Reproduced in Dacier, *Danseuse,* 59–60; also Vince, "With Entertainments of Dancing," 142–43. The patrons whom she attracted during her year as a freelance performer in Paris (1732–33) are discussed in Dacier, *Danseuse,* 100–122, and Vince, 173–88.

25. Xavier Boniface, M. Bayard, and M. Dumanoir, *Mademoiselle Sallé: Comédie en deux actes, mêlée de couplets* (Paris: Ch. Tresse, 1841).

26. See Antoine de Léris, "Fêtes d'Hébé," *Dictionnaire portatif des théâtres*

(Paris: C.A. Jombert, 1754), where Sallé's *entrée*, "La Danse," is described as being the best as well as the most applauded in that opera.

27. Dacier, *Danseuse*, reproduces these rare comments in his final two chapters, 221–317.

28. Vol. 15 of *Mémoires du Duc de Luynes sur la cour de Louis XV, 1735–1758* (Paris: Didot Frères, Fils & Cie., 1860–64), 171.

29. Reproduced in Dacier, *Danseuse*, 243–47.

30. The will and letter are reproduced in Dacier, *Danseuse*, 266–67 and 317.

31. For more information on these performers, see *A Biographical Dictionary of Actors, Actresses, Musicians, Dancers, Managers, and other Stage Personnel in London, 1660–1800*, 16 vols., ed. Philip H. Highfill Junior, Kalman A. Burnim, and Edward A. Langhans (Carbondale: Southern Illinois University Press, 1973–93). As is typical of minor theatrical dancers in London at this time, nothing is known about how their performances were received.

32. See *Mercure de France*, November 1736, 2552–53. François Parfaict and Claude Parfaict compliment this dancer in vol. 2 of *Mémoires pour servir à l'histoire des spectacles de la foire* (Paris: Briasson, 1743), 116. Both sources clearly refer to Mademoiselle Le Fèvre as a student of Sallé. According to Marian Hannah Winter, *The Pre-Romantic Ballet* (London: Pitman, 1974), 33, the interrelationships of the Lefevre dynasty of dancers are "impossible to sort out."

33. *Mercure de France*, May 1743, 1019.

34. French sources seldom provide the full name of dancers, preferring to distinguish members of the same family by labels such as *cadet/cadette* (the younger) or *aîné* (the elder). Where several siblings in one family were dancers, another distinguishing characteristic might have been adopted as a label: see the reference to Sallé's dancing partner Malter *l'anglais* below (he was the only one of several dancing brothers to have performed in London). For absolute clarity of identification, proper names and labels are given when known.

35. *Mercure de France*, July 1743, 1630–31.

36. The poem is reproduced in vol. 5 of [Babault et al.], *Annales dramatiques, ou Dictionnaire général des théâtres* (Paris: Henée, 1808–12), 298. Noverre, in *Letters*, trans. Beaumont, deemed Louise-Madéleine "the first dancer in the world" (Letter 8, 67).

37. The connection between this pantomimic scene and the intrigue of the opera itself was recognized by the *Mercure de France* in its review of the 1754 revival (February 1754, 189), as recounted in Dacier, *Danseuse*, 197–98.

38. See Vince, "With Entertainments of Dancing," 281–82; see also vol. 7 of *Annales dramatiques*, 525.

39. Sallé's first performance of *Les Caractères de la dance* occurred on 25 November 1725. *The London Stage, 1660–1800*, 11 vols., ed. Emmett L. Avery et al. (Carbondale: Southern Illinois University Press, 1960–68) notes that this dance "express'd all the different Movements in Dancing."

40. Winter, *Pre-Romantic Ballet*, 35.

41. *Mercure de France*, May 1732, 992–93, as reported in Claude Parfaict and François Parfaicts' *Dictionnaire des théâtres de Paris*, 7 vols. (1756; reprint, Geneva: Slatkin, 1967), 4:515.

42. *Mercure de France*, September 1732, 2003, as reproduced in Dacier, *Danseuse*, 78.

43. Parfaict and Parfaict, *Mémoires*, 2:23–24.

44. Dacier, *Danseuse*, 200; see also Vince, "With Entertainments of Dancing," 246–47.

45. See *Mercure de France*, April 1740, 766–67, and July 1740, 1630.

46. Winter, *Pre-Romantic Ballet*, 57.

47. Philip Cooke, discussed earlier, played the sculptor. The connection with Sallé is suggested by the wording of the press announcement (see *The London Stage* for 9 April 1746): "A Grand Ballet, *reviv'd*, call'd Pigmalion" (my emphasis). Newspaper advertisements often made reference to a work's earlier staging history *(in London):* the phrase "not acted these . . . years" was typical. Of the several works from the French comic repertory staged by Francisque Moylin's company at the Haymarket during the 1734–35 season, only *Arlequin Balourd; or, Harlequin Blunderer* is described as "Not Acted these Sixteen Years" (see *London Stage*, 27 December 1734): it was staged *in London* by Francisque's company in February 1719 and March 1720.

48. Noverre, *Letters*, trans. Beaumont, Letter 8, 67–68. An appendix to Dacier's *Danseuse* provides details about Sallé's partners during her Paris seasons. See also *The London Stage*.

49. Parfaict and Parfaict, *Mémoires*, 2:54.

50. As recorded in "Malter, Mons," *Biographical Dictionary of Actors*.

51. Pierre Bordes de Berchères, *Le Jardin de Delos ou Terpsichore a Londres . . .*, in *Crane Court, ou Le Nouveau temple d'Apollon a Londres. Ode a messieurs de la Société royale de Londres* (London: Idibus Maii, 1734). See also Vince, "With Entertainments of Dancing," 200–202, for further evidence of interest in the London press.

52. *Mercure de France*, April 1734, 772, as translated by Vince, "With Entertainments of Dancing," 202–3.

53. Louis de Cahusac, *La Danse ancienne et moderne ou Traité historique de la danse*, 3 vols. (La Haye: Jean Neaulme, 1754), 3:154–55, as translated in Vince, "With Entertainments of Dancing," 240 (my emphasis).

54. Battersby, *Gender and Genius*, especially 35–39, 100, 121.

55. Bruce Alan Brown, "Calzabigi, Ranieri de,'" in *The New Grove Dictionary of Opera*, 4 vols., ed. Stanley Sadie (London: Macmillan, 1992), 1:695.

56. Anon., "Dissertation sur les ballets pantomimes des anciens pour servir de programme au ballet pantomime tragique de *Sémiramis*," in Ranieri Calzabigi, *Scritti teatrali e letterari*, 2 vols., ed. Anna Laura Bellina (Rome: Salerno

Editrice, 1994), 1:170. I am grateful to Professor Brian Trowell for leading me to this reference.

57. [Calzabigi], "Dissertation," 1:174.

58. See "La Sculpture" from *Ballet Triomphe des Arts* (1700), *Amadis de Grèce* (1699; prologue, i), *l'Empire de l'Amour* (1733; third entrée). We also find dancing statues in several London productions, including the dramatic opera *The British Enchanters* (1706; act 1, scene 1), the pantomime *The Miser; or, Wagner and Abericock* (1727), and the masque, *Cephalus and Procris* (1730).

59. Lincoln Kirstein, *Four Centuries of Ballet: Fifty Masterworks* (New York: Dover, 1984), 106–9.

60. R. Aloys Mooser, *Annales de la musique et des musiciens en russie au XVIIIme siècle*, 3 vols. (Geneva: Montblanc, 1948–51), 2:133–41. Jean-Jacques Rousseau's *Pygmalion* (1775) was arguably an inspiration for works staged after its publication. Also cited is Susan Leigh Foster, "Pygmalion's No-Body and the Body of Dance," in *Performance and Cultural Politics*, ed. Elin Diamond (London: Routledge, 1996), 131–54.

61. See Dacier, *Danseuse*, 112–13.

62. For more on this production, see note 47 above.

63. Sibylle Dahms, in her article on Hilverding in *International Encyclopedia of Dance*, 6 vols., ed. Selma Jeanne Cohen et al. (Oxford: Oxford University Press, 1998), 3:364–65, suggests the following concerning his visit to Paris: "The Vienna court archives show that he was a dancing master from 1731 to 1734, a court dancer in 1735, and a ballet master from 1737 onward. Hilverding was probably in Paris from about 1735 to 1737 in order to study—financially supported by an imperial scholarship—with Michel Blondy and to learn about recent artistic tendencies in French ballet."

64. The *tragédies lyriques* are *Ariadne* (1672) and *Ariadne et Bacchus* (1696); the ballets that feature characters from this story are "l'Automne ou l'Amour paisible dans l'état du mariage" from *Ballet des Saisons* (1695) and "Bacchus et Ariadne" from *Les Amours des Dieux* (1727).

65. Marie-Françoise Christout, "Jean-Baptiste De Hesse," *International Encyclopedia of Dance*, 2:365.

66. Such an enquiry is not assisted by the fact that the Parfaicts' *Mémoires* was written before Sallé joined the Opéra-Comique. Émile Campardon, in his *Les Spectacles de la foire*, 2 vols. (Paris: Berger-Levrault, 1877), shows no awareness of her post-1741 activities (2:375–76); Antoine de Léris, *Dictionnaire portatif des théâtres* (Paris: C.A. Jombert, 1754) and the *Annales dramatiques*, suggests she spent her later years in England.

67. "*Zéphire et Flore:* a 'Galant' Early Ballet by Angiolini and Gluck," in *Opera and the Enlightenment*, ed. Thomas Bauman and Marita Petzoldt McClymonds (Cambridge: Cambridge University Press, 1995), 189–216, especially 197–200. For more on the descriptions for Sallé's ballet, see Sarah McCleave,

"English and French Theatrical Sources: The Repertoire of Marie Sallé," in *Dance and Music in French Baroque Theatre: Sources and Interpretations*, ed. Sarah McCleave (London: IAMS, 1998), 13–32, especially 22–26.

68. *Parodies* of Rameau's *Les Indes galantes* are identified in the article on "Indes galantes" in de Léris, *Dictionnaire portatif.*

69. "Bezons, La Foire de," in Parfaict and Parfaict, *Dictionnaire*, as translated in Winter, *Pre-Romantic Ballet*, 87.

70. See Noverre, *Letters*, trans. Beaumont, Letter 14, 149–52, for his description of *Les Jalousies*, and Letter 7, 54–55, for his discussion of previous *ballets en action*. Although Sallé never performed in *Les Fêtes grecques et romaines*, the role of Terpsichore was premiered by her teacher, Françoise Prévost, in 1723. Sallé took that role in Handel's prologue, *Terpsichore* (1734), which was based on *Les Fêtes grecques.*

71. Sallé would have had extended contact with Noverre during her period with the Opéra Comique in the mid-1740s; her apparent influence on him is of considerable significance and cannot be treated in sufficient depth here. For a preliminary consideration, see Sarah McCleave, "Marie Sallé and the Development of the *ballet en action*," *Journal of the Society for Musicology in Ireland* 2 (2007), http://www.music.ucc.ie/jsmi/.

72. An additional sphere of influence to consider is the impact Sallé may have had on composers with whom she worked. An in-depth study, however, of the respective musical styles of Handel and Rameau, her two chief collaborators, is beyond the scope of this article. Preliminary observations about Handel's response to Sallé (by writing different styles of dance music) and further remarks on Rameau's "gestural" style in *Les Indes galantes* will be expanded in an intended monograph on dance and issues of genre in the Baroque. See also Sarah McCleave, "Marie Sallé as Muse: Handel's Music for Mime," *The Consort* 51 (1995): 13–23; McCleave, "Sallé, Handel, Rameau and the Development of Narrative Dance Music," in *Die Beziehung von Musik und Choregraphie*, ed. Jörg Rothkamm and Michael Malkiewicz (Berlin: Vormerk, 2007), 107–21.

73. The most significant obstacle for this type of work is the lack of texts for Sallé's London pantomimes. Moreover, a detailed comparison of sources is beyond the scope of this study.

7

In Pursuit of the Dancer-Actress

Moira Goff

The London theater companies of the early eighteenth century included several women who were both dancers and actresses. They were not dancers who occasionally took minor acting roles, nor were they actresses who sometimes danced when required. These women not only danced regularly in the entr'actes and took leading roles in danced afterpieces but they also had their own acting roles, often leading ones, in which they appeared season after season. Some of them had begun as dancers, adding acting to their skills after a few seasons; others had started as actresses and had later taken up dancing as well. They are best described as dancer-actresses.

There had been dancing alongside drama in the London theaters from the Restoration onward, and actresses had danced as well as acted. The dancer-actress appears from the early 1700s, and she apparently disappears by about 1740. During this period, like most actresses, actors danced when the play required them to, but no leading actors danced in the entr'actes or afterpieces. Equally, no leading male dancers acted in mainpiece (or even afterpiece) plays. There were, thus, no men in the London theater companies who can be described as dancer-actors. By contrast, there were several women in the London theaters of the early eighteenth century who had dual careers as both dancers and actresses. This essay pursues the careers, particularly the dancing careers, of three of the most successful dancer-actresses: Margaret Bicknell, Elizabeth Younger, and Hester Santlow.

Between 1700 and 1730, when these three dancer-actresses were enjoying their stage careers, commentators and newspaper advertisements record how dance began to rival drama in its popularity with audiences. Dancing became ever more important in the London theaters, as the range and variety of entr'acte dances increased and pantomime afterpieces became a staple of the evening's entertainment. Dancing also became more expressive. John Weaver produced his first dramatic entertainments of dancing at Drury Lane, and his Lincoln's Inn Fields rival John Rich was quick to seize on his ideas. Weaver learned from, and exploited, the stage personalities and skills of Hester Santlow and Margaret Bicknell, as John Rich did those of Elizabeth Younger. This essay will investigate the evidence for their individual performance qualities and explore how their acting influenced their dancing. It will consider how both their stage personalities and their skills contributed to the development of expressive dancing on the London stage.

Margaret Bicknell

Margaret Bicknell's first recorded stage appearance was at Drury Lane on 20 August 1702, when she performed a solo *Scotch Dance*.[1] Performance records are very incomplete for the earliest years of the eighteenth century, so it is unlikely that this was her stage debut. On 1 July 1703 Mrs. Bicknell was billed in the acting role of Hoyden in John Vanbrugh's *The Relapse*. Again, it is unlikely that this was her debut as an actress, although she may well have begun her acting career during the 1702–3 season.[2]

From 1703/4 to 1705/6 Margaret Bicknell was billed only as a dancer; her repertory included a *Harlequin* duet, which she danced at Drury Lane on 22 December 1703. Her first billing of the 1706–7 season was at the Queen's Theater on 7 November 1706 as an actress, in the role of Edging in Colley Cibber's *The Careless Husband*. Mrs. Bicknell acted, but apparently did no dancing, at the Queen's Theater from 1706/7 to 1708/9. Her next billing as a dancer was not until 16 March

1710, still at the Queen's Theater, when she and John Thurmond Junior danced between the acts of George Farquhar's *The Recruiting Officer* (in which Mrs. Bicknell may have played the part of Rose).

Between 1706 and 1710 the Lord Chamberlain ordered several changes both to the genres of entertainment permitted at Drury Lane and the Queen's Theater and to the companies of the two theaters, trying to resolve the rivalry between drama and musical entertainments, particularly Italian opera.[3] Dancers were among those forced to change companies, and female dancers were particularly vulnerable as the number of players employed in the London theaters fell as a result of the Lord Chamberlain's actions. Margaret Bicknell was not the only female dancer who turned to acting in an attempt to ensure continued employment. During the 1710–11 season, when the theaters regained some stability, she moved back to Drury Lane, where she would spend the rest of her career both dancing and acting.

Margaret Bicknell's most important acting roles included Margery in William Wycherley's *The Country Wife* and Silvia in Farquhar's *The Recruiting Officer*, but her regular repertory also extended to Cherry in Farquhar's *The Beaux' Stratagem* (a role she created) and Pert in George Etherege's *The Man of Mode*. These were only a few of the roles she played season after season at Drury Lane.[4] Her dancing career extended beyond the entr'actes, for she danced as the Grace Aglaia in John Weaver's *The Loves of Mars and Venus* (1717), as a Nymph in his *Orpheus and Eurydice* (1718), and as Andromeda (Colombine) in his *The Shipwreck; or, Perseus and Andromeda* (1717). She also worked closely with the dancing master John Thurmond Junior from the 1718–19 season, appearing as Colombine in both *The Dumb Farce* (1719) and *The Escapes of Harlequin* (1722). Mrs. Bicknell's early death on 24 May 1723 sadly prevented her from dancing in Thurmond's phenomenally successful *Harlequin Doctor Faustus*, which opened at Drury Lane on 26 November 1723.

Elizabeth Younger

Margaret Bicknell's sister, Elizabeth Younger, was first mentioned in advertisements on 29 January 1711, when she played Lightning in *The Rehearsal* by George Villiers, Duke of Buckingham at Drury Lane, although she may have begun acting there as early as 1706.[5] By the 1712–13 season her roles at Drury Lane included Rose in *The Recruiting Officer* and Prue in William Congreve's *Love for Love*. When Mrs. Bicknell died, Mrs. Younger took over several of her sister's roles, including Silvia in *The Recruiting Officer*, which became part of her regular repertory. Elizabeth Younger's first billing as a dancer, again at Drury Lane, was on 3 May 1714, when the advertisements announced "A new *Saraband* and *Jig* by Miss Younger, being the first time of her Dancing alone on the Stage." Her entr'acte dances included a "Turkish Dance" created by the French dancing master Anthony L'Abbé in 1721 or 1722, which was recorded in Beauchamp-Feuillet notation and published.[6] For John Weaver she danced as the Grace Thalia in *The Loves of Mars and Venus*, and for John Thurmond Junior she appeared as a Punch Woman in *The Escapes of Harlequin* and as both Helen of Troy and Ceres in *Harlequin Doctor Faustus*.

Mrs. Younger disappeared from the stage for the whole of the 1724–25 season. When she returned, it was to Lincoln's Inn Fields, where she appeared as Margery in *The Country Wife* on 4 October 1725, "being the first Time of her Appearance on that Stage."[7] Elizabeth Younger quickly became one of the company's leading actresses, with a repertory that also included such roles as Hellena in Aphra Behn's *The Rover, Part 1*, Cordelia in Nahum Tate's *King Lear*, and Selima in Nicholas Rowe's *Tamerlane*. When the company opened the newly built Covent Garden Theater on 7 December 1732, she played Millamant in Congreve's *The Way of the World*.[8] At Lincoln's Inn Fields she no longer danced regularly in the entr'actes, but she did dance frequently in afterpieces, for she took over roles as a Mezzetin Woman and the Miller's Wife in *The Necromancer* (1723, Rich's riposte to *Harlequin Doctor Faustus*) and created the role of Colombine in *Apollo and Daphne* (1726), *The Rape of Proserpine* (1727), and *Perseus and Andromeda* (1730). Mrs. Younger left the stage for good at the end of the 1733–34 season.

Hester Santlow

The most successful of the dancer-actresses of the early eighteenth century was Hester Santlow, who made her debut as a dancer at Drury Lane on 28 February 1706. Although she worked within court as well as theater circles, dancing for Mr. Isaac whose ball dance "The Union" she performed before Queen Anne at Saint James's Palace in 1707, Mrs. Santlow (like Mrs. Bicknell) was affected by the Lord Chamberlain's orders, and she also became an actress. She made her acting debut on 3 December 1709 at Drury Lane, playing Prue in Congreve's *Love for Love*. The 1709–10 season was particularly successful for her, not least because of her creation of the title role in Charles Shadwell's *The Fair Quaker of Deal*.

By the 1710–11 season Hester Santlow was established as a leading actress with the Drury Lane company. Her repertory subsequently included such comic roles as Hellena in *The Rover, Part 1*, and Belinda in Vanbrugh's *The Provoked Wife*, and such tragic roles as Ophelia in *Hamlet* and Cordelia in Tate's *King Lear*.[9] Hester Santlow's dancing repertory is more fully recorded than that of any of her contemporaries because, as the leading dancer on the London stage, her performances were more often advertised in the newspapers. Her entr'acte dances ranged from a *passacaille* to a *Harlequin Dance;* she was so famous in the latter that her portrait was painted in Harlequin dress.[10] Seven of her dances were recorded and published in Beauchamp-Feuillet notation, from Isaac's "The Union" to the demanding solo "Passagalia of Venus & Adonis" created for her by Anthony L'Abbé.[11]

Mrs. Santlow worked very closely with John Weaver, for she created the roles of Venus in *The Loves of Mars and Venus,* Eurydice in *Orpheus and Eurydice,* and Helen of Troy in *The Judgment of Paris* (1733). She also danced in almost all of John Thurmond Junior's pantomime afterpieces at Drury Lane, including creating the roles of Diana in the Masque of the Deities in *Harlequin Doctor Faustus* and Daphne in *Apollo and Daphne* (1725). For Monsieur Roger, Drury Lane's dancing master from 1727/28 to 1730/31, she created Andromeda in the pantomime *Perseus and Andromeda* (1728; Roger devised the serious scenes and Weaver the comic scenes). Hester Santlow retired from the stage at the end of the 1732–33 season, following the death of her husband, the actor-manager Barton Booth, whom she had married in 1719.

Critical Accounts: Margaret Bicknell

Before the 1730s, little critical commentary on performances in the London theaters was published, so there are very few eyewitness accounts or appraisals to explain the individual appeal of each of the three dancer-actresses pursued in this essay. Mrs. Bicknell had the good fortune to become a favorite of Sir Richard Steele, who provides much of the evidence for her performance qualities. He first mentioned her in *The Tatler* for 16 April 1709, when he wrote of her appearance in the title role of *The Country Wife:* "Mrs. *Bignall* did her Part very happily, and had a certain Grace in her Rusticity, which gave us Hopes of seeing her a very Skilful Player, and in some Parts, supply our Loss of Mrs. *Verbruggen*."[12] Steele's reference to the popular comedy actress Susanna Verbruggen, who died in 1703, hints at Margaret Bicknell's performing style. She may have owed her casting in several roles that had belonged to Mrs. Verbruggen to Drury Lane's actor-manager Colley Cibber. He greatly admired Mrs. Verbruggen, and wrote in his *Apology* of her "Variety of Humour," and her ability to portray "the Lively, and the Desirable."[13] Mrs. Bicknell evidently had a similar vivacity in performance.

Steele provided a puff for Mrs. Bicknell's forthcoming benefit in *The Spectator* of 5 May 1712:

> It would be a great Improvement, as well as Embellishment to the Theater, if Dancing were more regarded, and taught to all the Actors. One who has the Advantage of such an agreeable girlish Person as Mrs. *Bicknell*, joyned with her Capacity of Imitation, could in proper Gesture and Motion represent all the decent Characters of Female Life. An amiable Modesty in one Aspect of a Dancer, an assumed Confidence in another, a sudden Joy in another, a falling off with an Impatience of being beheld, a Return towards the Audience with an unsteady Resolution to approach them, and a well-acted Sollicitude to please, would revive in the Company all the fine Touches of Mind raised in observing all the Objects of Affection or Passion they had before beheld.

He added "Mrs. *Bicknell* has the only Capacity for this sort of Dancing of any on the Stage."[14] It is unclear whether Steele saw Mrs. Bicknell's "Capacity of Imitation" as part of her acting or her dancing skills, although his reference to "Gesture and Motion" suggests the latter. His mention of the danced representation of "Characters of Female Life" anticipates by a few years Françoise Prévost's *Caractères de la danse.*[15]

Critical Accounts: Elizabeth Younger

Elizabeth Younger had as long a career as her sister, but there are virtually no eyewitness accounts of her as either a dancer or an actress. Thomas Davies, writing many years later, said dismissively that she was "a general actress, and sometimes appeared in tragedy, though, I think, not to advantage," although he conceded that "Mrs. Younger's Millamant was spritely."[16] She obviously shared some performance qualities with Mrs. Bicknell, several of whose roles she inherited, and with Mrs. Santlow, for they were rivals in a number of roles after Mrs. Younger moved to Lincoln's Inn Fields.

One source for Elizabeth Younger's performance style is the published notation for the "Turkish Dance," which L'Abbé created for her and Monsieur Denoyer during the latter's first visit to London. L'Abbé's dance is to three pieces of music from the fourth *entrée*, "La Turquie," in Campra's 1697 *opéra-ballet L'Europe galante* and may well have been inspired by its story of rivalry in the harem.[17] The "Türkish Dance" begins with the couple side by side, as if ready for the conventional opening to a duet. Instead, Denoyer launches into a bombastic solo, full of jumps and beats, many incorporating turns, and including such virtuoso steps as a *tour en l'air* with an *entrechat six*. He dances away from, toward, and at one point right around, his partner, perhaps showing "the haughtiness and supreme authority of the *Sultan*."[18] Mrs. Younger's reactions (if any) to Denoyer's feats of virtuosity are not recorded by the notation. Her solo, to the second piece of music, makes use of some of the same choreographic material but has no virtuoso steps. Its small jumps and little beats are understated, and it could be performed in a languid or seductive style, in keeping with "the passionate nature of the *Sultanas*" depicted in *L'Europe galante*.[19]

On the last repeat of her music, Mrs. Younger is joined by Denoyer for a duet that uses the same vocabulary of steps. Their duet continues with the third piece of music, but it changes its character completely. They advance downstage with flat-footed steps previously used in Denoyer's solo and then perform lots of small, complex jumps, with added beats and quarter or half turns. In turn, they each perform steps with *cabrioles* (rarely included in notated dances for women). The duet is spirited, even combative, and ends as the two dancers, holding inside hands, travel sideways toward stage left and stop suddenly, with their right feet in the air. L'Abbé's "Türkish Dance" clearly shows Elizabeth Younger's command of both the elegance of the serious style and the lively, energetic footwork of comic dancing.

Critical Accounts: Hester Santlow

Mrs. Santlow's performances as an actress and particularly as a dancer received much attention in newspapers, periodicals, and other works. She was greatly admired by her fellow professionals as well as by audiences. In his preface to his translation of Pierre Rameau's *Le Maître a danser*, published in 1728, the dancing master John Essex wrote of:

> the incomparable Mrs. *Booth* [i.e., Hester Santlow], in whom Art and Nature are so beautifully wove together, . . . that the Produce of the many different Characters she represents is the Wonder and Admiration of the present Age, and will scarce be credited by the Succeeding. I shall beg leave to mention the *Chaconne, Saraband, Menuet,* in which she appears with that Grace, Softness, and Address none can look on but with Attention, Pleasure, and Surprise. She far excels all that went before her, and must be the just Subject of Imitation to all that dare attempt to copy after her. Besides all these, the *Harlequin* is beyond Description, and the *Hussar* another opposite Character in which she has no Rival.[20]

Essex's praise was intended to draw a comparison with Rameau's description of the French dancer Françoise Prévost in his original preface to the treatise. Rameau had written of Prévost: "She justly deserves to be regarded as Terpsichore the Muse, . . . and has all the Advantages over Proteus in the Fable. She at Pleasure assumes all manner of Shapes."[21] His reference to "Proteus," like Essex's references to "the many different Characters" represented by Hester Santlow, was intended to call attention to the dancer's acting abilities.[22]

Barton Booth tried to evoke his wife's performance qualities in his "Ode on Mira, Dancing."[23] He wrote of her "Order and Grace together join'd, / Sweetness with Majesty combin'd," and exclaimed "Gods! how divine an Air / Harmonious Gesture gives the Fair!" He described how "She whirls around! she bounds! she springs! / As if Jove's messenger had lent her Wings." Booth's "Ode" pictures Hester Santlow as Venus moving "to a slow and melting Air," as Daphne whose "swift Feet outstript the Wind," and as Diana who "charms the Sight."[24] As well as grace and softness, Mrs. Santlow evidently had speed and vigor. Booth was obviously enraptured by Hester Santlow's sensuality when she danced.

Some of Mrs. Santlow's expressive ability, and her technical command, can be glimpsed in L'Abbé's solo "Passagalia of Venus & Adonis" created between 1715 and 1718.[25] The choreography suggests that L'Abbé may have intended Mrs. Santlow to represent different characters or imitate various passions as she danced.[26] He made much use of ornamentation and variation, by adding small jumps and beats and quarter, half, or even three-quarter turns to steps, adding to the expressive

potential of the "Passagalia," but at the same time displaying Hester
Santlow's technical strength. The dance's vocabulary includes a *demi-
entrechat* and a *demi cabriole en tournant un demi tour,* both familiar from the
notated dances for men but rarely found in those for women. L'Abbé's
"Passagalia of Venus & Adonis" demonstrates Hester Santlow's range
and variety of expression as a dancer.

John Weaver and Eighteenth-Century English Acting

In his *An Essay Towards an History of Dancing* of 1712, Weaver described
"*Scenical Dancing*" as "a faint Imitation of the *Roman Pantomimes*" that
"explains whole *Stories* by *Action.*" He wrote "should we form our Notions of these *Pantomimes* from those Representations we have among
us, we should be apt to imagine an *Actor* rather describ'd here than a
Dancer."[27] There are many parallels between acting and the expressive
dancing Weaver designed for *The Loves of Mars and Venus.* Several of the
gestures he described in his scenario are related to gestures discussed by
Quintilian in his *Institutio Oratoria.*[28] The link between rhetoric and acting is made clear by Charles Gildon in his *The Life of Mr. Thomas Betterton,* published in 1710, a work that has much in common with Weaver's
Essay.[29] In his advice to actors, Gildon referred almost entirely to tragedy. He indicated that tragic acting style was formal and dignified, with
gestures drawn from rhetoric, bodily presentation based on classical and
classically influenced statuary and paintings, and facial expressions derived from the work of artists like Charles Le Brun.[30] Comic acting style
was little mentioned by commentators in the early eighteenth century,
but it was apparently close to the conventions governing everyday behavior in polite society, albeit with some exaggeration, and thus far less
solemn than the tragic.[31]

The London theaters put on fifty or more plays each season, a sched-
ule that necessarily meant limited rehearsal periods.[32] Plays changed
nightly, and even though many were stock plays repeated season after
season, actresses needed shortcuts if they were to sustain such a repertory. Actresses had particular "lines," that is they played particular types
of tragic and comic roles (although these were not necessarily narrowly
defined); this made it easier for them to learn and rehearse what were
very similar parts in a number of different plays.[33] When an actress succeeded to a part that had been created by her predecessor, she tried to

follow the earlier actress's performance; because tradition was an important part of performance style, an actress did not need to create afresh every new role she acquired.[34] Weaver, Mrs. Bicknell, Mrs. Younger, and Mrs. Santlow were all part of this system.

As an actress, Mrs. Santlow's "lines" included pathetic heroines in tragedy and witty heroines in genteel comedy. By the 1716–17 season her tragic roles included Cydaria in John Dryden's *The Indian Emperor* and Selima in Rowe's *Tamerlane,* while her comic roles included Harriet in Etherege's *The Man of Mode* and Angelica in Farquhar's *The Constant Couple.*[35] All four provide hints about Hester Santlow's danced portrayal of Venus. Cydaria was originally played by Nell Gwyn, and Harriet was probably created by Elizabeth Barry (who later became London's leading tragedienne).[36] Angelica was created by Jane Rogers, who also specialized in pathetic heroines.[37] Both Selima and Harriet were played by Anne Bracegirdle, who also acted and sang as Venus in Peter Anthony Motteux's masque *The Loves of Mars and Venus,* Weaver's principal source for his first dramatic entertainment of dancing.[38]

The action of Weaver's *The Loves of Mars and Venus* unfolds in six scenes, and Venus appears in scenes 2, 4, and 6. In scene 2 Venus introduces herself to the audience by dancing a *passacaille,* in which she is joined by the Graces and the Hour. The dance is hardly over before Vulcan enters, and he and Venus proceed to quarrel in a "*Dance* being altogether of the *Pantomimic* Kind." Vulcan begins by expressing "Admiration" for his wife, but their mute exchange becomes ever more acrimonious, until Venus, with an expression of "Contempt; *and* Disdain," finally leaves the stage.[39] In *The Constant Couple* Angelica quarrels with Sir Harry Wildair; the pretexts differ from those in *The Loves of Mars and Venus,* but their dispute involves some of the same passions. Sir Harry declares, "your Beauty ravishes my Eye," but Angelica soon ripostes that it is "possible to make me detest and scorn you"; she finally exits, hurling an insult at him as she leaves.[40] (See figure 7.1.) A scene in *The Man of Mode* hints at how the "Coquetry . . . seen in affected Airs" that Venus assumes in scene 2 might have been played.[41] Harriet and Young Bellair are feigning courtship, and he gives her some advice on how to act the part: "Clap your hand upon your bosom, hold down your gown. Shrug a little, draw up your breasts and let 'em fall again, gently, with a sigh or two."[42]

In scene 4 Mars and Venus meet, he with "Gallantry; Respect; Ardent Love; and Adoration" and she with "An Affected Bashfulness; reciprocal Love; and wishing Looks."[43] Their encounter recalls scenes within both *The Indian Emperor* and *Tamerlane.* In Dryden's play, the

Figure 7.1. Sir Harry Wildair and Angelica are the couple top right in this frontispiece from George Farquhar, The Constant Couple (London: B. Lintott, 1711). Reprinted by permission of the British Library.

"Spanish General" Cortez has hardly entered on the scene before he "spies the Ladies and goes to them, entertaining *Cydaria* with Courtship in dumb show"; Cydaria, Montezuma's daughter, immediately falls in love with him.[44] Weaver refers to scene 4 of *The Loves of Mars and Venus* as "representing Love and War" in which "Strength, and Softness, reciprocally, and alternately are seen in their full Power."[45] This contrast is seen in Rowe's *Tamerlane,* in which Selima, daughter of Bajazet, is in love with Axalla, "an Italian Prince, General and Favorite of *Tamerlane.*" In their first love scene together, she exclaims "Oh! help me to resolve against this Tenderness" shortly before "Sinking into his Arms," and he declares "The noble ardour of the War, with Love / Returning, brightly burns within my Breast" before he is forced to return to the battle raging offstage.[46] *The Loves of Mars and Venus* ends conventionally with a "Grand Dance" after Neptune, accompanied by other gods and goddesses, persuades Vulcan to forgive the lovers.[47] Throughout Weaver's dramatic entertainment of dancing, Hester Santlow moved constantly back and forth between acting and dancing.

Colombine in England

As two of the three Graces in *The Loves of Mars and Venus,* Mrs. Bicknell and Mrs. Younger apparently did little other than dance, but Weaver (like Sir Richard Steele) must have seen Mrs. Bicknell's expressive potential, for he cast her as Andromeda (Colombine) alongside himself as Perseus (Harlequin) in *The Shipwreck; or, Perseus and Andromeda,* his comic counterpart to *The Loves of Mars and Venus* first given at Drury Lane on 2 April 1717. No description of the story or the action in *The Shipwreck* survives, but the advertised cast list points to another of the influences on Weaver, the *commedia dell'arte.* Margaret Bicknell was possibly the first English actress to play Colombine.

The role of Colombine had been developed by Catherine Biancolelli, daughter of the famous Harlequin Dominique, in plays like *Arlequin Empereur dans la Lune* (1684) and *Colombine Avocat Pour et Contre* (1685). Her Colombine evolved into a witty, cynical, resourceful, amoral, and definitely French *servante* who was more than a match for Harlequin and all the other characters she encountered.[48] Unlike Harlequin, Colombine seems to have been slow to cross the Channel; she is conspicuous by her absence in plays such as the *Emperor of the Moon* (1687), Aphra Behn's adaptation of *Arlequin Empereur dans la Lune.*[49] She may have arrived in

London with the dancer-actors Joseph Sorin and Richard Baxter, who appeared together in a *Night Scene by a Harlequin and Scaramouche, after the Italian Manner* at Drury Lane on 22 August 1702. Sorin and Baxter were later invited to return to London by Sir Richard Steele, and on 4 April 1716 they gave an afterpiece at Drury Lane entitled *The Whimsical Death of Harlequin*. In the intervening years they had been playing in France, in a repertory that included such plays as Lesage's *Arlequin-Colombine ou Colombine-Arlequin*.[50] It seems likely that Sorin and Baxter introduced Weaver, and Margaret Bicknell, to a French Colombine who both acted and danced.

It is not easy to recover the English Colombine. After *The Shipwreck,* Mrs. Bicknell played Colombine in John Thurmond Junior's afterpieces *The Dumb Farce* (1719) and *The Escapes of Harlequin* (1722). No scenarios of either were published, but the cast list for *The Dumb Farce* includes such characters as Geronte, Octave, and Angelique, as well as Harlequin and Colombine, linking it to scenarios of the *commedia dell'arte*.[51] It could well have been inspired by *La Foire de St. Germain,* which had been given by a visiting troupe of French comedians for their opening performance at Lincoln's Inn Fields on 7 November 1718 and was published in an English translation that same year.[52]

Mrs. Bicknell was a comic actress, whose "lines" included waiting women, who were anything but subservient, as well as their mistresses. She had no significant roles in tragedies. In *The Fair of St. Germain* Colombine is very much the character created by Catherine Biancolelli, aiding and abetting the young lovers Angelica and Octavio against the Doctor (Angelica's guardian, who wants to marry her), with the help of Harlequin. The role resembles others from Mrs. Bicknell's acting repertory, for example Pert, who is waiting woman to Mrs. Loveit in *The Man of Mode*.[53] Both are witty, free with their advice to their mistresses, and cynical about love. Colombine declares to Angelica, "Love is but an indifferent kind of Diversion to those scrupulous people that know not how to extract the Quintessence of it," and when she learns of the designs of the Doctor she observes that: "A Guardian's marrying his Ward is, indeed, one short Way of making up his Accompts. But if the Guardian is old, she generally finds great Errors in the Reck'ning."[54] In her first exchange with Mrs. Loveit, Pert advises her to "Hate . . . that base man Mr. Dorimant, who makes you torment and vex yourself continually," a little later giving her opinion that "A modish man is always very busy when he is in pursuit of a new mistress."[55] Like Mrs. Santlow, Mrs. Bicknell could draw on her acting repertory for her roles in danced afterpieces.

Elizabeth Younger shared some of her sister's acting roles and hence her "lines," but she had a wider range in comedy and (like Hester Santlow) played some of the softer tragic roles. Her dancing career at Lincoln's Inn Fields resembled that of her sister rather than Mrs. Santlow's, partly because Rich's company made few serious attempts to emulate Weaver's dramatic entertainments of dancing (although it did parody them). When it came to pantomime afterpieces, Rich had no scruples about copying and trying, usually successfully, to outdo Drury Lane. Nevertheless, there were significant differences between the pantomimes at the two rival theaters. Most of the pantomimes at both Drury Lane and Lincoln's Inn Fields had double plots that were quite separate from one another; one was a serious plot (usually involving classical deities) that unfolded in scenes that alternated with those of the second comic plot (involving *commedia dell'arte* characters). At Drury Lane the serious plot was almost invariably danced. At Lincoln's Inn Fields, the serious plot was always sung and had added divertissements of dancing, rather like French opera.

The comic plots in the Lincoln's Inn Fields pantomimes offered many opportunities for expressive dancing and gesture. One of the first afterpiece dancing roles taken by Elizabeth Younger, after her move to Lincoln's Inn Fields, was the Miller's Wife in *The Necromancer*.[56] The published scenario of the pantomime provides a vivid outline of the opening to the scene in which she appears: "The Miller's Wife comes down the Stairs from the Mill, and dances; in the Interim her Husband enters, and in a very angry Manner is for driving her up again; she endeavours to perswade him from it; but he persisting; she in a very obsequious Manner leaves him, and is going up; he mollified at her Behaviour, calls her back, is reconcil'd, and dances with her."[57] There was no counterpart to this scene in Drury Lane's *Harlequin Doctor Faustus*, although the wordless quarrel of the Miller and his Wife is reminiscent of that between Vulcan and Venus in *The Loves of Mars and Venus*.

Mrs. Younger was Colombine to John Rich's Harlequin in a number of pantomimes at Lincoln's Inn Fields. The published libretti record only the sung serious parts of these afterpieces, but the comic part of *Perseus and Andromeda* was so popular that it enjoyed a separate life of its own; it was later performed and a scenario published in the provinces.[58] Colombine in this pantomime is similar in some respects to the witty heroines of genteel comedy, even as she encourages Harlequin in a series of outrageous tricks. The nine comic scenes are concerned with

Harlequin's attempts to win Colombine "Daughter to the Spanish Merchant" against the disapproval of the Spaniard and the rivalry of her other lover, the Petit Maître.[59] The comic action was celebrated for the transformations of John Rich as Harlequin, who spent much of his time disguised as a dog.

The action of *The Tricks of Harlequin* begins with a letter Harlequin wants to send to Colombine. In scene 3, transformed into a dog, Harlequin "gives it to *Colombine,* and she strokes him." Almost immediately he misbehaves, "*Harlequin* walks round, holds up one Leg and pisses on the *Petit Maitre*"; hardly surprisingly, the Petit Maître and the "dog" get into a fracas and the Spaniard goes to kill Harlequin, but "*Colombine,* by Action, begs he would not, intimating 'tis her favorite Dog." Scene 4 changes to a different mood, as "*Harlequin, Colombine,* and several *Shepherds* and *Shepherdesses*" come together for a dance, although the pastoral atmosphere is shattered when the Spaniard discovers them and Harlequin transforms himself into a statue of Mercury and rises above his pursuer on a cupola.[60] These were among the scenes conflated in a satirical engraving showing not Mrs. Younger but Mrs. Laguerre (another dancer-actress), with her skirts tucked up to her knees, dancing with Francis Nivelon who played the Spaniard.[61] (See figure 7.2.) In scene 8 "*Harlequin* sees *Colombine* in the Balcony, he makes love to her in dumb Shew, she returns it," but she has some darker passions to express before the comic plot reaches its happy ending. Shortly afterward: "The *Petit Maitre* meets them [Harlequin and Colombine] and draws his Sword; *Colombine* runs off frighten'd. They fight; *Harlequin* falls. Re-enter *Colombine* who mourns over him." In the final comic scene of *Perseus and Andromeda* the Shepherds and Shepherdesses return, "who, kneel to the *Spaniard,* and, by Action, begs [*sic*] him to forgive *Harlequin;* he agrees, and they all join in a Grand Dance."[62] Rich was probably echoing the final scene in *The Loves of Mars and Venus.*

The comic scenes in *Perseus and Andromeda* present a world not so very far removed from that of the mainpiece comedies given at Lincoln's Inn Fields. In the course of her career, Elizabeth Younger played two leading roles in *The Country Wife* (which, despite the indelicacies of its plot, held its place on the London stage into the eighteenth century), the witty worldly Alithea, and the "Country Wife" Margery.[63] In *Perseus and Andromeda,* the Petit Maître is reminiscent of Alithea's fashionable and self-absorbed suitor Sparkish, while the Spaniard's jealous care of his daughter recalls Pinchwife's jealousy over his wife; Colombine unites

Figure 7.2. Mrs. Laguerre and Francis Nivelon appear alongside John Rich (as both a dog and Mercury) in *Perseus and Andromeda*, in this frontispiece from James Miller, *Harlequin-Horace: or, the Art of Modern Poetry* (London: L. Gilliver, 1731). Reprinted by permission of the British Library.

facets of Alithea's city sophistication with Margery's country guile. Such comparisons cannot be pushed too far, but Elizabeth Younger could certainly draw on her acting in both comic and tragic roles, as well as her dancing skills, when she played Colombine for John Rich.

Conclusion

The dancer-actresses Margaret Bicknell, Elizabeth Younger, and Hester Santlow all enjoyed great popularity, and very successful careers, because of their acting and dancing skills and their engaging stage personalities. They worked in theaters where, even though drama was the dominant form of entertainment, plays were performed side by side with dances and mutual influences were unavoidable. As both actresses and dancers they needed to deploy all their beauty, charm, and sexual allure. Dancing, no less than acting, was subject to the pressures of the repertory system of the London stage, and it was inevitable that, with limited rehearsal time, dancers who were also actresses would draw on their acting skills when they played dancing roles in afterpieces. The relationship between the two art forms was seen and remarked on by contemporaries, not least because nearly every evening they could see dancer-actresses both acting and dancing in the London theaters.

During the first third of the eighteenth century, dance began to close the gap with drama in terms of its sophistication and its popularity with audiences. Dancing on the London stage could already be exacting in style and technique, but it became expressive of "*Actions, Manners,* and *Passions*" as well.[64] Mrs. Bicknell's dancing is difficult to recover, but the notated dances of Mrs. Younger and Mrs. Santlow show them to have mastered the technique of dancing practiced at the Paris Opera and exploited its expressive potential. The experiments of Françoise Prévost, if they were not directly known in London, were certainly emulated there. In London, too, *commedia dell'arte* enjoyed renewed popularity through the performances of Sorin and Baxter. All three dancer-actresses included *commedia dell'arte* characters in their dancing repertory, and they must have learned much from the performances of the two visitors from France.

Drama and *commedia dell'arte* were two of the most significant influences on John Weaver when he came to produce his dramatic entertainments of dancing. Weaver may have theorized about the pantomimes of classical antiquity, but in practice he brought together contemporary acting and dancing to create dance works that were independent of both plays and operas. Hester Santlow used her skills and experience as an actress in both comedy and tragedy and deployed her stage personality to create serious roles in dramatic entertainments of dancing at Drury Lane. Margaret Bicknell and Elizabeth Younger did the same to create their English versions of Colombine in pantomimes at Drury Lane and Lincoln's Inn Fields, respectively. The roles created by these women were integral to the phenomenal success of these new afterpiece genres. It is natural to conclude that they were collaborators with, rather than merely interpreters for, John Weaver, John Rich, and others. Indeed, it is possible to claim that expressive dancing developed on the London stage as quickly as it did because of the accomplished performances of the dancer-actresses Margaret Bicknell, Elizabeth Younger, and Hester Santlow.

Notes

1. Information about performances in the London theaters, including quotations from advertisements, is taken from *The London Stage, 1660–1800*, part 2, *1700–1729*, ed. Emmett L. Avery, and part 3, *1729–1747*, ed. Arthur H. Scouten (Carbondale: Southern Illinois University Press, 1960, 1965). Biographical information about players in the London theaters is taken from Philip H. Highfill Jr., Kalman A. Burnim, and Edward A. Langhans, *A Biographical Dictionary of Actors, Actresses, Musicians, Dancers, Managers & Other Stage Personnel in London, 1660–1800* (Carbondale: Southern Illinois University Press, 1973–93).

2. In the London theaters, seasons usually ran from September to the following May or June.

3. For a summary of these events, see Curtis A. Price, "The Critical Decade for English Music Drama, 1700–1710," *Harvard Library Bulletin* 26 (1978): 38–76.

4. Between 1703 and 1723 Mrs. Bicknell played fifty-five acting roles in fifty-one plays; about a third of the roles formed her regular repertory. Each season she played, on average, fifteen to eighteen acting roles.

5. In John Banks's *Virtue Betrayed; or Anna Bullen*, given at Drury Lane on 27 March 1706, the role of Princess Elizabeth was played "by the Child," who has been identified as Elizabeth Younger. See John Genest, *Some Account of the English Stage from the Restoration in 1660 to 1830* (Bath: H. E. Carrington, 1832), 2, 340.

6. See Meredith Ellis Little and Carol G. Marsh, *La Danse Noble: An Inventory of Dances and Sources* (Williamstown, MA: Broude Brothers, 1992), [c1725]-Lab.

7. Avery, *London Stage*, part 2, 834.

8. Between 1713 and 1734 Mrs. Younger played ninety-eight acting roles in

seventy-eight plays; about a quarter of the roles formed her regular repertory. Each season she played, on average, eighteen to twenty acting roles.

9. Between 1709 and 1733 Hester Santlow played sixty-five roles in sixty-two plays; about a third of the roles formed her regular repertory. Each season she played, on average, eighteen to twenty acting roles.

10. The portrait is now in the Theater Collections of the Victoria and Albert Museum, London. See Geoffrey Ashton, *Catalogue of Paintings at the Theater Museum, London*, ed. James Fowler (London: Victoria and Albert Museum, Society for Theater Research, 1992), 7–8.

11. See Little and Marsh, *Danse Noble*, [1707]-Unn, [1708]-Slt, [c1725]-Lab, [1731]-Prw.

12. *The Tatler*, ed. Donald F. Bond (Oxford: Clarendon Press, 1987), 1, 31 (italics in original).

13. *An Apology for the Life of Colley Cibber*, ed. B. R. S. Fone (Ann Arbor: University of Michigan Press, 1968), 94, 95.

14. *The Spectator*, ed. Donald F. Bond (Oxford: Clarendon Press, 1965), 3, 395–96 (italics in original).

15. For an account of Prévost's solo, see Pierre Aubry and Émile Dacier, *Les Caractères de la Danse* (Paris: H. Champion, 1905).

16. Thomas Davies, *Dramatic Miscellanies* (London: the Author, 1783–84), 3, 368, 373.

17. *La Belle Dance: Catalogue raisonné fait en l'an 1995*, comp. Francine Lancelot (Paris: Van Dieren, 1996), FL/1725.1/13.

18. Original plot summary for *L'Europe galante*. James R. Anthony, *French Baroque Music from Beaujoyeulx to Rameau* (Portland, OR: Amadeus Press, 1997), 171.

19. Anthony, *French Baroque Music*, 171.

20. Pierre Rameau, *The Dancing-Master: or, the Art of Dancing Explained*, trans. John Essex (London: [J. Essex and] J. Brotherton, 1728), xv, xvi (italics in original).

21. Rameau, *Dancing-Master*, xxvi.

22. For early comparisons between actors and Proteus, see Joseph R. Roach, *The Player's Passion* (Newark, NJ: University of Delaware Press, 1985), 41.

23. Benjamin Victor, *Memoirs of the Life of Barton Booth, Esq.* (London: J. Watts, 1733), 49–51.

24. Victor declared that "The Ode on Dancing was wrote in the year 1718, and left incorrect." *Memoirs*, 35. The references to Hester Santlow as Daphne and Diana suggest that Booth may have revised the poem at a later date.

25. For the date of creation of the "Passagalia," see Moira Goff, "Art and Nature Join'd: Hester Santlow and the Development of Dancing on the London Stage, 1700–1737" (doctoral thesis, University of Kent at Canterbury, 2000), 191–92.

26. Goff, "Art and Nature Join'd," 198–99.

27. John Weaver, *An Essay Towards an History of Dancing* (London: Jacob Tonson, 1712), 168, 147 (italics in original).

28. John Weaver, *The Loves of Mars and Venus* (London: W. Mears, J. Browne, 1717), 21–23, 28. Quintilian, *The Orator's Education*, ed. and trans. Donald A. Russell (Cambridge, MA: Harvard University Press, 2001), 5, 85–183. There is no published research tracing the various sources Weaver used for his gestures.

29. Charles Gildon, *The Life of Mr. Thomas Betterton* (London: Robert Gosling, 1710). The relationship between the two works is explored in Richard Ralph, *The Life and Works of John Weaver* (London: Dance Books, 1985), 135–36. For the relationship between acting and rhetoric, see also Roach, *Player's Passion*, chapter 1.

30. For example, see Gildon, *Life of Mr. Thomas Betterton*, 25–27, 37.

31. Peter Holland, *The Ornament of Action* (Cambridge: Cambridge University Press, 1979), 57–58.

32. Avery, *London Stage*, part 2, cxxvii; Tiffany Stern, *Rehearsal from Shakespeare to Sheridan* (Oxford: Clarendon Press, 2000), 203–5.

33. For "lines" see Holland, *Ornament of Action*, 77–81.

34. Stern, *Rehearsal*, 212–14. Actresses, and dancers, would also draw on their individual skills and personalities in performance. Improvisation was another important means by which they could cope with the pressures of an ever-changing repertory, although it cannot be examined in this essay. Improvisation, or "caprice," in dancing is explored by Edmund Fairfax, *The Styles of Eighteenth-Century Ballet* (Lanham, MD: Scarecrow Press, 2003), chapter 6. However, as his text demonstrates, there is very little evidence from the early 1700s. The available sources suggest that improvisation, in the early years of the century at least, encompassed ornamentation and variation as well as (if not rather than) the impromptu invention of steps, in parallel with musical practice. Eighteenth-century dance improvisation needs further research and careful interpretation of the surviving sources.

35. Her debuts in all these roles were at Drury Lane: Cydaria, 27 January 1711; Selima, probably 5 November 1716, although no cast was listed until 27 December 1716; Harriet, 22 February 1711; Angelica, 11 October 1714.

36. Elizabeth Howe, *The First English Actresses* (Cambridge: Cambridge University Press, 1992), 80, 151.

37. Howe, *English Actresses*, 104, 189.

38. Howe, *English Actresses*, 182; Mrs. Bracegirdle was billed as Harriet at the Queen's Theater on 9 November 1706. For Weaver's use of Motteux's masque, see Ralph, *John Weaver*, 53.

39. Weaver, *Loves*, 20, 24 (italics in original).

40. George Farquhar, *The Constant Couple* (London: B. Lintott, 1711), 30–31.

41. Weaver, *Loves*, 22.

42. George Etherege, "The Man of Mode," in *Restoration and Eighteenth-Century Comedy*, ed. Scott McMillin (New York: W. W. Norton, 1973), 79–153; quotation, 106.

43. Weaver, *Loves*, 25.

44. John Dryden, *The Indian Emperor* (London: J. Tonson, W. Feales, 1732), 12, 22 (italics reversed).

45. Weaver, *Loves*, 25.

46. Nicholas Rowe, *Tamerlane* (London: J. Tonson, J. Brown, 1717), A6v, 16, 17 (italics in original).

47. Weaver, *Loves*, 27.

48. Virginia Scott, *The Commedia dell'Arte in Paris, 1644–1697* (Charlottesville: University Press of Virginia, 1990), 255, 294, 301, 306.

49. *The Works of Aphra Behn*, ed. Janet Todd (London: William Pickering, 1992–96), 7, 153–207 (158, dramatis personae).

50. Émile Campardon, *Les Spectacles de la foire*, 2 vols. (Paris: Berger-Levrault, 1877), 1:100–101.

51. *The Dumb Farce* was first performed at Drury Lane on 12 February 1719.

52. Jean-François Regnard and Charles Rivière de Fresny, *The Fair of St. Germain*, trans. J. Ozell (London: W. Chetwood, J. Roberts, 1718). The title page declares: "As it is Acted at the Theatre in *Little Lincoln's-Inn-Fields*, by the *French* Company of Comedians" (italics in original). The scenario had originally been played by the Comédie Italienne in Paris in 1695. This version is discussed by Scott, *Commedia dell'arte*, 376–77.

53. Mrs. Bicknell was first billed as Pert at Queen's Theater on 18 January 1707.

54. Regnard and Fresny, *Fair of St. Germain*, 4, 5.

55. Etherege, "Man of Mode," 96, 97.

56. Mrs. Younger first danced in *The Necromancer* on 3 November 1725.

57. "The Necromancer," in *An Exact Description of the Two Fam'd Entertainments of Harlequin Doctor Faustus* (London: T. Payne, 1724), 19–35; quotation, 29.

58. *The Tricks of Harlequin: or, the Spaniard Outwitted* (Derby, 1739). The title page describes the text as the "Comic Part of the celebrated Entertainment of Perseus and Andromeda."

59. *Tricks of Harlequin*, unnumbered [2], "Persons Names."

60. *Tricks of Harlequin*, 9–10, 13 (italics in original).

61. The engraving was published as the frontispiece to James Miller, *Harlequin-Horace: or, the Art of Modern Poetry* (London: L. Gilliver, 1731). See also Frederick George Stephens, *Catalogue of Political and Personal Satires Preserved in the Department of Prints and Drawings in the British Museum*, vol. 2, *1689–1733* (1873; reprint, London: British Museum Publications, 1978), no. 1718.

62. *Tricks of Harlequin*, 17, 18, 20 (italics in original).

63. See William Wycherley, "The Country Wife," in McMillin, *Restoration and Eighteenth-Century Comedy*, 3–78.

64. Weaver, *Essay*, 160: "Stage-Dancing was at first design'd for *Imitation;* . . . plainly and intelligibly representing *Actions, Manners,* and *Passions*" (italics in original).

WORLDVIEWS

8

Elisabeth of Spalbeek: Dancing the Passion

KAREN SILEN

In the middle of the thirteenth century, the young Elisabeth of Spalbeek became widely known for her danced reenactments of the Lord's Passion.[1] Elisabeth's supporters understood her dances as a divine revelation received directly from God for the purposes of inspiring her audiences and renewing their faith. Her performances, revered by her religious superiors, were held in a specially built round chapel. This site became the destination of the faithful who came from across Europe to observe her dances. In 1267 Abbot Philip of Clairvaux carefully recorded Elisabeth's performances in a document known as the "Life of Elisabeth of Spalbeek."[2] This report provides a rare and detailed description of dance practice before the fifteenth century as well as an unusual glimpse of an individual dancer known to a wide audience.

Compared to most thirteenth-century records of dance, Elisabeth's "Life" describes a surprising range of movements, including backbends, falls to the floor, and amazing feats of balance. It also reports that Elisabeth endured self-flagellation and bore signs of the stigmata during the performances, which took place while Elisabeth was in an ecstatic state.[3] While her dances are remarkable on their own, our perception and appreciation of them can be greatly enhanced by viewing them within their social and historical contexts. Elisabeth's dancing may be seen as a choreographic response to a specific set of cultural beliefs and conditions that limited women's roles in orthodox religion and as a manipulation of those beliefs. Her ecstatic states infused her words and dances with divine authority, albeit an authority that required sanction from her immediate clerical supervisors. That evidence of Elisabeth's dances survives is a testament both to the power and success of her performances and to their usefulness to members of the clerical hierarchy that carefully monitored, preserved, and promoted them.

Elisabeth was a visionary, or mystic, living in the late thirteenth century in the diocese of Liège in the southern Low Countries. She was part of a much greater historical movement, one that is now under investigation by scholars in a number of fields. Hagiographical texts such as Elisabeth's "Life" are celebrated as a fruitful source for the study of medieval culture and society.[4] Research into the lives of female visionaries has revealed information about how these women lived, worked, practiced their religious beliefs, and depicted themselves through their own writing or were depicted by their male hagiographers. However, while several scholars have remarked on the role of dance in their religious practices, no studies have yet focused primarily on the dancing of these women.

This essay is a first step toward reconstructing Elisabeth's dance and its meaning and it identifies some of the ways that her performances embodied cultural beliefs and performance practices of her day. The incomplete nature of many medieval sources and lack of in-depth studies make it impossible to know whether Elisabeth's "Life" records new dance practices or whether it is simply an unusually detailed description of dance practices that already existed. What is certain is that the "Life" provides details about an individual performer in a period we know very little about and that it points to new types of sources and methods for investigating early dance history. Elisabeth's "Life" also raises some important questions about how to define dance when analyzing sources originally designed for very different purposes than as records of dance.

Thirteenth-Century French Flanders and the Beguines

One of the most striking social and religious phenomena of the High Middle Ages was the large number of lay men and women devoted to living a life in harmony with their religious beliefs but outside convent and monastery walls. By the late twelfth century, and increasingly in the thirteenth century, large groups of men and women formed associations and communities to pray and to live simply. Donating their possessions and money, they devoted their lives to aiding the sick and the poor.[5] In the southern Low Countries where Elisabeth lived, women who lived religious lives, whether in groups or alone, were known as Beguines.

According to historian Walter Simons a number of conditions appear to have contributed to these changes in lay religiosity that occurred especially in the Low Countries and northern Italy. Among these conditions are social changes such as increased urbanization, changing marriage and hereditary patterns, discontent with an outdated church structure that no longer served the needs of contemporary people, and a lack of religious education among secular clerics, especially local parish priests. The new mendicant (begging) orders such as the Franciscans and to a lesser extent the Dominicans, which emphasized the imitation of Christ and the apostles, were also influential in spreading these beliefs and practices, especially in towns and cities. By giving away their own possessions and devoting their lives to preaching and ministering to the poor, mendicants served a powerful need in society as they modeled this increasingly popular form of Christian behavior.[6]

Many individuals, however, wished to imitate Christ at a deeper level than by following the example of his good works. Sermons and devotional works instructed Christians to meditate on Christ's Passion and his suffering with the aim of imagining oneself present at the event.[7] Aiding the imagination, numerous devotional works, song lyrics, and works of visual art provided vivid and explicit depictions of a bleeding Christ hanging upon the cross. One writer even urged readers to act out the story of Christ's last hours,[8] a practice that had long been taken up both inside the Church and out. Dramatic performances of the Passion involved acting, singing, costumes, and elaborate stage sets, making vivid and tactile the story of Christ's death and redemption.[9]

For some people, however, imagining Christ's pain and suffering did not provide the degree of closeness to God for which they strove, and increasingly lay people as well as those in religious orders sought additional means to merge with Christ. In order to fully identify with Christ's suffering, they undertook the experience of pain themselves.[10] This, at least, is how many current scholars interpret the ascetic practices that were widespread in the late Middle Ages. Carolyn Walker Bynum is perhaps the best-known scholar to have argued that these practices ought not to be interpreted by twentieth-century standards as signs of self-loathing or as a disregard for the body; to do so misinterprets what such practices meant to medieval men and women.[11] She argues instead that "they strove not to eradicate body but to merge their own humiliating and painful flesh with that flesh whose agony, espoused by choice, was salvation. Luxuriating in Christ's physicality, they found there the lifting up—the redemption—of their own."[12] Saints' lives detail some of the most extreme forms of these practices, but their authors claim that the descriptions are intended only to impress readers and listeners with the miracles performed (or perhaps endured) by saints and holy men and women. One medieval writer (known to have sent scourges to fellow clerics) advised moderation. "There is no need to compete with Christ. To do so would be vain; moreover . . . it is tedious to have to wash blood stains from one's clothes."[13] The frequency with which writers advise against imitating these practices suggests that they were in fact widely adopted.[14] The most well known of these practices are flagellation, fasting, and wearing hair shirts, but others included sleep deprivation and praying barefoot in winter.[15]

The wish to merge with Christ, engaging in ascetic practices, and focusing on Christ's life and suffering have all been identified with a particular kind of spirituality that was practiced in the southern Low Countries, beginning in the late twelfth century, by female visionaries and mystics.[16] Women like Elisabeth, whether semireligious Beguines or Cistercian nuns, sought a direct experience of God. They relied on practices that had been used by monks for centuries to put themselves into a state of trance, rapture, or ecstasy.[17] Often these ecstatic states were accompanied by visions. Reports of saints' lives also tell of women who heard heavenly voices or received prophecies. Many contemporaries perceived these women as divinely inspired or, as in Elisabeth's case, possessed by God.

According to many hagiographers, the result of a person's internal unification with God could be read in a number of outward physical signs, including states of trance or receiving the stigmata.[18] Some of the more extreme signs reported by hagiographers included bloating, levitation, elongation of the body, the "gift of tears" (uncontrollable crying), convulsions, frenetic shouting, climbing trees, vomiting fire, and wandering naked.[19] In comparison with these reports, Elisabeth's dances appear modest, indeed.

Dancing, too, was recognized as an expression of rapture. Images of dancing women were used to indicate the state of the female soul in a state of ecstasy,[20] and hagiographers described their subjects' dancing as a result of their union with God,[21] as the following example about Beatrice of Nazareth shows. "When time for Communion came, not only was her mind filled with inner spiritual sweetness, but the delight breaking out in all the members of her body, like an inebriating nectar, made her move excitedly in a kind of spiritual dance."[22]

In many respects, Elisabeth resembled other female mystics of her day; like them she exhibited characteristics of a trance state, she danced, she beat herself, and she received the stigmata. But Elisabeth differed from them as well; her trances (as far as we know) did not lead to visions but to a bodily reenactment of Christ's Passion. Her performances encompassed both mystical and theatrical practices of her day, but differed significantly from these. Like professional performers or clerical actors, she performed parts of the story of Christ's Passion, but she did so not as a role player, but as a result of divine inspiration and possession. To her followers, Elisabeth not only portrayed Christ's sufferings but she participated in them; her pain as well as her representation of Christ's story were perceived as external manifestations of God's presence in her body.[23]

Elisabeth's Dances

Philip of Clairvaux begins his description of Elisabeth's dances with a very telling passage. Each day, he says, after rising and dressing, Elisabeth starts her performance by performing an interpretation of Psalm 150, which states:

> Praise ye the Lord. Praise God in his sanctuary: praise him
>   in the firmament of his power.
> Praise him for his mighty acts: praise him according to his
>   excellent greatness.
> Praise him with the sound of the trumpet: praise him with
>   the psaltery and harp.
> Praise Him with timbrel and dance; praise Him with
>   stringed instruments and organs.
> Praise Him upon the loud cymbals; praise Him upon
>   high sounding cymbals.

> Let every thing that hath breath praise the Lord. Praise ye
> the Lord.[24]

According to Philip, Elisabeth demonstrates the meaning of the psalm by playing her body as if it were a musical instrument; instead of singing the psalm with her voice, she performs it by striking herself on the jaws repeatedly, "creating a loud and harmonious constancy of sound . . . as if playing on beautiful-sounding timbrels and cymbals."[25] Philip's interpretation of Elisabeth's self-inflicted beatings as an embodiment of the words of the psalm (an interpretation he repeats later in the "Life") offers a key to understanding her entire performance. Through these ascetic practices, Elisabeth's ardent devotion is given bodily expression and her emotional and spiritual state is revealed. Elisabeth's body also provides the perfect receptacle for God's miracle on earth in the union between the divine and human, evident in her performance of Christ's last hours on earth. Having set the stage, literally and figuratively, Philip then describes the rest of her performance.

Although the story of the Passion plays a central role in Elisabeth's dances, it is somewhat surprising to find how little of the dances appears to be taken up by the story. Rather, the most striking feature of Elisabeth's performances is their use of time: the dances merge the Passion narrative with church time, the division of the day into the Divine Office. Elisabeth's performances are broken up into seven distinct dances, performed over the course of the day.[26] As the day progresses, she advances through the narrative, performing successive parts of the story, along with many other movements, as described below.

Elisabeth's dances follow the structure of the Divine Office within each of the liturgical hours as well. She performs different kinds of movements or movement sequences to correspond with different sections of each hour. Just as her religious counterparts sing or chant psalms, Elisabeth enacts the psalm cited above; joining in prayers, she assumes specific prayer positions; and she enacts the different stages of the Passion story in place of readings or lessons.[27] And just as the celebration of each liturgical hour contains different variations and sequences of these key elements, Elisabeth varies her danced interpretations of these sections throughout each of the seven performances.[28]

In addition to describing this basic structure, Philip records that Elisabeth begins each dance section by rising from her bed, quickly and joyfully. Similarly, she ends each performance in the same way, by lowering herself backward onto the ground, and rolling over and over as if trying to catch her breath until finally stopping in a quiet and peaceful "ecstasy," when she is carried by her mother and sisters into a small antechamber where she rests until the next performance.[29]

Philip also details some specific movements and movement sequences that are either performed between the different sections or as part of them. Some of these movements include slapping and hitting herself (sometimes with whips) and movements requiring extraordinary strength and coordination. In this latter category he reports that she lowers herself backward to the floor from a standing position and ends face to the floor, without aid of hands or feet; also, from a cross-position she swings her torso like a pendulum while balanced with one foot on top of another.[30]

Although each dance section contains the same elements used in different sequences, the primary difference between them is the incorporation of a different segment of the Passion story. In some cases the narrative element is used as a choreographic theme for dance movements, interspersed with other danced sections; at other times Elisabeth portrays the story more literally, in a kind of pantomime. (See figure 8.1.) During the first hour (matins), for instance, Elisabeth portrays Christ being beaten by the crowd, acting in both the role of Christ and that of his tormentors, whereas during prime (the second hour of the daily office), Elisabeth holds her arms behind her back while performing a variety of movements. Philip writes that by using this position of the arms, Elisabeth represents Christ being led as a criminal through the streets. During the next hour (terce), the period when Jesus was bound to a pillar, Elisabeth holds her arms rigidly in front of her with arms bent at the elbows and fingertips on opposite elbows, again performing sequences of movements, all the while keeping her arms in this position. For the hours of sext, none, and vespers, the three hours when Christ was believed to have hung on the cross, Elisabeth stands with one foot pressed on top of the other and holding her arms out from her sides, forming a cross with her body, while performing a startling range of movements, including two described above: lowering to and rising from the floor (without using her arms) and swinging her torso. In the last of these three hours, vespers, Elisabeth portrays Jesus dying as described in the Gospel,[31] with her head rolling from side to side, at last resting on the

HOURS OF DIVINE OFFICE	APPROXIMATE STARTING TIMES	ELEMENTS OF THE PASSION NARRATIVE IN ELISABETH'S PERFORMANCES	KEY ELEMENTS IN ELISABETH'S PERFORMANCE OF THE PASSION NARRATIVE
Matins Lauds	12:00 a.m. 3:00 a.m.	Jesus beaten by the crowd	Beginning her performance during matins and continuing straight through lauds, Elisabeth moves as a person being beaten and as if she is striking someone else.
Prime	6:00 a.m.	Jesus being led through the streets as a criminal	Elisabeth holds her arms behind her back while performing a range of movements.
Terce	9:00 a.m.	Jesus tied to a column	Elisabeth keeps her arms rigidly in front of her body, with arms bent at the elbows and fingers touching opposite elbows, while performing a variety of movements.
Sext None Vespers	Noon 3 p.m. 4:30 p.m.	Jesus hanging on the cross and dying	For each of the three hours of sext, none, and vespers Elisabeth remains with her arms outstretched in a cross position while she performs a series of movements. During vespers, while still standing in the cross position, she rolls her head from side to side, finally resting it on her right shoulder.
Compline	5:00 p.m.	Jesus buried in a tomb	Elisabeth holds herself in a burial position, halfway between sitting and lying.

Note: The only information Philip of Clairvaux provides in his "Vita Elisabeth sanctimonialis in Erkenrode" about the timing of Elisabeth's performances is that they began at midnight. The times given here are estimated, based on information taken from Roger E. Reynolds, "Divine Office," in *Dictionary of the Middle Ages*, vol. 4, ed. Joseph Reese Strayer (New York: Scribner, 1982), 221–31. In the thirteenth century, the starting times and length of each hour varied according to time of year, location, and day of the week.

Figure 8.1. Approximate timing of Elisabeth's performances.

right. Finally, during the hour of compline, Elisabeth represents Jesus in death by holding herself in a burial position, halfway between sitting and lying.[32]

In addition to these movements, Philip describes other elements of her performance, including her costume, which consists of an undergarment (a tunic of wool) covered by a white linen garment that hangs to just above the ground.[33] She also incorporates a cross and diptych in her work. Intriguingly, Philip writes that Elisabeth performed in a chapel specially built for her performances, but he provides almost no details, except that it was built by Elisabeth's relative and local protector, the Benedictine abbot William of Saint-Truiden. Apparently the chapel still stands. It is believed to have been circular in shape originally, but it was expanded at various times over the centuries to accommodate the increased popularity of the Elisabeth cult. These additions enlarged the chapel and altered its shape.[34] It was later adorned with frescos. Elisabeth is perhaps the only thirteenth-century Beguine saint to have "such a comprehensive program of architecture and imagery," according to Walter Simons and Joanna Ziegler.[35] But like so many aspects of Philip's report, the specific ways that Elisabeth used this space remain a mystery.

For Philip, one of the most important elements of Elisabeth's performance is the blood that she sheds from her hands, feet, and side—places corresponding to Christ's wounds on the cross. Elisabeth also reportedly bled from her eyes and fingertips. According to Thomas Bestul, audiences were familiar with bleeding fingertips from current methods of torture. "Among the commonplaces found no earlier than in the Passion narratives of the thirteenth century is the nonbiblical detail that when Christ was arrested, his hands were bound so tightly that blood burst from beneath the nails."[36] No doubt these details added drama and authenticity to Elisabeth's performances.

Based on this description, it appears that Elisabeth embraced a remarkable range of contemporary theatrical practices, religious symbols, and ritual gestures in her dances, powerfully communicating her authority as a vehicle for God's Word. Philip's report "stages" her performances on the written page, carefully selecting, elaborating, and explaining aspects of the dances for an audience steeped in the religious practices and traditions of their age. Although many of the specific movements of Elisabeth's performances remain elusive to us, Philip's report nevertheless provides other information about how the dances were performed, promoted, and received.

Analysis

Evident in the above synopsis of Philip's account are many rich and interesting details of Elisabeth's dances. In examining these details, however, it is important to recognize that Philip, typical of hagiographical writers, elaborates only that which documents and supports a representation of Elisabeth as a holy woman. His purpose is to record a miracle, not a dance. The brevity of movement description is one of the major limitations of medieval documents as records of historical dance practices. But just as it would be wrong to assume that Philip reports every aspect of Elisabeth's performance, it would be equally incorrect to suppose that if he does not record specific elements or practices they did not exist. For example, Philip does not refer to current dance practices, to a vocabulary of named dance movements or steps, to floor patterns, rhythm, or even musical accompaniment. It is impossible to distinguish which details he considers unimportant to his rhetorical purposes, which are too obvious to mention or beyond his expertise to describe, and which are unknown to him or do not yet exist. The "Life" alone cannot answer every question about medieval dance practices, even Elisabeth's, but understanding Philip's stated aims helps to illuminate what movements he chooses to record and how he categorizes them.[37]

According to Philip, proof of divine possession appears both in Elisabeth's movements and in her person. He describes movements that appear to fit into two categories. Movements that are familiar to Philip (and likely to his readers) from religious practices and imagery include gestures (beating and self-flagellation and drawing the sign of the cross on different parts of her body) and certain bodily shapes (various prayer positions and the cross). Other movements impress Philip because they appear difficult to perform and require either immense strength or coordination, such as Elisabeth's lowering herself to the ground from a standing position, without using hands or feet. On two occasions he remarks that Elisabeth moves as if she is being led; that is, she does not appear to be moving herself but moves as if "from outside." All of these elements, he claims, provide evidence that she moves as a result of God's will, because when Elisabeth is not in an ecstatic state, she is too weak to move and must be carried from place to place.[38]

Philip also emphasizes movement qualities in Elisabeth's performance. She moves with confidence in a manner that is "composed . . . moderate and light"; her movements are never indecent, and she never stumbles. Her movement qualities cover the spectrum from completely bound to swinging, pendular movements of the whole body, with shaking, beating, and striking movements falling somewhere in between. It is also clear that many of the movements, in addition to great strength, require control, flexibility, and practice. Elisabeth can and does repeat movements frequently but "in exacting detail." That these characteristics were understood as evidence of God's presence is not unusual for this period; Philip's concern for physical self-control and orderly movements stems from a centuries-long and well-documented tradition that instructed monks to moderate their movements to reflect the inner state of their saintly souls.[39]

By the third quarter of the thirteenth century, unlike earlier in the century, women claiming divine inspiration faced intense scrutiny. Philip reveals that he had been initially skeptical of reports about Elisabeth's performances. After all, he and his audience were sure to have known that possession states could just as likely result from demonic intervention or human fraud as from divine inspiration. Once thoroughly convinced, however, Philip carefully delineates in the "Life" all the signs by which he and his audience can be assured of Elisabeth's sanctity.[40]

Philip goes one step further, outlining the various ways that Elisabeth and her performances reflected and promoted orthodox Christian positions on confession and ex-communicants (defending the first and rejecting the latter).[41] His emphasis on Elisabeth's physical weakness, youth, sexual purity, and years of self-flagellation are intended to provide evidence of her spiritual purity and suitability as a vessel for God's presence.[42] And though the stigmata—bleeding at what were thought to have been the sites of Christ's wounds—was a sign of God's presence, Philip seems to anticipate the possibility of objections to it by inserting a long passage on women's right to receive the stigmata, a right equal to that of any man, including Saint Francis of Assisi.[43] Despite his care, Elisabeth's single known critic from this time, Gilbert of Tournai, ridicules Beguines generally and Elisabeth specifically. "Among this type of silly women was one who achieved a semipublic reputation for being marked with Christ's stigmata. If this is true, it should not be rumored in secret, but let it be known openly. If, however, it is not true, let this hypocrisy and simulation be thwarted."[44] Scholars have argued that Gilbert's condemnation of Elisabeth's stigmata was territorial, a defense of the monopoly Saint Francis held over the miracle. Gilbert and the rest of the Order of Friars Minor were known to zealously fight off any "competitive claims to this miracle whenever and wherever they arose."[45]

While the account of Elisabeth's performance provides many details about her dances and how they were perceived and promoted, it also leaves many questions unanswered. Perhaps the most perplexing absence in Philip's description is his failure to describe any sound or musical accompaniment except those Elisabeth makes herself, either by the beating of her palms on her flesh, or the variety of wordless sounds she makes with her voice. At one point he reports that she "joins in" the prayers with her own movements,[46] suggesting that the monks and abbot who are witnessing Elisabeth's performances may be singing or chanting psalms, reciting prayers, and otherwise following their usual observation of the hours in accompaniment to her dances, but this is not stated explicitly.

Philip also avoids categorizing Elisabeth's performance in terms of performance practices of his day; he does not refer to it as a drama, pantomime, or dance, but only as evidence of God's magnificent grace and power. His failure to specify performance genres or musical accompaniment raises the question of whether Elisabeth's performances ought, in fact, to be classified as dance, either by medieval or twenty-first-century definitions of the word. Although a definitive decision about how to categorize Elisabeth's performances is beyond the scope of this paper, it is a fruitful direction for discussion, revealing some of the more subtle aspects of Elisabeth's performance.

Both the *American Heritage* and *Oxford Concise Dictionary* define dance as moving rhythmically "usually to music," alone or in groups, and using fixed or improvised steps and gestures.[47] The essential part of the definition is rhythmical motion, although it is unstated whether the rhythm must be metrical or not. Philip does not indicate whether Elisabeth's movements are in any sense rhythmical. He does write that Elisabeth's performance involves much repetition of movements and sounds, and he compares Elisabeth's body with a musical instrument, suggesting that the sounds she makes by repeatedly hitting herself form a rhythm that is analogous to his notion of music, whether rhythmical or not. Since musical notation of the period did not indicate rhythm or meter, it is not surprising that Philip neglected these details. More importantly, rhythm was unimportant to his argument that Elisabeth's movements were a sign of God's presence.

It may be argued that relying solely on recent dictionary definitions of dance is misleading and that a more appropriate concern is whether medieval audiences conceived of Elisabeth's performances as dance. Erika Bourguignon writes that dance ethnologists often classify structured movement systems as "dance" only when labeled such by the culture in which the dance is created and performed.[48] Unfortunately, Philip does not reveal how he, Elisabeth, or her audiences perceived Elisabeth's movements in relation to contemporary performance practices. Looking beyond Elisabeth's "Life" to other hagiographical texts[49] to determine a definition of dance reveals that aspects of Elisabeth's performance are consistent with those of Beatrice of Nazareth: "Sometimes when Beatrice was occupied in holy meditations, prudently inspecting the divine wonders with the eye of contemplation, and sometimes when she was giving her mind a little rest and was not meditating, the consolation of divine grace would suddenly present itself, so inebriating and flooding her heart with an ineffable joy that not only would the nectar-like taste refresh her inwardly with much delight, but also outwardly effervescing into bodily form, it would stir her up to a spiritual dance, in which she would excitedly strike parts of her body."[50] Again, no mention is made of rhythmical movement or music, although Beatrice's repeated self-striking is considered by her hagiographer to be a divinely inspired dance. From this example it appears that musical accompaniment for ecstatic dancers is either unimportant or non-existent: female visionaries move as the result of internal stimuli brought on by divine inspiration and intervention, not as a response to external sounds.

On a more practical note, it would seem odd if Beatrice *were* dancing to music. Ecstatic states were often unpredictable, and musicians could not always be at hand to provide musical accompaniment for spontaneous mystical encounters. In fact, it is possible that the lack of musical accompaniment served as a sign of an authentic ecstatic state, since those in a true rapture were known to be oblivious to the external world or to their physical senses. On the other hand, Elisabeth's performances were anticipated and even staged, posing no difficulties to locating musicians or singers in advance. And because Philip writes that Elisabeth "joined" in the prayers with her movements, performing before a group of monks who would likely have been accustomed to singing the hours of the Divine Office, it is conceivable that dancer and singers performed the offices simultaneously. What we cannot know from Philip's account is whether music was absent altogether or simply irrelevant to his case.

Whether Elisabeth's performances are envisioned to be the result of her sanctity, her choreography, or a collaborative effort between clerical supervisors and performer, Elisabeth's dance was intended as a form of bodily communication. And in order to communicate, Elisabeth's performances incorporated bodily signs that would have been familiar to an audience of clerics. These included gestures and positions from religious ritual as well as wordless dramatic action structured in an understandable and acceptable format. Some readers of Elisabeth's "Life" may envision her performances as a kind of pantomime or ritual rather than a dance. But even as her performances contained elements of pantomime, along with familiar gestures and ritual actions, it is difficult to place Elisabeth's movements in any category except dance. The Passion narrative served as a structure for her performances and provided thematic material for her movements to differentiate each hour, but the result is neither a pantomime nor a series of ritualistic gestures. By performing these movements in a new context, Elisabeth infused them with new meaning. Instead of signifying that she was engaged in an act of prayer or participating in a ritual, her movements revealed God's presence moving her—literally—to convey Christ's suffering. As a means of bodily communication and personal expression incorporating and transforming different sign systems, using repetition, and developing sequences of movements thematically, Elisabeth's performance shares similarities with twenty-first-century concert dance practices. Elisabeth's audiences may well have recognized her performances as dance for many of the same reasons that we would today, but this cannot be ascertained; while medieval hagiographers recognized dance when they saw it, their interest in writing about it revolved around its use as evidence of the Divine.

Conclusion

For Elisabeth and other female visionaries, there was no certain road to acceptance or sainthood; signs meant different things to different individuals and groups. Determining whether a woman was divinely possessed was not achieved by objective criteria. "Above all" writes Nancy Caciola, "discernment [the distinguishing of divine from satanic possession] was an ideological act, an interpretation inflected by local mentalities, the observer's self-interest, and the exigencies of power."[51] Although we know little about the responses of Elisabeth's audience beyond Philip, it would be surprising if, given the cultural climate of the period, Elisabeth and her dances were not interpreted differently by different observers.[52]

The advantages that trance states (at least those sanctioned as holy) could provide for medieval women were as evident to medieval audiences as they are to us today. In a society and religious power structure that often regarded women as incapable of intellectual or spiritual power, women who achieved a trance state could be perceived as having direct access to God. Such women rose to an elevated status and gained privileges typically denied them. In many cases, to be taken seriously, religious women needed to attribute their voice, their vision, their writing, their music, and their dance to God. Even then they required clerical authorization.[53]

Among the many details missing from Philip's report is any mention of Elisabeth's experience. Through the hagiographic lens, bodies (women's as well as men's) appear only as signs to be read and used for ideological purposes. Was she simply a vessel to be filled with God's (or Philip's) purposes? Was she a fraud, who manipulated well-known signs to increase her social status and prestige? Or might we consider Elisabeth in a different light: as a Hildegard von Bingen of dance, or as a thirteenth-century Martha Graham, manipulating her body and what it symbolized to claim authority and create a new form of dance? Opinions differ now, as they did seven hundred years ago.[54]

One of the most intriguing and confounding aspects of Philip's description is the revelation of a conception of dance as a uniquely personal form of religious expression and communication, albeit through the (then) socially accepted form of an ecstatic state. In many ways, Elisabeth's dances more closely resemble examples of twenty-first-century art or concert dance than the court dance tradition at the heart of most early dance research. Although infused with elements—blood, self-inflicted pain, the enactment of Christ hanging on the cross—that are in many respects alien to modern sensibilities, these elements were essential signs of her divine possession and inspiration to medieval audiences. Beyond these elements, however, Philip's report reveals a number of characteristics about Elisabeth's dances that strike a familiar note to present-day audiences of dance. Elisabeth's dances included narrative and pantomime, they were highly structured, and each of the seven dances in her daily cycle used the same elements in different sequences and with some variation (an example of the musical and choreographic structure called "theme and variation"). The dances incorporated gestures, bodily shapes, falls and rises, a range of movement qualities, rhythms played out on different parts of the body, and technically diffi-cult movements. An important component of the dance's communica-tion was drawn from the way the movements were performed, with an emphasis on self-control, lightness, and effortlessness. Finally, Philip's description and interpretation of the dances rely on a conception of the body as a sign to be read as the external manifestation of an internal state.

The similarities between Elisabeth's dances of possession and late twentieth-century concert dance traditions raise interesting questions about the historical and cultural links between the two periods. While they deserve more consideration than is possible in the present paper, the similarities can be explained in part because of the methods used in my investigation: the application of late-twentieth-century research and forms of dance analysis to medieval practices. I hope this study also strongly suggests that there are more similarities between past and present performance traditions than between recent concert dance and the courtly social dances at the heart of many early dance studies. Elisa-beth's dances belonged to a world that was in dialogue with that of the courts: secular and religious circles shared many beliefs, conceptions of dancing bodies, and bodily practices, although sometimes interpret-ing them in very different ways. But dance movements designed for the stage, in the thirteenth as much as in the twenty-first century, share only some characteristics with those considered appropriate to the ballroom or the dance floor.

Philip's report of Elisabeth's dances significantly broadens and en-riches our picture of medieval dance. It reveals how dance could incor-porate religious symbols, rituals, gestures and conceptions of the human body to make Christ's Passion vivid for the faithful, and claim divine au-thority for the performer. The fragmented nature of medieval sources makes it impossible to know whether Elisabeth's performances had any direct impact on dance practices in her time, but word of her dances continued to spread over the course of several centuries through hand-copied manuscripts of Elisabeth's "Life." For Philip, Elisabeth's dances were miraculous because they revealed God's presence visible for all to see. For us, the miracle is that a record of Elisabeth's dances has sur-vived for over seven hundred years, and through her dances a window has been opened onto the past, revealing a world both familiar and very different from our own.

Notes

This essay is a preliminary study for a chapter of my dissertation on dance practice and theory in France and French Flanders; most of the topics and sources introduced here are addressed in far more detail in the larger study. I would like to express my appreciation for the generosity shown by Joanna E. Ziegler and Edward Vodoklys for sharing with me their early translation of Elisabeth's "Life," which will be published by Peregrina Press. My deepest thanks go to Steven Justice and James Whitta for their comments on early drafts of this essay, and to Dr. Whitta for his gracious assistance with my own translation of the text. Even with their help, however, I am fully to blame for any errors in translation or interpretation.

1. Acknowledgment for the discovery of Elisabeth's dances goes to Joanna E. Ziegler. Although Philip of Clairvaux's text, "Vita Elisabeth sanctimonialis in Erkenrode," was known to scholars, Ziegler's careful analysis of the "Life" and her attempts to translate it into movement revealed that Elisabeth's movements ought to be categorized as dance, rather than pantomime, as previously assumed. See Walter Simons and Joanna E. Ziegler, "Phenomenal Religion in the Thirteenth Century and Its Image: Elisabeth of Spalbeek and the Passion Cult," *Studies in Church History* 27 (1990): 117–26; and Susan Rodgers and Joanna E. Ziegler, "Elisabeth of Spalbeek's Trance Dance of Faith: A Performance Theory Interpretation from Anthropological and Art Historical Perspectives," in *Performance and Transformation: New Approaches to Late Medieval Spirituality*, ed. Mary A. Suydam and Joanna E. Ziegler (New York: St. Martin's Press, 1999), 299–355.

2. Philip of Clairvaux, "Vita Elisabeth sanctimonialis in Erkenrode," in *Catalogus codicum hagiographicorum bibliothecae Regiae Bruxellensis* (Brussels: Polleunis, Ceuterick et Lefebure, 1886), 363–78 (hereafter cited as "Life.") The fact that at least ten medieval manuscript copies of the "Life" circulated and that it was translated into Middle English attests to a continued interest in Elisabeth and her dances for at least two centuries after her death. See Walter Simons, "Reading a Saint's Body: Rapture and Bodily Movement in the 'Vitae' of Thirteenth-Century Beguines," in *Framing Medieval Bodies*, ed. Sarah Kay and Miri Rubin (Manchester, NY: Manchester University Press, 1994), 10.

3. For descriptions of medieval dance practice, see Christopher Page, *Voices and Instruments of the Middle Ages: Instrumental Practice and Songs in France, 1100–1300* (Berkeley: University of California Press, 1986), 114–15. I use the words "ecstatic," "rapture," "trance," and "possession" to reflect medieval categories for women's behavior rather than "altered state of consciousness." See, however, Erika Bourguignon, "Trance Dance," in *The International Encyclopedia of Dance*, 6 vols., ed. Selma J. Cohen (New York: Oxford University Press, 1998), 6:184–88.

4. For discussions of the use of hagiography as historical documents, see Amy Hollywood, *The Soul as Virgin Wife: Mechthild of Magdeburg, Marguerite Porete, and Meister Eckhart* (Notre Dame, IN: University of Notre Dame Press, 1995), 27–39; Nancy Caciola, *Discerning Spirits: Divine and Demonic Possession in the Middle Ages* (Ithaca, NY: Cornell University Press, 2003), 21; and Catherine M. Mooney, ed., *Gendered Voices: Medieval Saints and Their Interpreters* (Philadelphia: University of Pennsylvania Press, 1999).

5. See Walter Simons, *Cities of Ladies* (Philadelphia: University of Pennsylvania Press, 2001); and Hollywood, *Soul as Virgin Wife*, 39.

6. Simons, *Cities of Ladies*, 1–20.

7. Thomas H. Bestul, *Texts of the Passion: Latin Devotional Literature and Medieval Society* (Philadelphia: University of Pennsylvania Press, 1996), 1, 147.

8. Auctor Incertus [Beda?], *De meditatione passionis Christi per septem diei horas libellum*, in *Patrologiae cursus completus. Series Latina*, 221 vols., ed. J.-P. Migne (Paris, 1841–66), 94:561–68, cited in Caciola, *Discerning Spirits*, 116.

9. For early examples in Latin and vernacular languages, see David Bevington, *Medieval Drama* (Boston: Houghton Mifflin, 1975).

10. Caroline Walker Bynum, *Holy Feast and Holy Fast: The Religious Significance of Food to Medieval Women* (Berkeley: University of California Press, 1987), 210.

11. Bynum, *Holy Feast*, 108.

12. Bynum, *Holy Feast*, 246.

13. Jeffrey F. Hamburger here refers to the Italian Dominican, Venturino da Bergamo, whose works are published in G. Clementi, *Il B. Venturino da Bergamo dell'ordine de' Predicatori (1304–1346); Storia e documenti* (Rome: Tipografia Vaticana, 1904), reprinted as *Un Santo patriota, il B. Venturino da Bergamo dell'ordine de' Predicatori (1304–1346): Storia e documenti* (Rome: Desclée, 1909). Specifically in this passage, Clementi (in *Il B. Venturino da Bergamo*, pt. 2, p. 127) is cited by Hamburger in *The Visual and the Visionary: Art and Female Spirituality in Late Medieval Germany* (New York: Zone Books, 1998), 304 (citations 553, n.98).

14. Bynum, *Holy Feast*, 84.

15. Bynum, *Holy Feast*, 78–79. She adds (210): "Reading the lives of fourteenth- and fifteenth-century women saints greatly expands one's knowledge of Latin synonyms for whip, thong, flail, chain, etc."

16. Caciola, *Discerning Spirits*, 15. See also Barbara Newman, "Possessed by the Spirit: Devout Women, Demoniacs, and the Apostolic Life in the Thirteenth Century," *Speculum* 73, no. 3 (July 1998): 733–70.

17. Simons, *Reading a Saint's Body*, 16.

18. Simons, *Reading a Saint's Body*, 15.

19. Caciola, *Discerning Spirits*, 68–69.

20. Simons, *Reading a Saint's Body*, 17–18; Jeffrey F. Hamburger, *The Rothschild Canticles* (New Haven, CT: Yale University Press, 1990), 58.

21. For Beatrice, Elisabeth, and other visionary women, receiving the host in Communion often brought on an ecstatic state. Carolyn Walker Bynum explains the significance of the host in the high Middle Ages: "The food on the altar was the God who became man; it was bleeding and broken flesh. Hunger was unquenchable desire; it was suffering. To eat God, therefore, was finally to become suffering flesh with his suffering flesh; it was to imitate the cross" (*Holy Feast*, 54).

22. *The Life of Beatrice of Nazareth, 1200–1268,* trans. and annotated by Roger De Ganck (Kalamazoo, MI: Cistercian Publications, 1991), 102–3.

23. The lives and rituals of female visionaries can also be seen as types of performance; see, for example, the many articles in Suydam and Zeigler, *Performance and Transformation.*

24. Psalm 150 from *The Psalms,* with introduction and critical notes by Rev. A. C. Jennings, M.A. (London: MacMillan and Co., 1885), 392. As in most of Philip's references to biblical passages, the entire psalm is not quoted but is referred to, with the assumption that readers would know the entire passage by heart.

25. Philip, "Life," 364.

26. Philip, "Life," 363. Philip says that she performs seven times a day, beginning with the night office, or matins, at midnight and proceeding through the daily offices of prime, terce, sext, none, vespers, and compline. Lauds (mentioned on page 366) is combined with matins.

27. Philip, "Life," 364.

28. For information about the Divine Office, see Dom Pierre Salmon, *The Breviary through the Centuries* (Collegeville, MN: The Liturgical Press, 1962). For medieval practices specifically, see Roger E. Reynolds, "Divine Office," *Dictionary of the Middle Ages,* 13 vols. (New York: Scribner, 1982–89), 4:221–31.

29. Philip, "Life," 364, 365, 369.

30. Exactly how she performs these movements is unclear. Among the many questions raised by Philip's description is whether Elisabeth is a contortionist, whether she is or appears to be levitating (levitation being one of the miracles allegedly performed by several female visionaries), or whether the mechanics of Elisabeth's movements, and the words to describe them, simply elude Philip. Given the difficulty of describing complex movements, Elisabeth's "Life" may well be a case where readers need not assume that the hagiographer's claimed inability to write what he sees is merely an expected trope.

31. Mt 8:20; Lk 9:58.

32. Philip writes that he observed additional variations on Good Friday when she included representations of Mary and Saint John the Evangelist ("Life," 379).

33. Philip, "Life," 364.

34. For information on the chapel see Simons and Ziegler, "Phenomenal Religion," 118–20. At some point after her death frescos were painted depicting other saints, testifying "to Elisabeth's exemplary behaviour as a semi-religious, living devoutly under the supervision of the Cistercian Order" (122). The frescos were painted sometime between 1350 and 1500.

35. Simons and Ziegler, "Phenomenal Religion," 122.

36. Bestul, *Texts of the Passion*, 155.

37. Philip states that his purpose is to record God's miraculous presence in Elisabeth ("Life," 363–64).

38. Philip, "Life," 364–70.

39. Simons (*Reading a Saint's Body*, 13–15) traces this tradition from the ancient Greeks through the early Christian Fathers and into thirteenth-century prayer manuals.

40. Philip says he decided to view Elisabeth's performances in order to see for himself whether the reports he had heard were true but he found that the truth exceeded them ("Life," 363–64). On the art of discerning among spiritual fraud, demonic possession, and divine possession, see Caciola's *Discerning Spirits*, and Newman, "Possessed by the Spirit." Newman also compares clerical attitudes towards possessed women in the late twelfth and thirteenth centuries.

41. Philip, "Life," 374–75.

42. Philip, "Life," 363–64.

43. Philip, "Life," 373.

44. A. Stroick, "Collectio de scandalis ecclesiae," *Archivum Franciscanum Historicum* 24 (1931): 61–62. Cited by Simons and Ziegler, "Phenomenal Religion," 123, and quoted in Caciola, *Discerning Spirits*, 118.

45. Caciola, *Discerning Spirits*, 119.

46. Philip, "Life," 365–66.

47. Bourguignon, "Trance Dance,"186.

48. *The American Heritage Dictionary of the English Language* (Boston: Houghton Mifflin Company, 1992), 472; and *The Concise Oxford Dictionary of Current English* (Oxford: Clarendon Press, 1990), 292.

49. Although it is rare for the movements of female mystics to be classified as dancing, Philip's description of Elisabeth is consistent with many other accounts of divine possession and inspiration, as noted above. See also Simons, *Reading a Saint's Body*, 15.

50. De Ganck, *Life of Beatrice of Nazareth*, 232–33. In the courtly tradition at this time, most descriptions of dancing refer to dancers who accompanied themselves by singing while they danced.

51. Caciola, *Discerning Spirits*, 125.

52. We do know that Elisabeth was surrounded by controversy some ten years after Philip wrote his "Life." She was then established as a prophetess, sought out by King Philip III of France. Two different sources provide

completely different impressions of her, offering no further information about her dances (Caciola, *Discerning Spirits*, 113–25).

53. Newman, in "Possessed by the Spirit," 760–62, and Rodgers and Ziegler, in "Elisabeth of Spalbeek's Trance Dance of Faith," 303–6, discuss different ways that medieval women may have benefited by exhibiting signs of possession.

54. On hagiographical writings, see Newman, "Possessed by the Spirit," 734. Caciola finds Elisabeth a "cipher" and is much more skeptical than Ziegler or Simons.

9

Galanterie and *Gloire:* Women's Will and the Eighteenth-Century Worldview in *Les Indes galantes*

JOELLEN A. MEGLIN

The title of the *opéra-ballet Les Indes galantes* is intriguing. What did French codes of etiquette, subtleties of conversation, and sexual in-nuendo *(galanterie)* have to do with the encounter between two worlds, Europe and *les Indes* (the latter encompassing *indiens* and *indiennes* from the Orient and the New World, sanguinely blurred in an exotic extrava-ganza)? Everything, it turns out. The 1735 *opéra-ballet* was a mapping of *galanterie* onto *les Indes* at the same time that it was a mapping of *les Indes* onto *galanterie*. In other words, the stuff of gender relations was used to narrate encounters between diverse peoples and the stuff of national character was used to narrate gender relations. By "stuff" is meant rep-resentations, since these things are, of course, imagined entities or cul-tural constructs.

In a close reading of the libretto of *Les Indes galantes,* one can analyze the discourse of *galanterie* (and its implied counterpart—*gloire*), exploring implicit gender and geopolitical connotations as they were embedded in semiotic structures of this *opéra-ballet*. These structures included narra-tive, lyrics, music, dance, *merveilles* (marvels or special effects), costumes, and scenic design. In particular, this research focuses on the prologue

and the *entrée*, *Les Incas du Pérou* (The Incas of Peru), placing aural, kines-
thetic, and visual iconography vis-à-vis key period texts to explore how
the sensuous elements of the *opéra-ballet* resonated with intellectual and
critical discourses of the times.[1] Hence, the emphases of this study are
both textual and contextual, exploring the nature of woman and "curious" others as they were constructed in the *opéra-ballet*.

Analyses of the ballet of the *ancien régime* have typically made the
king's body the central axis of inquiry (both figuratively and literally).
Art historian Sarah R. Cohen has theorized "the artful body," discovering the aesthetics of artifice and the politics of bodily display in an aristocratic ideal embraced by Louis XIV.[2] Musicologist Susan McClary
has encapsulated the literature with the viewpoint that Louis XIV used
music and dance as part of an "absolutist agenda" for the purpose of
social control: "to regulate—indeed, literally to *synchronize*—the bodies
and behaviors of his courtiers."[3] What is missing from analyses that center the origins of the noble style solely in court culture is the contribution of salon culture, with its women-centered ethos. It is difficult to
reconcile approaches that revolve around the king with statements like
those of Jacques Barzun, for example, who, in quoting La Rochefoucauld, has observed that the *honnête homme* was "he who does not make a
point of anything in regard to himself *(qui ne se pique de rien)*. It was a social ideal that found expression in related phrases: *la bonne compagnie, le
beau monde, les gens comme il faut*. This ideal was due to the influence of
women. They were the arbiters of taste and the judges of comport-
ment, exercising that preciseness that La Rochefoucauld noted in their
speech. The salon was a staged play and they were the critics."[4]

Similarly, in her extensive study of salon culture in seventeenth-
century France, Carolyn C. Lougee has argued that not only were
women the overseers of social grace, disbursing the "parfum de l'aristo-
cratie" to meritorious newcomers, but, as intriguers at court and partners in unequal marriages *(mésalliances)*, they also played a dynamic role
in social mobility. These social changes instigated a strenuous debate on
woman's place: advocates of women observed their beneficent, civiliz-
ing influence; detractors claimed they had disruptive, chaotic, perni-
cious effects on society.[5] The first salons had begun in the early seventeenth century, well before Louis XIV's court, creating the mold for
polite society, refinement of mien, manners, and conduct, and, most especially, the art of conversation.[6] Led by women throughout the seventeenth and eighteenth centuries, they were a formidable force in the

demonstration, debate, and critical reception of all manner of ideas—
scientific, philosophical, literary, and political, according to the tenor
of the times. Literary critic Joan DeJean has suggested that the culture
of aristocratic self-containment and "interiority" arose, at least in part,
from the conduct of nobles who had rebelled against the monarchy,
lost, and found intellectual haven in the salons.[7] *Les Indes galantes* evoked
a particular brand of *galanterie* with deep roots in seventeenth-century
salon practice, discourses, and literature.

Galanterie and a Woman's Map of Human Relations

The prologue of *Les Indes galantes* opens in the pleasure gardens of Hebé
(Divinity of Youth), who invokes couples from four European nations
(France, Italy, Spain, and Poland) to participate in the "brilliant Games
of Terpsicore." The lyrics are replete with the language of *galanterie—
douceur* (sweetness, gentleness), *tendresse, l'Amour*—and phrases, as will become apparent, reminiscent of Madeleine Scudéry, the geometer of *tendresse:* "For a tender heart discretion augments the sweetness of the
blessings."[8] But the sound of drums and trumpets silences the sound of
bagpipes, interrupting the gracious Dance of the Lovers, a *musette*. Bellonne, the Roman goddess of war (figure 9.1), enters—and with her the
language of *la Gloire*—and her entourage of flag-bearing warriors lures
Hebé's devotees away to war.

Among the meanings of the word *gloire*, according to Antoine
Furetière's *Dictionnaire universel* (1690), were "God's majesty, the glimpse
of his power and infinite grandeur" and a "borrowed" definition of
"worldly honor . . . praises given to the merit, knowledge, and virtue of
men."[9] In the *opéra-ballet*, Bellonne represents an all-too-human, belli-
cose reflection of *gloire*—military splendor. A man played this goddess, in
spite of her female persona, at least in the 1735, 1736, 1761, and 1765
productions.[10] Certainly, Louis XIV, in his public image as the Greek
god Apollo, had "borrowed" majesty, power, grandeur, and glory as a
worldly, but classically (historically) legitimated, reflection of the sun.
What is more, the young monarch had played la Guerre (War) in the
grand finale of *Les Noces de Pélée et de Thétis* (The Nuptials of Peleus and
Thetis, 1654). Jérôme de La Gorce suggests that his costume was that
of a triumphant hero and that it prepared the public for a new military
campaign, as did the verse of the libretto: "To have a good peace it is

Figure 9.1. A 1761 costume sketch shows Bellonne, a role for bass voice in Jean-Philippe Rameau's score, as a female warrior. Such images of amazons or *fortes femmes* originated in the regencies of Marie de Médicis and Anne of Austria in the first half of the seventeenth century (DeJean, *Tender Geographies*, 19–42). Reprinted by permission of the Bibliothèque nationale de France, Paris.

necessary to have a good war."[11] Robert M. Isherwood goes so far as to say that "music was the medium by which the king's grandeur and his glorious adventures were recounted to all the estates."[12] This use of the term *gloire*, counterpoised with *galanterie*, permits exploration of the gendered oppositions inherent in the libretto and its divergent sources of authority in the ethos and practices of court and salon cultures.[13]

To return to the libretto, Hebé calls upon l'Amour (Cupid), who promptly descends on clouds—a god on a machine *(deus ex machina)*, representing a *gloire* of quite a different kind.[14] But once again there was a gender reversal: a woman played the "Son of Venus" (a role for soprano voice in Jean-Philippe Rameau's score), at least in 1735 and 1736.[15] Hebé asks that Cupid's arrows be sent to the far corners of the earth to recompense for the European hearts she has lost.[16] Thus, the Pleasures fly away to the exotic Indies and take up arms in a symbolic commingling of pleasure and conquest.

This conflation of the language of sexual conquest with that of military conquest was less strange than one might expect, being a literary commonplace of the era. The prologue followed a formula borrowed from what some music historians consider the first *opéra-ballet*, André Campra and Antoine Houdar de La Motte's 1697 *L'Europe galante*. Here, the Graces, the Pleasures, and the Laughs are busily forging Cupid's arrows under Venus's supervision, when Discord interrupts their dance. (Note the connotation of "musical dissonance" alongside the meaning of "dissension or strife" in the allegorical character's name.) What ensues is a musical battle between Venus and Discord, where each threatens to claim more hearts in Europe. "To my bloody altars all come to sacrifice," sings Discord, and Venus counters, "Love has in Europe a new glory / . . . It reigns in the middle of war. / In spite of your vain efforts it brings together two hearts / Who will some day make the destiny of the earth."[17] The lyrics seem to echo the theories of seventeenth-century advocates of women who predicted that greater public influence on women's part promised a new epoch of peace.[18] One can also infer a plaintive subtext—a desire for peace in a nation depleted by war toward the end of Louis XIV's long reign. Indeed, the *opéra-ballet* germinated, originally as a fin-de-siècle form, in the period of austerity, persecution of Protestants, disastrous wars, and famine that marked the twilight of Louis XIV's reign. Then came the Regency (1715–23), with its return of pleasure and promiscuity and resurgence of salons. The early reign of Louis XV, whose skillful first minister, Cardinal Fleury, favored diplomacy over war, was a period of relative prosperity, monetary stability, reduced religious persecution, and reduced censorship as well as cultural brilliance.[19] It was in this climate—one that judged Louis XIV harshly—combined with a ballet milieu in which women were achieving preeminence on the stage, that Rameau's *opéra-ballet* flourished.[20]

But gallantry and glory had already been potently mixed in another genre, one that parodied the sexual-heroic prowess of the Sun King. Historian Peter Burke has documented the use of war as a metaphor for sex in the "reverse of the medal," subversive images of Louis XIV devised vis-à-vis "the official campaign to present the king as a hero."[21] Robert Darnton, who has charted the history of political libel in pre-Revolutionary France, has found in the last decades of the seventeenth century the emergence of a new genre, the politico-sexual biography of prominent historical figures—the great men and women of court. According to Darnton, the originator of the form was the libertine courtier, Roger de Rabutin, Comte de Bussy. His *Histoire amoureuse des Gaules*, written around 1659–60, satirized the sexual affairs of women of court, but its sequels, written anonymously and attributed to Rabutin, were far more indicting of Louis XIV's absolute monarchy.[22] They were later collected in a five-volume epic, *La France galante*, subtitled *Histoires amoureuses de la cour de Louis XIV*, published in Cologne in 1688 and 1689.[23]

Were these titles fortuitous: *La France galante* (1688), *L'Europe galante* (1697), and *Les Indes galantes* (1735)? The chronological sequence, the expanding geographical *topos* in the titles, and the juxtaposition of grand-scale historical events and sexual liaisons in subject matter suggests otherwise. The interplay of sexual and geopolitical themes is evident in an edition of *La France galante* published in 1696. It contains, in addition to the title work, the following sequels: *France Becomes Italian, with Other Disorders of the Court; Royal Divorce, or Civil War in the Family of the Great Alexander* [Louis XIV]; *Continuation of Gallant France, or the Last Disorders of the Court; The Loves of His Royal Highness the Dauphin with the Countess of Rourre* (figure 9.2).[24] In one sequel, *Le Grand Alcandre Frustré* (The Great Alexander Frustrated), Louis XVI is depicted as a tongue-tied wimp in the presence of the only chaste woman in the court (besides the queen, of course), whom he would like to seduce. "Have you found up to now anything that dared to resist you: cities, chateaux, fortresses, enemies, everything renders itself to you, everything bends under your laws, and you fear that the heart of a woman dares to hold out against a King

Figure 9.2. The satirical side of *galanterie* is apparent in a frontispiece for *Les Amours de Monseigneur le Dauphin avec la Comtesse de Rourre*, from an edition of *La France Galante, ou Histoires Amoureuses de la Cour* published in Cologne in 1696. Reprinted by permission of Elzevier Collection, University of Pennsylvania Library.

always victorious?" coaches the duke of La Feuillade, his confidante and go-between.[25]

This is not to suggest that *L'Europe galante* or *Les Indes galantes* were of a satirical vein but, rather, that there was an historical connection between gallantry and an illicit literature. Moreover, these *opéra-ballet*s had linkages with a salon genre of French literature, which at its very roots defined itself in opposition to Louis XIV's patriarchal and absolute monarchy. But before proceeding with gallantry's subversive side, it is well to consider it as a discourse invoking a host of meanings.

According to Furetière's *Dictionnaire universel*, published in 1690, the word *galant* (feminine: *galante*) had four distinct meanings: (1) (adjective) a "civil gentleman, knowledgeable in the workings of his profession"; (2) (adjective) "a man who has the air of the Court or agreeable manners, who tries to please, particularly the beautiful sex," or, applied to a woman, one "who knows how to live, how to choose and receive her company," or, applied to a fête, "a rejoicing of gentle people"; (3) (noun) a "lover who gives himself entirely over to the service of a mistress," or a man who is "skillful, adroit, dangerous, in that he is savvy in his affairs"; (4) (noun) "he who entertains a woman or girl, with whom he has some illicit commerce," or "a Courtesan."[26] These definitions reveal that the concept of the *homme galant* overlapped that of the *honnête home*—the gentleman or courtier who, on the one hand, had mastered aristocratic codes of etiquette, being polite, elegant, self-disciplined, and self-contained; on the other hand, he could adroitly penetrate and manipulate these codes and demonstrate wit in high social circles.[27] The man had class, either by noble birthright or by acquired merit, and his aplomb was especially apparent where women were concerned. Indeed, *galanterie* as the specific ability to please the ladies had become a synecdoche for the ability to please society in general. It embraced a spectrum of meanings and attitudes, often of opposing valences, that in some ways intersected with the *querelle des femmes* (women's quarrel), the longstanding debate on women's worth.[28] Thus, *galanterie* embodied sometimes an idealistic, eulogistic flavor, sometimes a satirical, cynical flavor. As an adjective appended to a person, place, or thing, *galant(e)* might reflect women's concerns or signify something addressed to their tastes. But it might also be used (in what was the precursor of eighteenth-century libertine literature) as a term of mockery to expose licentious behavior, skillful intriguing at court, and the overlap between sexual liaisons and power. Examining the full range of denotative and connotative meanings implicit in *galanterie* reveals its precise meanings in *Les Indes galantes.* Because the prologue and four *entrées* of *Les Indes galantes* portrayed women's prerogative in their narratives and women's privileging of sentiment in an aesthetics of subtle coloration, this *opéra-ballet* was addressed to women and their sympathizers, and it professed a point of view that was designed to please and serve them.

What may seem like merely an array of meanings in a dictionary actually represents a discourse that emerged over time, accumulating inflections, ironies, and sometimes even inversions. This explains the existence of what Alain Viala has termed "a *galanterie* of distinction and a *galanterie* of debauchery."[29] In its distinguished past, *galanterie* started as a social ethos, *l'art de plaire*, and reemerged as a literary aesthetic that advocated writing and reading as an essential part of sociability.[30] Viala charts the course of *galanterie* from its inception in Castiglione and Della Casa, to its acme in France from 1650 to 1670 (Scudéry, Villedieu, La Fontaine), to its adoption by Louis XIV's court in *fêtes galantes* and comedy ballets by Molière. He notes among its specific referents a fête or *divertissement* "given in honor of a lady or ladies"; moreover, of particular relevance for this study, he suggests that *galanterie* was eventually applied to notions of French hegemony in Europe as an implicit statement of the preeminence of French taste and culture.[31]

To understand the particular gallantry at work in *Les Indes galantes*, it is useful to explore its heyday in the mid-seventeenth century and what has been characterized as the very roots of the French novel. Joan DeJean locates these origins at a time when history and fiction partook of one another in a critical moment, during the Fronde (1648–53), the series of civil uprisings stirred by the *parlements* and the nobles to limit the power of the monarchy built up under Richelieu and Mazarin.[32] During the Fronde the leadership of noblewomen like the duchesses of Longueville and Montpensier was legendary. Overlapping these years, between 1649 and 1653, the ten volumes of Madeleine de Scudéry's *Artamène, ou le Grand Cyrus*, dedicated to the duchesse of Longueville, were published in which the characters and events of the Fronde were read by its readership. As DeJean says, "the bond forged thereby between prose fiction and political subversion marks the origin of the modern French novel."[33] *Artemène* is considered the pinnacle of the *roman héroïque* (romance).[34] Note that the subtitle of *Les Indes galantes* is *Ballet héroïque*, and it, too, situates women at the center of historical affairs.

What immediately followed these events, the flowering of the culture of the *précieuses*, is the bedrock of the gallant *opéra-ballet*.[35] The hallmarks of this culture, according to DeJean, are a literary-linguistic code and "a code to govern male-female relations."[36] DeJean argues that the new novel evolved directly out of salon culture with its valuing of conversation as a form and its practice of collaborative writing. Scudéry's ten-volume *Clélie, Histoire romaine* (1654–60) became the bestseller of the century. Its celebrated *Carte de Tendre* (Map of Tenderness) was a primer in gallantry, revealing, from a woman's perspective, the way a man should treat a woman. The *Carte de Tendre* is interesting because its mapping out of intimate matters of male-female relations gave them a broader significance, endowed them with repercussions for society, and transcribed them into a worldview. In this geography of sentiment the personal was indeed political, and female governance was at the heart of civilization. It is this very use of the male-female relation as a metaphor for the conduct of human relations, what is more the placing of female prerogative at the center of civilization, that is evident in *Les Indes galantes.*

A document published in 1668 under the title of *la Carte géographique de la Cour* (Geographic Map of the Court), described under the title of *la Carte du pays de Braquerie* (Map of the Country of Gallants of the Court) in the memoirs of Bussy-Rabutin and invented by himself and the Prince de Conti sometime in late 1654, was probably a satirical answer to Scudéry's *Carte de Tendre*. The *Carte du pays de Braquerie* reveals the other side of the debate in the *querelle des femmes*, particularly the animosity the *précieuses* inspired in some quarters: "In the Country of the Gallant Dames there are many rivers. The principal ones are the Slut and the Coquette; the *Précieuse* separates the Country of Gallant Dames from the Country of Prudery. The source of all these rivers comes from the Country of the Husbands. The largest and most mercantile is the Slut, which disappears with the others in the Sea of Cuckoldom."[37] The authors proceed with a description of each city (read: woman) in terms of its shifting "governors" and changing commerce. The metaphor of geography as sentiment is parodied with salacious intent. By considering both sides of the debate on women's worth and her place in society (implicit in the discourse on *galanterie*), one sees clearly the "feminist" implications of *Les Indes galantes.*[38]

Recall that the prologue sets up the pretext for the four *entrées*, for their tenuous unity amid boundless diversity of plot, spectacle, and decor. Love is the universal principle:[39] "Is there a heart in the Universe that does not owe you homage?" the libretto asks rhetorically.[40] The mapping of the sentiments of the human heart will chart an understanding of

the character of other civilizations—Peruvian, Turkish, Persian, and
Amerindian—even as these civilizations will lend new compass to the
uncharted terrain of the heart. In professing love as an organizing principle of the universe, the *opéra-ballet* was invoking a Neoplatonic plat-
form championed in seventeenth-century salons. Here, a cult of *sociabilité* (sociability, good fellowship), built upon ideals of "social salvation, of
love as a cosmologically cohesive force, and of woman as guide to salvation," put women at the center of civilized society.[41] How was French
feminine culture, particularly its gender etiquette infused with *galanterie*,
made into a fine cultural export as part of an expansionist, colonialist
worldview in the *opéra-ballet?*

Les Incas du Pérou and the Lovable Conqueror

In the first *entrée, Les Incas du Pérou* (The Incas of Peru),[42] an Inca princess, Phani-Pallas,[43] forms a love bond with the Spanish conqueror
Dom-Carlos. The high priest of the Festival of the Sun, Huascar, tries
to persuade her that the Gods have ordained her marriage instead to
him, later stirring up a volcano with the help of his henchmen as proof.
Phani's aria, "Viens, Hymen, viens m'unir au Vainqueur que j'adore; /
Forme tes noeuds, enchaîne-moi" (Come, Hymen, come unite me with
the Vanquisher whom I adore; / Form your bonds, enchain me),[44] could
be read from the perspective of the early twenty-first century as the
feminized voice of a colonized people. Never has the word "enchaîne"
produced a lovelier enchaining of sound (melisma). But oddly, a similar
posture of adoration of the conquistador is found in one of the acknowledged sources of the *opéra-ballet,* Garcilaso de la Vega's *Histoire des
Yncas;* oddly because Garcilaso was part-Inca and part-Spanish.[45]

Garcilaso attributes the fall of the Inca Empire to the war between
two brothers, Huascar and Atahuallpa, provoked by the latter's treach-
ery. Moreover, he argues that the Incas worshipped the Spaniards as
gods because Huaina Cápac (father of the brothers) had prophesied their
coming as well as the triumph of Christianity. "This adoration lasted
until the avarice, lust, cruelty, and rigor with which many of them treated
the Indians undeceived them."[46] The use of the name Huascar for the
high priest in *Les Incas du Pérou* is interesting in light of the fact that Garcilaso presents "Huáscar" as the legitimate ruler of the Inca Empire and
far more sympathetically than Atahuallpa. In addition, Phani-Pallas

would owe her name to *palla*—"a woman of the royal blood"—also described in Garcilaso.[47]

This dual perspective, both admiring and criticizing the conqueror, found its way into *Les Incas du Pérou*. True, the Spanish bore the brunt of the criticism; nevertheless, the barbarity of the European mercantile system (in which France held a large stake) stood exposed, well in the tradition of the sociopolitical critique that inspired so many Enlightenment narratives.[48] In Huascar's recitative one hears the (imagined) voice of the oppressed: "It's gold that eagerly, / Never satiating himself, these Barbarians devour; / Gold that on our altars is only ornament, / Is the only God that our tyrants adore."[49] Indeed, Jean-Philippe Rameau's prelude to the adoration of the sun, through the use of *le stile anticuo*—an antiquated style of polyphony—creates a mournful, ecclesiastical feeling with sighing figures and fugal imitations[50] that underlines the sense of a culture being relegated to antiquity. The prelude immediately follows Huascar's invocation: "Sun, they have destroyed your superb asylums, / Only the temple of our hearts remains for you: / Deign to hear us in these tranquil deserts, / Zeal is for the Gods the most precious honor."[51]

As the Festival of the Sun progresses and the imagery celebrating *le Soleil* thickens, the *opéra-ballet* evokes *le Roi-soleil*, in particular, Louis XIV's religious fanaticism, inspired by Madame de Maintenon, toward the end of his reign. Huascar's costume, with its man-in-the-sun motif and gold ornamentation radiating from the center, reinforces the implicit comparison.[52] The high priest's chant grows increasingly irrational, mingling images of *l'Amour* (sent from the prologue) with images of *l'Astre du jour* (the Star of the Day), and his *égarements* (aberrations) seem to conjure the *tremblement de terre* (in French an earthquake trembles like a spurned lover), represented by a vigorous tremolo in the strings (see figure 9.3). This is an example of a *merveille*—a modern marvel at that, as the librettist Louis Fuselier claims in the foreword: "The Volcano that serves as the Knot of this American *Entrée* is not an invention as fabulous as the Operations of Magic. These flaming Mountains are common in *les Indes*."[53] "Dans les abîmes de la Terre, / Les vents se declarent la guerre!" (In the abysses of the Earth, / The winds declare war!),[54] bellows the Choir, at once recalling the warrior persona of Louis XIV and projecting the fault for war onto the colonized. A seemingly vindictive Nature interrupts the well-ordered equanimity of the Dance of the Peruvian men and women.[55]

Figure 9.3. A *tremblement de terre* (earthquake) from the manuscript copy of Jean-Philippe Rameau's score for *Les Indes galantes*—just one of a series of *merveilles* in which musical and scenic innovation was blended with exotic "curiosity" in this *opéra-ballet*. Reprinted by permission of the Bibliothèque nationale de France, Paris.

Surely, this aberrant Apollo needs a lesson in gallantry. For as James Munro explains Scudéry's code of *tendresse,* its essence is the ability to moderate one's passion and desire out of concern for the well-being of another. In this light, *tendre amitié* (tender friendship) is to be valued as much as *tendre amour,* and both are governed by a quality of solicitude for or empathy with the other.[56] Huascar's emotional excesses serve no good end, either social or amorous. *Galanterie* is social grace in the deepest sense, based in the ability to see the world from someone else's perspective. It depends upon one's *sensibilité,* or one's ability to project oneself into another's experience, to feel vicariously their emotions.[57] This was one of the things that made *Les Indes galantes,* gallant: the *opéra-ballet* extended the woman-centered ethos of *sensibilité* to its view of other civilizations. For in each of the four *entrées,* the sense of pathos goes to the exotic other, and in each case, the sense of social bonds (or relations between nations) via the metaphor of love bond is mediated through the prerogative of a woman.

Ultimately Huascar realizes his crime and pleads for the volcano to vomit a boulder to crush him. The volcano obliges, thus allowing this character to command the pathos of the play. Clearly, the emotional power (and meanings) of the *entrée* resides in a complex interplay of narrative, lyrics, musical chromatics, spectacle, and dance. This is not marvel for the sake of marvel; as Philippe Beaussant puts it: "It is this double movement of the music, in which the grandly picturesque descriptive aspect comes to engender a pathetic moment, that is remarkable here."[58]

If *Les Incas du Pérou* ennobled conquest through the language of sexual love, it also ennobled sexual love through the language of conquest. This *entrée* may be compared in its duality of meanings to the very popular ballroom dance of the period called "Aimable Vainqueur,"[59] which could simultaneously mean the Gentle Conqueror of Hearts[60] (a metaphor for Love) or the Amiable Conqueror—an oxymoron that expresses the questionable notion of the conqueror having the best interests of the conquered at heart. Arguably, the meanings of the *entrée* were thus accessible to its spectators through their own embodied experience.[61] Reconstructions of "Aimable Vainqueur" reveal its beautiful synchronicity, deferential hesitations (imitations in musical terms), permutations of symmetry, and overriding sweetness and softness *(douceur),* all of which suggest inner feeling expressed in mutual accord.[62] Pierre Rameau, in his *Le Maître à danser* (1725), uses "Aimable Vainqueur" as an example of the aesthetics of *danse de Ville* (ballroom dance) as a whole, as well as a particular step *(coupez du mouvement)*. "Examples of this step are given in the Aimable Vainqueur, which is a very beautiful ballroom dance. They are placed there in different manners and so appropriately *(à propos)* that it seems that the leg expresses the notes [of music]; which proves that harmony *(accord)* or rather imitation of the Music in the dance, since one must imitate the gentleness *(douceur)* of its sounds with gentle and gracious steps."[63] The very structure of the movement here, and especially the relationship between the music and the dance, seem to evoke the salon ethos of skilled conversation, sensitivity, mutual accord, grace, gentility, and gentleness.[64] *Galanterie* may be thought of as intemperate passion subdued (both in the ballroom and in the *opéra-ballet*), and this was its precise evocation in *Les Incas du Pérou*, when the unruly passions of the Inca priest were quite literally blotted out, while the Inca princess found her noble ideal in the Spanish conqueror.[65]

But *galanterie* was rendered au courant only insofar as it intersected with the worldview in the eighteenth century. Consider the *vraisemblance* (verisimilitude) of *Les Inca du Pérou* and its modernity for its day. Religious rituals from around the world had caught the public imagination with the publication between 1723 and 1743 of the eleven-volume work *Les Cérémonies et coutumes religieuses de tous les peuples du monde* (The Ceremonies and Religious Customs of the Various Nations of the Known World), illustrated with over 170 copper plate engravings by Bernard Picart (1673–1733).[66] Notice the discourse of the curious, but realize, too, that Catholicism and Protestantism were equally paraded in this display of strange custom and spectacle. *Les Cérémonies* was done in typical Enlightenment encyclopedic style (although it predated Diderot and d'Alembert's *L'Encyclopédie*, 1751–72, by a number of years), as evinced by its attempt to catalogue all the religions of the known world, enhanced by numerous illustrative plates. Even though its text was a rehashing of the substance of other authors (notably Garcilaso), whom it dutifully credits, and at least some of its visual images were refurbished ones from earlier works,[67] its very layout suggests cross-cultural comparison. It was this same cosmopolitan spirit that was echoed in the *opéra-ballet* and infused it with modernity. The third volume, "Containing the Ceremonies of the Idolatrous Nations," which included Inca ceremonies, was published in English translation in 1734, one year prior to the premiere of *Les Indes galantes*.[68] When Fuselier says, "The ceremonies and festivals of the Peruvians were superb,"[69] one wonders if his imagination (and Jean-Philippe Rameau's) were not jogged by Picart's lush renderings (see figure 9.4).

Figure 9.4. Bernard Picart's engraving for what the text, quoting Garcilaso, describes as a solemn feast in which the Incas worshipped the Father of Light as "the sole, supreme, and universal God" (193). From the English translation of *Les Cérémonies et coutumes religieuses de tous les peuples du monde*, volume 3, published in 1734. The Sun God's face radiates wavy lines of gold, evoking images of Louis XIV. This imagery was reflected in the costume design for Huascar in the 1751 production of *Les Incas du Pérou*. Reprinted by permission of the Founders Collection, University of Pennsylvania Library.

Certainly, the Festival of the Sun, with its grand pagan mass[70] and numerous dance divertissements, was a high point of this *opéra-ballet*.

In the 1736 version of the libretto, there are three indications for dances during this *Feste du Soleil:* (1) after the first invocation, "Soleil, on a détruit tes superbes aziles," to Rameau's nostalgic prelude to the adoration of the sun, "The Princesses and the Incas perform their adoration to the Sun"; (2) after the second invocation, the memorable "Brillant Soleil," they perform the "Dance of the Peruvian men and women"; and (3) immediately before the earthquake, "They dance."[71] A libretto for a production of *Les Incas* staged at Fontainebleau in 1754, which lists "Sr. [Antoine Bandieri de] Laval" as the *Maître des Ballets du Roi*, indicates another dance after the third invocation, "Clair flambeau du monde"

(Clear flame of the world).[72] A libretto for a production staged at Versailles in 1765, attributing the ballets to Monsieur Laval, father and son, appears to have been the personal copy of the latter, with "M. LaVal fils" handwritten inside as well as the phrase "the entrances, exits of the Dance and the airs of the Ballets."[73] Handwritten notes after the choir's third reprise of "Clair flambeau" indicate a "Loure en Rondeau" and beside the final indication "they dance," "3 gavottes."[74] As the dances progress from nostalgic and reverential, to solemn and stately, to dignified and deferential, and, finally, to gracious and lilting, one senses the influence of Amour, also apparent in the lyrics. In Inca dance, at least according to how their customs were portrayed in *Les Incas du Pérou,* couple dancing, with its shared axis of symmetry, complementary action, and balance (of power) between men and women, was the sine qua non of civilization.

Even as women's novels had influenced the themes and tone of *Les Indes galantes,*[75] the *opéra-ballet* may have inspired at least one famous novel written by a woman. In 1747 Madame de Graffigny (who in 1743 had enjoyed a restaging of *Les Indes galantes,* read Fuselier's libretto, and laughed at a parody in the form of an *opéra comique*) published *Lettres d'une péruvienne* (Letters of a Peruvian Woman).[76] Indeed, this epistolary novel contains a bit of poetic justice: when Graffigny's exotic heroine visits the opera, she discovers that music and dance seem to be natural, universal languages (high praises in the Enlightenment), for they communicate passion, compassion, and understanding with an immediacy that words can only imperfectly approximate as inherently arbitrary signs.[77] In the novel, Zilia retains her independence and Inca identity by refusing to marry a Frenchman who has rescued her from Spanish captors. (She offers him *amitié* rather than *amour.*) While Phani chooses the Spanish conqueror, Zilia chooses to remain faithful first to Aza, her Inca equal, and later, when that is no longer feasible, to her Inca identity.[78] Nevertheless, the plot in both *opéra-ballet entrée* and novel turns around a woman's constancy that wins out in the end. Moreover, this constancy is given geopolitical import as it symbolizes encounters between nations and diverse peoples. Audiences viewing later productions of *Les Incas du Pérou* (1751, 1761, 1771) in all likelihood identified Phani with the Peruvian princess from Graffigny's best seller.

Themes of the triumph of constancy, the power of friendship *(amitié),* and the virtue of tenderness recur in the other three *entrées* of *Les Indes galantes.* For instance, in the second *entrée, Le Turc généreux,* love prevails over interracial desire and the polygamous advances of a sultan. Fuselier created the character of the Turk after a real model drawn from a newspaper story, he avowed, a Bacha with exceptional "tenderness." The generous Turk repudiated the stereotype of the brutal and lascivious Turk. In its rewriting of the conventional story of the noble European woman taken captive by pirates and delivered into white slavery in a Turkish harem,[79] this *entrée* also embraced the cultural relativity of the eighteenth-century *philosophes. Amitié* and *reconnaissance,* the chance to return a benevolent act, motivate Fuselier's "virtuous Bacha," a character based upon "an illustrious Original"—Visir Topal Osman, whose story appeared in the January 1734 edition of the *Mercure de France:* "A Turk like Topal Osman is not an imaginary Hero; & when he loves, he is susceptible to a nobler & more delicate tenderness than that of the Orientals."[80] Thus, *tendresse,* with its tempering of passion, was exported to the Orient. Still, as in the other *entrées,* Rameau found occasion for a *merveille*—here, a storm, whose furious winds, waves, and thunder are a meteorological metaphor for Emilie's unheeded heart, before gallantry provides a denouement.

The third *entrée* of the *opéra-ballet, Les Fleurs, Feste persane* (Persian Flower Festival), with its famous *Ballet des fleurs* (Ballet of the Flowers) featuring Marie Sallé, deserves its own analysis, for which there is not space here. In this ballet-within-an-*opéra-ballet* (a nesting of forms that in itself evokes the aesthetics of gallantry), we are once again in the empire of love. An anthropomorphized garden is a metaphor for human sentiment. Zéphire's tenderness prevails over Borée's brashness, as the gentle West Wind displaces the stormy North Wind and renders homage to La Rose, the Queen (Sallé). It was precisely the very public nature of the homage that made the personal political here.

A detailed analysis of *Les Sauvages,* a new *entrée* added to the *opéra-ballet* in 1736, is published elsewhere, exploring both its representation of *les sauvages* (Native Americans) and its thematic intersections with the discourse of *galanterie.*[81] Suffice it to say that, in this *entrée* Zima, a daughter of the chief of a *sauvage* nation, remains true to her *sauvage* lover, Adario, and rejects his European counterparts: Damon, a flighty Frenchman, and Don Alvar, a jealous Spaniard. In preferring tender friendship to impassioned and inconstant love, she specifically invokes the discourse of *tendresse.* Thus, in this final *entrée* of *Les Indes galantes,* female prerogative was placed at the center of the critique of European mores; moreover, female desire and matters of the heart served as the model for affairs of state. The ceremony of the Grand Calumet of Peace furthered the metaphor: gallant relations between the sexes promoted gallant (diplomatic) relations between peoples. The narrative fiction contained what Joan DeJean refers to as "tender geographies, the fact that in [women's novels of the seventeenth century] affairs of the heart are portrayed as indissociable from affairs of state."[82]

Conclusion

This close reading of *Les Indes galantes* is framed with key discourses relating to the gentler sex, discourses clustered around *galanterie* and its close associates: *sensibilité, tendresse, douceur, sentiment, sociabilité.* Considering both sides of the debate on women's worth—the coinages of the advocates and the detractors of the *précieuses,* the usages of the champions and the satirists of *galanterie,* its bifurcated connotations of social grace and sexual slander—one must conclude that, not only did *Les Indes galantes* enter into these discourses, but it took the "feminist" side. In this *opéra-ballet,* women acted as the regulators of social grace, bespeaking a salon-centered agenda as opposed to an absolutist one.

Undoubtedly, there was a complex interplay of passion, pathos, and prerogative in *Les Indes galantes.* A character might typify male prerogative, yet not occupy the emotional center of the production—a spot reserved for female and conquered (feminized) male subjects. Situated within the grand anthropological project of the eighteenth century, and incorporating the ethos of *sensibilité,* this 1735 *opéra-ballet* opened up a space for alternative views and imagined otherness.[83] Through its representation of diverse peoples, not to mention its collaborative layers of production elements (music, lyrics, dance, marvels, costumes, and decor), *Les Indes galantes* created a dynamic performance text that resists resolution into simple, unitary meanings. But one thing is abundantly clear: as performers and dramatis personae, women in the public space played out their stake in the conduct of human relations worldwide.

Notes

An early version of this research was presented at the Society of Dance History Scholars conference in Eugene, Oregon, June 20, 1998, as "Women in the Public Space of the *Opéra-ballet:* The Play of Passion, Pathos, and Prerogative."

I received funding for yet an earlier version of the project under the aegis of a National Endowment for the Humanities Summer Seminar led by Madeleine Gutwirth and Carol Blum at Stony Brook, New York, in 1996. I would also like to thank John Pollack, Public Services Specialist of the Annenberg Rare Book and Manuscript Library of the University of Pennsylvania, as well as the entire staff of the Bibliothèque de l'Opéra in Paris.

1. My method relies on the premises of discourse analysis, as articulated by historian Robert Darnton. In discourse analysis, analysis of texts and intertextuality are the key focuses of historical investigation; the historian of intellectual history reconstructs discourses, which may be seen as ongoing debates. I extrapolate these concepts to the *opéra-ballet*, which I see as a performance medium that engaged the discourses of its era in literary fiction and nonfiction. See Darnton, *The Forbidden Best-Sellers of Pre-Revolutionary France* (New York: Norton, 1996), 169–80.

2. Sarah R. Cohen, *Art, Dance, and the Body in French Culture of the Ancien Régime* (Cambridge: Cambridge University Press, 2000).

3. Susan McClary, "Music, the Pythagoreans, and the Body," in *Choreographing History*, ed. Susan Leigh Foster (Bloomington: Indiana University Press, 1995), 90 (italics in the original). A key source here is Robert M. Isherwood, *Music in the Service of the King: France in the Seventeenth Century* (Ithaca, NY: Cornell University Press, 1973).

4. Jacques Barzun, *From Dawn to Decadence: 500 Years of Western Cultural Life, 1500 to the Present* (New York: HarperCollins, 2000), 351.

5. Carolyn C. Lougee, *Le Paradis des Femmes: Women, Salons, and Social Stratification in Seventeenth-Century France* (Princeton, NJ: Princeton University Press, 1976), esp. parts 1 and 2; quotation, 53.

6. An Italian woman, the marquise de Rambouillet, seeking an alternative to the rustic court of Henry IV, created the first salon in 1610. It was known at the time as the *chambre bleue* or *ruelle*, words that implied the intimacy of the space. See Joan DeJean, "The Salons, 'Preciosity,' and the Sphere of Women's Influence," in *A New History of French Literature*, ed. Denis Hollier (Cambridge, MA: Harvard University Press, 1989), 297–303.

7. Joan DeJean, *Tender Geographies: Women and the Origins of the Novel in France* (New York: Columbia University Press, 1991), 71–82.

8. "Les Jeux brillants de Terpsicore"; "Il est pour un tendre coeur / Des biens dont le secret augmente la douceur." *Les Indes galantes, Ballet heroique. Représenté par l'Academie Royale de Musique; Pour la premiere fois, le Mardy 23. Aoust 1735. Remis avec la nouvelle entrée des Sauvages, Le Samedy dixiéme [sic] Mars 1736* ([Paris]: Jean-Baptiste-Christophe Ballard, 1736), 3, 5. According to Théodore de Lajarte, *Les Indes galantes* premiered on 23 August 1735, had 28 consecutive representations, and was remounted, in whole or in part, on 10 or 11 March

1736 (at this time the *entrée Les Sauvages* was added), 28 May 1743, 9 February 1744, 8 June 1751, 14 July 1761 (29 representations), and 5 December 1771. In addition, the *entrée Les Sauvages* was staged as a fragment on 20 July 1762, 16 July 1773, and 25 July 1773. Thus, this *opéra-ballet* remained in the repertory for almost forty years. See Lajarte, *Bibliothèque musicale du Théatre de l'Opéra: Catalogue historique, chronologique, anecdotique* (Hildesheim: Georg Olms Verlag, 1969), 175–78.

9. "Majesté de Dieu, la veuë de sa puissance, de sa grandeur infinie" and "par emprunt," "l'honneur mondain, . . . la loüange qu'on donne au merite, au sçavoir & à la vertu des homes." Antoine Furetière, *Dictionnaire universel*, 3 vols. (1690; reprint, Geneva: Slatkine, 1970), vol. 2.

10. M. Cuignier played Bellonne in 1735 and 1736, Mr. Jaubert in 1761, Le Sieur Durand in 1765. In addition to the 1736 libretto of *Les Indes galantes* (2), see *Les Indes galantes, ballet heroïque: Représenté pour la premiere fois, par l'Academie Royale de Musique, le Mardy vingt-troisième d'Aoust 1735* ([Paris]: Ballard, 1735), 2; *Les Indes galantes, Ballet-Héroïque: Réprésenté, pour la première fois, par L'Academie-Royale de Musique, en 1735. Repris en 1743. Pour la seconde fois, le Mardi 8 Juin, 1751. Et remis au Théâtre le Mardi 14 Juillet 1761* (Paris: Lormel, 1761), 10; *Prologue des Indes galantes. Représenté devant Leurs Majestés à Versailles le Samedi 16 Février 1765* ([Paris]: Christophe Ballard, 1765).

11. "Pour avoir une bonne paix / Qu'il fallait une bonne guerre." Jérôme de La Gorce, *Féeries d'opéra: Décors, machines et costumes en France 1645–1765* (Paris: Éditions du patrimoine, 1997), 52.

12. Isherwood, *Music in the Service of the King*, 352.

13. Several scholars interpret such oppositions as originating solely in the politics and propaganda machine of absolutism. According to Thomas E. Kaiser, Isherwood argues that court musicians vacillated between tropes of love and glory to accommodate Louis XIV's shifting peace and war policies. Indeed, *Le Salon de la Guerre* (with its images of Bellone and La Discorde painted on the cupola) and *Le Salon de la Paix* at Versailles evoked and reflected this dual imagery. In the eighteenth century, says Kaiser, Louis XV's royal image-makers reverted to the "pastoral image of monarchy based on love, harmony, and peace"; hence, his sobriquet given in 1744, *Louis le Bien-Aimé* (well-loved). See "Louis *le Bien-Aimé* and the Rhetoric of the Royal Body," in *From the Royal to the Republican Body: Incorporating the Political in Seventeenth- and Eighteenth-Century France*, ed. Sara E. Melzer and Kathryn Norberg (Berkeley: University of California Press, 1998), 131–61; quotation, 134.

14. In Furetière's *Dictionnaire universel*, under the first definition of *gloire* is an application to painting and opera: "a highly illuminated spot, an imperfect representation of celestial *glory*" (un lieu fort esclairé, une representation imparfaite de la *gloire* celeste). Noverre refers to this sort of *gloire* in the context of a discussion of theatrical machinery and the marvelous. An example of this machinery

is illustrated in the Plates of the *Encyclopédie*. See Cyril W. Beaumont, trans., *Letters on Dancing and Ballets by Jean Georges Noverre* (1803; reprint, New York: Dance Horizons, 1966), 34 and opposing illustration.

15. "Fils de Venus," in *Indes galantes* (1736), 6. Mlle Petitpas in 1735 and 1736.

16. Here the prologue makes an oblique reference to the War of Polish Succession (1733–38), in which France intervened.

17. "A mes sanglans autels tout vient sacrifier"; "L'Amour a dans l'Europe une nouvelle gloire. / . . . Il regne au milieu de la guerre. / Malgré tes vains efforts il rassemble deux coeurs / Qui feront quelque jour le destin de la terre." *L'Europe galante: Ballet représenté par l'Academie Royale de Musique; Pour la première fois le vingt-quatrième d'Octobre 1697. Repris en 1703. 1715. 1724. & 1736. Et remis le Mardi 9 May 1747* ([Paris: la Veuve de Delormel], 1747), 7–8.

18. See Lougee, *Le Paradis des femmes*, 20, 32–34.

19. On Cardinal Fleury and the early reign of Louis XV see Emmanuel Le Roy Ladurie, *The Ancien Régime: A History of France, 1610–1774*, trans. Mark Greengrass (Oxford: Blackwell, 1996), esp. chapter 8.

20. Le Roy Ladurie, *The Ancien Régime*, 341; Cohen, *Art, Dance, and the Body*, 258. Georgia Cowart has argued that, since its inception, the opera in France had been associated with women, and the rhetoric of opera criticism appropriated that of *querelle des femmes*. "Of Women, Sex, and Folly: Opera under the Old Regime," *Cambridge Opera Journal* 6, no. 3 (1994): 205–20.

21. Peter Burke, *The Fabrication of Louis XIV* (New Haven, CT: Yale University Press, 1992), 142.

22. Darnton, *Forbidden Best-Sellers*, 210–11. Much of the libelous literature was published in Amsterdam and The Hague, which had large populations of Huguenots expelled from France after the Revocation of the Edict of Nantes in 1685.

23. Darnton, *Forbidden Best-Sellers*, 211; Library of Congress, *The National Union Catalog, Pre-1956 Imprints* (London: Mansell, 1968–81), 217.

24. *La France devenuë Italienne, avec les autres desordres de la Cour; Le Divorce Royal, ou guerre civile dans la Famille du grand Alcandre; Suite de la France Galante, ou les derniers dereglemens de la Cour; Les Amours de Monseigneur le Dauphin avec la Comtesse de Rourre. La France Galante, ou Histoires Amoureuses de la Cour, Nouvelle edition, Beaucoup augmentée, & enrichie des Figures* (Cologne: Pierre Marteau, 1696). Robert Darnton notes that the complete collection of seventeen novellas was not published as *La France galante* until 1737. *Forbidden Best-Sellers*, 421.

25. "Avez-vous trouvé jusques ici quelque chose qui osât vous résister: villes, châteaux, forteresses, ennemis, tout se rend à vous, tout plie sous vos lois, et vous craignez que le coeur d'une femme ose tenir contre un Roi toujours victorieux?" Bussy Rabutin, *Histoire amoureuse des Gaules*, 4 vols., ed. Paul Boiteau (Paris: Jannet [etc.], 1856–76), vol. 4, *Suivie des Romans historico-satiriques du XVIIe siècle*, ed. C.-L. Livet (Paris: Paul Daffis, 1876), 8.

26. (1) "homme honneste, civil, sçavant dans les choses de sa profession"; (2) "un homme qui a l'air de la Cour, les manieres agreables, qui tâche à plaire, & particulierement au beau sexe"; "qui sçait vivre, qui sçait bien choisir & recevoir son monde"; "une resjouïssance d'honnestes gens"; (3) "amant qui se donne tout entier au service d'une maistresse"; "habile, adroit, dangereux, qu'il entend bien ses affaires"; (4) "celuy qui entretient une femme ou une fille, avec laquelle il a quelque commerce illicite"; "une Courtisane." Furetière, *Dictionnaire universel.*

27. See Georges Van den Abbeele, "Moralists and the Legacy of Cartesianism," 332–33, and Thomas Crow, "Fêtes galantes," 404–5, in Hollier, *A New History of French Literature.*

28. On the *querelle des femmes,* see Joan Kelly, "Early Feminist Theory and the *Querelle des Femmes,* 1400–1789," *Signs: Journal of Women in Culture and Society* 8, no. 1 (1982): 4–28.

29. Alain Viala, "*Les Signes Galants:* A Historical Reevaluation of *Galanterie,*" trans. Daryl Lee, *Yale French Studies* 92, *Exploring the Conversible World,* ed. Elena Russo (1997): 12.

30. Viala's analysis of the social ethos/aesthetics of *galanterie* bears comparison with the production values of the *opéra-ballet:* gallant works tended to mix genres, to subscribe to worldly diversion or *divertissement,* to incorporate game-like envelopes like the play (or fête or ballet) within a play; to maintain a graceful (amateur) attitude toward playing, and to advocate a noble ideal eschewing self-love.

31. Viala, "*Les Signes Galants,*" 11–29; quotation, 14. Viala attributes the decline of aesthetic gallantry to attacks by the Ancients (classicists) on its mixing and engendering of genres (the novel, for example), as well as a return to the debauched side of gallantry in the eighteenth-century guise of libertinage. See also Walter E. Rex, "Sunset Years," in Hollier, *A New History of French Literature,* 396–402, and Joan DeJean, *Tender Geographies,* 135–40, for descriptions of the *roman galant, nouvelle galante, histoire galante,* and other gallant genres in the last two decades of the seventeenth century.

32. Information on the relationship between the Fronde and Madeleine de Scudéry's novels is drawn from Joan DeJean, *Tender Geographies,* esp. chapters 1 and 2.

33. DeJean, *Tender Geographies,* 45.

34. DeJean, *Tender Geographies,* 5.

35. Preciosity was a literary-linguistic movement (zenith 1654–61) that arose as part of a second wave of salon culture. The *précieuses* were much satirized as a result of prejudices against learned women (cf. Molière's *Les Précieuses ridicules,* 1659); nevertheless, their close analysis of human motivation and conduct, especially in love, made a major contribution to French literature (cf. Madame de Lafayette's *La Princesse de Clèves,* 1678). DeJean encapsulates the precious

aesthetic: "conversation instead of action and an ever more intricate analysis of the human heart" ("The Salons," 302). Note the compatibility of this aesthetic with the new genre of the *opéra-ballet*. Lougee notes that by the 1660s the word *précieuse* had come to mean, quite simply, "a woman who frequents a salon, a member of Parisian polite society" (*Le Paradis des Femmes*, 7).

36. DeJean, *Tender Geographies*, 51.

37. "Dans le pays des Braques il y a plusieurs rivières. Les principales sont: la Carogne et la Coquette; la Précieuse sépare les Braques de la Prudomagne. La source de toutes ces rivières vient du pays des Cornutes. La plus grosse et la plus marchande est la Carogne, qui va se perdre avec les autres dans la mer de Cocuage." See Boiteau, *Histoire amoureuse des Gaules*, 401–16.

38. For a discussion of "feminist" and "anti-feminist" perspectives of the *précieuse*, see Lougee, *Le Paradis des Femmes*, parts 1 and 2.

39. Stephen Greenblatt has argued that, in an historical retreat from multiplicity toward universality, dance was perceived as a universal language in the late seventeenth century. I would add that *galanterie* was a perfect vehicle with which to represent the notion of fundamental unities (as well as to imply French hegemony), in part as a result of its pervasive conventions in French culture. The idea of essential human commonality, whether embodied in gallant relations or otherwise, was central to Enlightenment humanism. See "Toward a Universal Language of Motion: Reflections on a Seventeenth-Century Muscle Man," in *Choreographing History*, ed. Susan Leigh Foster (Bloomington: Indiana University Press, 1995), 25–31.

40. "Est-il un coeur dans l'Univers / Qui ne vous doive son hommage." *Les Indes galantes* (1736), 6.

41. Lougee, *Le Paradis des Femmes*, 39.

42. With the exception of *Les Sauvages*, *Les Incas du Pérou* was the most popular *entrée* of *Les Indes galantes*, being remounted as "a fragment" (without the other *entrées*) in 1744 and 1771. The order of the *entrées* varied from production to production. The 1735 production began with *Le Turc généreux*. In this study, I follow the order specified in the 1736 libretto. See Lajarte, *Bibliothèque musicale*, 176–77.

43. Costume design illustrated in de La Gorce, *Féeries d'opéra*, 142–43.

44. *Les Indes galantes* (1736), 11.

45. Louis Fuselier, the librettist of *Les Indes galantes*, cites "Garcilasso [*sic*] de la Véga, Inca, Historien du Perou" in his foreword (iv). Garcilaso (1539–1616) was the son of a Spanish noble conquistador and an Inca princess (a cousin of the last two Inca rulers). He received a classical education and spent his adulthood in Spain; however, in his boyhood he had heard tales of Inca (oral) history from relatives on his mother's side. See Garcilaso de la Vega, El Inca, *Royal Commentaries of the Incas and General History of Peru*, trans. and ed. Harold V. Livermore (part 1 originally published in Spanish in 1609; part 2 in 1616–17; reprint,

Austin: University of Texas Press, 1966). Although Garcilaso used official, written Spanish sources in compiling his history, his work must be considered bicultural in perspective, especially because it addresses cultural misunderstandings due to language difficulties as well as differing interpretations of the facts and competing versions of the truth. Moreover, the work must be read in the context of the Spanish Inquisition.

46. Garcilaso de la Vega, *Royal Commentaries*, 725.

47. Garcilaso de la Vega, *Royal Commentaries*, 615.

48. English Showalter Jr. describes the species of cultural relativity that abounded in late seventeenth- and early eighteenth-century French texts: they "regularly compare cultures, decentering the perspective of the French reader and viewing French civilization as if it were foreign, at a moment when the French, just emerging from the glorious Century of Louis XIV, liked to consider themselves the most powerful and most advanced nation in the world." See "Intricacies of Literary Production," in Hollier, *A New History of French Literature*, 430. Montesquieu's *Lettres persanes* (Persian Letters, 1721) epitomized this practice and probably influenced the topicality of the harem setting in the third *entrée* of the opera ballet, *Les Fleurs, Fêtes persanes*.

49. "C'est l'or qu'avec empressement, / Sans jamais s'assouvir, ces Barbares dévorent; / L'or qui de nos Autels ne fait que l'ornement, / Est le seul Dieu que nos Tyrans adorent." *Les Indes galantes*, 13.

50. Musicologist Steven Zohn, associate professor of music history, Temple University, provided the musical analysis for my interpretation of the relation between music and text here.

51. "Soleil, on a détruit tes superbes aziles, / Il ne te reste plus de temple que nos coeurs: / Daigne nous écouter dans ces Déserts tranquilles, / Le zele est pour les Dieux le plus cher des honneurs." *Les Indes galantes* (1736), 15.

52. Costume design reproduced in de La Gorce, *Féeries d'opéra*, 141–42.

53. "Le Volcan qui sert au Noeud de cette Entrée Américaine n'est pas une invention aussi fabuleuse que les Operations de la Magie. Ces Montagnes enflamées sont communes dans les Indes." *Les Indes galantes* (1736), "Avertissement," v.

54. *Les Indes galantes* (1736), 17.

55. Although indicators of a culturally advanced society, the dances in this *entrée* still convey a sense of the strange and marvelous. See Philippe Beaussant, "*Les Indes galantes:* Commentaire littéraire et musical," in Jean-Philippe Rameau, *Rameau, Les Indes galantes* (Paris: L'Avant-Scène, 1982), 49.

56. James S. Munro, *Mademoiselle de Scudéry and the* Carte de Tendre (Durham, NC: University of Durham, 1986), 54–61.

57. Munro, *Mademoiselle de Scudéry*, 56.

58. Beaussant, "*Les Indes galantes*," 49.

59. "Aimable Vainqueur" was choreographed as a ballroom dance by Louis Pécour to an air from Campra's *tragédie-lyrique Hésione* (premiered 20 December 1700) and published by Raoul Auger Feuillet in 1701. The music is a *loure* in triple meter. See Wendy Hilton, *Dance and Music of Court and Theater: Selected Writings of Wendy Hilton* (Stuyvesant, NY: Pendragon Press, 1997), 437. That this dance was still performed well into the eighteenth century is verified by Giovanni-Andrea Gallini's *A Treatise on the Art of Dancing*, published in London in 1762 (reprint, New York: Broude Brothers, 1967). Gallini cites the "Louvre" (the dance's other name), along with the minuet, as the two dances most in fashion throughout Europe (*Treatise*, 177–78). He attributes the ability of the dance to please particularly to the "just concert of motions" within the couple.

60. Hilton, *Dance and Music of Court and Theater*, 437.

61. Indeed, in the compact-disc recording of Jean-Philippe Rameau's *Les Indes galantes* performed by Les Arts Florissants, directed by William Christie, and its accompanying version of the libretto, there is a direct reference to "aimables vainqueurs" in the *air gracieux* that follows the *loure en rondeau* performed during the Festival of the Sun. Since "Aimable Vainqueur" was a well-known *loure*, it is likely that the librettist and the composer intended to create a subliminal, or even quite conscious, association here (HMC 901367–9 [Arles: Harmonia Mundi, 1991], 68). See also Jean-Philippe Rameau, *Oeuvres Complètes, Publiées sous la Direction de C. Saint-Saëns, tome VII, Les Indes galantes, ballet héroïque en trios entrées et un prologue avec une nouvelle entrée, paroles de Fuzelier, édition revisée par Paul Dukas* (Paris: A. Durand et fils, 1902), 201; and Beaussant, "*Les Indes galantes*," 49.

62. Hilton has described the dance as "a unique blend of gently expressed nobility, tenderness, and tranquility. Partners keep eye contact almost throughout, turning away from each other only to return" (*Dance and Music of Court and Theater*, 437). Deda Cristina Colonna has demonstrated the use of reflection and rotation symmetry in its figures. See "Variation and Persistence in the Notation of the *Loure 'Aimable Vainqueur*,'" in *Proceedings, Society of Dance History Scholars*, Proceedings of the Twenty-First Annual Conference, University of Oregon, Eugene, OR, 18–21 June, comp. Linda J. Tomko (Riverside, CA: Society of Dance History Scholars, 1998), 285–94. My interpretation of the dance is based, in part, upon my own reconstruction of it in collaboration with Laura Katz and Tresa Randall, performed on 21–22 June 2002 at the Dance & the City: Urban and Urbane conference of the Society of Dance History Scholars in Philadelphia.

63. " . . . on donne des exemples de ce pas dans l'Aimable Vainqueur; qui est une fort belle danse de Ville, ils y sont placez de différentes manieres & si à propos, qu'il semble que la jambe exprime les notes; ce qui prouve cet accord ou plutôt cette imitation de la Musique avec la danse, puisque l'on doit imiter la douceur de ses sons par des pas doux & gracieux." Pierre Rameau, *Le Maître à*

danser (Paris, 1725; reprint, New York: Broude Brothers, 1967), 141. Rameau also describes what he calls a *pas de Sissonne coupé*, again giving an example from "Aimable Vainqueur," in which the force of a jump is moderated and the motion arrested: "at the first jump you land on your two feet without bending the knees; but you bend afterward to make the second jump" *(au premier saut vous retombez sur vos deux pieds, sans que les genoux soient pliez; mais vous pliez après pour faire le second saut)* (158).

64. It is beyond the scope of this study to compare the aesthetics of *la belle danse* according to Rameau's 1725 dancing manual with the aesthetics of *galanterie*. I shall simply mention that Rameau advises the dancer to soften his steps to conform to women's tempered manner and to create that mutual accord that he considers to be one of the chief beauties of the dance (*Maître à danser*, 106–7). His analysis of the usage of the *fleuret* similarly reflects the influence of women (*Maître à danser*, 122–23).

65. However, a noblewoman's discretion was once again satirized in a parody of *Les Indes galantes* written by Favart, featuring Madame Favart as Phani-Palla, and produced in response to the 1751 production of the *opéra-ballet*. As the love scene between the principals is reduced to mere seduction, Carlos responds to Phani's hesitations thus: "Eh! I've told you a hundred times, / Phani, beautiful Princess, / These words are too bourgeois, / Bear your nobility better." *(Eh! je vous l'ai dit cent fois, / Phani, belle Princesse, / Ces propos sont trop bourgeois, / Soutenez mieux noblesse.) Les Indes dansantes, Parodie des Indes galantes; Représentée pour la premiere fois par les Comédiens Italiens Ordinaires du Roi, le Lundi 26 Juillet 1751*, 4th ed. (Paris: N. Duchesne, 1759), 34.

66. The English translation was subtitled "Together with Historical Annotations and Several Curious Discourses Equally Instructive and Entertaining" (London: Claude Du Bosc, 1734). See also Gordon N. Ray, *The Art of the French Illustrated Book, 1700 to 1914* (New York: Pierpont Morgan Library with Dover Publications, 1986), 7.

67. Compare *One Hundred Prints Representing Different Nations of the Levant*. Jean Baptiste van Moor made the original tableaux for *Recueil de cent estampes representant differentes nations du Levant*, which Mr. Le Hay engraved (Paris, 1714). Charles Ferriol directed the project and published an explication to accompany the prints in 1715.

68. Also notable was the French expedition to Peru in 1735, making that country a topic of popular interest. See Le Roy Ladurie, *The Ancien Régime*, 371.

69. "Les Cerémonies & les Fêtes des Peruviens étoient superbes." *Les Indes galantes* (1736), "Avertissement," v.

70. Beaussant, "*Les Indes galantes*," 45.

71. "Les Pallas et les Incas font leur adoration au Soleil"; "Danse de Peruviens et Peruviennes"; "On danse." *Les Indes galantes* (1736), 15–17.

72. *Fragments représentés devant le Roi a Fontainebleau, le octobre 1754* (Sainte Cécile: Ballard), 25.

73. "Les entrees, sorties de la Danse et les airs des Ballets." *Les Incas du Perou, Acte de Ballet, Representé devant Leurs Majestés à Versailles le Mercredi 30 Janvier 1765* ([Paris]: Ballard, 1765). "Les Ballets sont de la composition de MM. Laval, Pere & Fils, Maîtres des Ballets de Sa Majesté."

74. *Les Incas* (1765), 17–18. See also Beaussant, "*Les Indes galantes*," 49. That the *loure*, specifically "Aimable Vainqueur," remained in fashion through the 1760s is testified to by Giovanni-Andrea Gallini, Director of the Dances at the Royal Theatre in the Haymarket, in *Treatise*, 177–78.

75. Besides the genres and novels mentioned above, there were *histoires galantes*, novels that merged historical fact and fiction in an almost inextricable blend, which comprised the dominant trend in the period from the late 1680s to 1715. DeJean has theorized works of this genre, also called *histoire secrète, mémoires secrets, nouvelle galante, annales galantes,* and *histoire des amours,* as precursors to histories of private life. In portraying the sexual intrigues of famous men, casting *galanterie* as the "soul" of the French and foreign courts (*Tender Geographies*, 138), and revealing women to be "the prime movers of history" (137), they were both derided and praised vis-à-vis official versions of history (135–40). Some of these novels portrayed the sexual indiscretions of powerful clerics, comparable with Huascar in *Les Incas*.

76. See *Correspondance de Madame de Graffigny*, 10 vols., ed. English Showalter et al. (Oxford: Voltaire Foundation, 1996), 4:303, 314–15, 318, 387–88, 398–89. The novelist seems to have enjoyed Favart's *L'Ambigu de la folie ou le Ballet des dindons* (Medley of Folly or the Ballet of the Turkeys), premiered 31 August 1743 at the Saint-Laurent fair theater, most of all. Other scholars have pointed to Voltaire's 1736 play *Alzire* and an expedition to Peru that returned to France in 1745 as influences on Graffigny. See Janet Gurkin Altman, "Making Room for 'Peru': Graffigny's Novel Reconsidered," in *Dilemmes du roman: Essays in Honor of Georges May*, ed. Catherine Lafarge (Saratoga, CA: Anma Libre, 1989), 40.

77. Françoise de Graffigny, *Lettres d'une péruvienne, Lettres portugaises, Lettres d'une péruvienne et autres romans d'amour par letters* (1747; reprint, Paris: Flammarion, 1983), 297–98.

78. Altman argues that the novel envisions "lovers as partners equally responsible for a nation," thus entering the "discourse of the equal partner in politics" ("Making Room for 'Peru,'" 43). In this, it departs from the traditional sentimental plot, which according to the "passion model" (42) has one or both lovers being consumed, isolated from society, and sacrificed. While the narrative of the *opéra-ballet entrée, Les Incas,* still conforms to the passion model, that of the final *entrée, Les Sauvages,* enters the discourse of equal partners in nationhood.

79. See, for example, the story within a story entitled "La force de l'amitié," in Alain-René Lesage, *Le Diable boiteux*, 2nd ed., ed. Roger Laufer (1707; reprint, Paris: Mouton, 1970). Lesage rewrites the *précieuse* conflict between *amour* and *amitié* in terms of male bonding.

80. "vertueux Bacha"; "un illustre Original"; "Un Turc semblable à Topal Osman, n'est pas un Héros imaginaire; & quand il aime, il est susceptible d'une tendresse plus noble & plus délicate que celle des Orientaux"; *Les Indes galantes* (1736), iv.

81. Joellen A. Meglin, "*Sauvages*, Sex Roles, and Semiotics: Representations of Native Americans in the French Ballet, 1736–1837; Part One: The Eighteenth Century," *Dance Chronicle: Studies in Dance and the Related Arts* 23, no. 2 (2000): 87–132.

82. DeJean, *Tender Geographies*, 4.

83. Similarly, many philosophic novels of the Enlightenment sought alternative perspectives in a thinly veiled critique of French society: Montesquieu's *Lettres persanes* (1721), Graffigny's *Lettres d'une Péruvienne* (1747), Voltaire's *L'Ingénu* (1767), and Diderot's *Supplément au Voyage de Bougainville* (1796) are examples of this literary tradition.

CONTRIBUTORS

Régine Astier is a leading authority in the reconstruction and performance of baroque dance, a field that she has helped develop worldwide since her first United States concert in 1968. She is an independent researcher and writer best known for her biographies of prominent French dancers of the *Ancien Régime*. In 1993 she founded the Conservatory of Baroque Dance for children aged ten to eighteen, followed by two performing groups, *Les petits* and *Les grands baladins du Roy*.

Lynn Matluck Brooks is the Arthur and Katherine Shadek Humanities Professor at Franklin & Marshall College. She holds degrees from the University of Wisconsin–Madison and Temple University and is a Certified Movement Analyst (Laban/Bartenieff Institute of Movement Studies). Her doctoral research was supported by a Fulbright/Hayes Grant for study in Spain, and she has held grants from the Pennsylvania Council on the Arts and the National Endowment for the Humanities. Brooks wrote performance reviews for *Dance Magazine* and edited *Dance Research Journal* (1994 through 1999). She has written three books and many scholarly articles on dance history subjects. In 2008 she assumes the co-editorship of *Dance Chronicle, Studies in Dance and the Related Arts*.

Anne Daye lectures in dance history at Laban, the London dance conservatory. As chairman of the Dolmetsch Dance Society, she has contributed to the growth of research, teaching, publication, and participation in dance from the fifteenth to nineteenth centuries. Her investigation into the Stuart masque combines documentary research, practical reconstruction, and literary analysis, and is currently in preparation as a doctoral thesis on the professional dance within the antimasque.

Angene Feves specializes in the reconstruction, teaching, and performance of Renaissance and Baroque dances. In 2000 her introduction to the

257

seventeenth-century manuscript "Instruction pour dancer" was published in Germany. She has also written articles for the *International Encyclopedia of Dance* and for *Dance Chronicle*. She oversaw production and wrote instruction books for the cassette recordings *Homage to Amor* and *Dances for a Noble Gathering*, compilations of dances from Fabritio Caroso's works.

MOIRA GOFF researches and reconstructs the dance of the early eighteenth century. She has published widely and has danced in Europe and the United States, as well as in the United Kingdom. Her research specialty is dance on the London stage from 1660 to 1760, and in 2001 she was awarded a doctorate for her thesis on the English dancer-actress Hester Santlow. Her book on Santlow's life and career has recently been accepted for publication.

NATHALIE LECOMTE (Ph.D., University of Paris, Panthéon-Sorbonne) is an independent researcher. She directed historians and wrote articles for the *Dictionnaire de la musique en France aux XVIIe et XVIIIe siècles* (1992) and *Dictionnaire de la danse* (1999). She also contributed to the critical edition of Louis Cahusac's *Traité historique de la danse* (2004). She is currently working on a book about the dance troupe of the Paris Opera from 1699 to 1733.

SARAH MCCLEAVE has been lecturer in the School of Music, Queen's University, Belfast, since 1998. Her research focuses on dance and drama in London and Paris of the 1720s to 1740s. She has published work in *The New Grove Dictionary of Music and Musicians* (2001), the *Göttinger Händel Beiträge*, *Consort*, and the Cambridge University Press *Companion to Early Opera* (forthcoming). She is currently working on a book based on her doctoral dissertation (King's College, London, 1993) entitled *Handel and the Dance: His London Operas in Context*.

JOELLEN A. MEGLIN is associate professor of dance at Temple University, where she was coordinator of doctoral studies in dance from 1997 to 2006. She directs Sprezzatura, a chamber dance ensemble that has performed, in London, Long Island, and Philadelphia, works ranging from eighteenth-century Baroque dance and twentieth-century modern dance classics to her own choreography. Her research has been published frequently in *Dance Chronicle* and *Studies in Dance History* monographs as well as presented nationally and internationally. She is a recent recipient of a Newberry Library Fellowship to pursue her research on American choreographer Ruth Page. In 2008 she assumes co-editorship of *Dance Chronicle, Studies in Dance and the Related Arts*.

KAREN SILEN is presently working on a dissertation at the University of California, Berkeley, on dance practice and theory in late thirteenth-century France and French Flanders. She has lectured on medieval performance, dance analysis, and contemporary and early dance at UC–Berkeley, Stanford University, and Mills College. Her published works include "Dance" in *Women and Gender in Medieval Europe: An Encyclopedia* (2006), and "Dance in Late-Thirteenth-Century Paris" in *Dance, Spectacle, and the Body Politick: Dance in Society from 1250 to 1750* (forthcoming).

BARBARA SPARTI is a dance historian specializing in fifteenth- to seventeenth-century Italian dance. She has performed and choreographed period works for theater and opera. She was visiting professor at the University of California, Los Angeles, and guest lecturer and choreographer at the University of California, Santa Cruz; Princeton University; and in Israel. Besides her edition and translation of Guglielmo Ebreo's 1463 dance treatise *On the Practice or Art of Dancing* (1993) and her introduction to a newly discovered 1614 dance treatise, *Mastro da Ballo* (2004), she publishes on questions regarding style and aesthetics, dance music, Jewish dancing masters, improvisation, the *moresca*, and Italian baroque dance.

INDEX

Numbers in italics refer to figures.

Accademia de' Lincei, 66–67
"Aimable Vainqueur," 241–42, 253n59, 253–54nn61–63, 255n74
Aldridge, Robert, 175
allegorical subjects and roles: in fifteenth-century Italian dance spectacles, 26, 27, 30, 34, 40; in Paris Opera ballets, 116–17, 232
"Alta Orsina" (Caroso), 59
Altemps, Cornelia Orsina, 59
Ambrosio, Giovanni, 21
Angiolini, Gasparo, 173, 175
Anne of Austria, Queen of France, 84
Anne of Denmark, Queen of England, 72, 78, 87–88
Apollo and Daphne (Thurmond), 186, 187
Arbeau, Thoinot, 49
Ariadne and Bacchus (Gallet), 175
Artenice (Racan), 5, 76
Astier, Régine, 7–8; article by, 123–44; contributor's note, 257
Auretti, Anne, 169
Auretti, Janneton, 169–70
autonomy, legal freedom of Paris Opera dancers, 106, 129, 142

Bacchus and Ariadne (Sallé), 161, 171, 173–75
Le Baillet des Fleur (Lany), 175
Il ballarino (Caroso), 50, 51, 53–54, 57, 58, 59, 60, 61

Ballet dansé par les Roi pour la Reine (French court ballet), 74
Le Ballet de la Reyne dansé par les Nymphes des Jardins (French court ballet), 74, 84
Ballet des Fleurs (Sallé), 171, 175, 245
Balon, Claude, 102, 113, 116, 128, 131, 134, 145, 146, 147, 148, 151, 152, 155n17, 161
"Barriera" (Caroso), 58, 69n16
"Barriera Nuova" (Caroso), 58–59
Barzun, Jacques, 229
"Bassa Honorata" (Battistino), 61
"Bassa Honorata" (Caroso), 60
"Bassa Romana" (Battistino), 59
Bassompierre, François Le Maréchal de, 76–77, 84
Battersby, Christine, 162, 165, 172–73
Battistino, Messer, 51–52, 53, 54, 57, 58, 59, 69n16
Baxter, Richard, 195
Beatrice of Nazareth, 219
Beauchamp, Pierre, 91
Beaussant, Philippe, 241
The Beaux' Stratagem (Farquhar), 185
Beguines, 208–10, 215, 217
Behn, Aphra, 186, 194
"Le Bellezze d'Olimpia" (Caroso), 51, 54
Bernard, Pierre-Joseph, 163, 165
Besford, Esther, 175
Bestul, Thomas, 215

Biancolelli, Catherine, 194, 195
Bicknell, Margaret, 9, 184–85, 186, 187–
    88, 192, 194–95, 199–200
Blamont, Colin de, 170
Blondy, Michel, 107, 113, 116, 137–38,
    142, 158n60, 161
Bocan, Mr. (Jacques Cordier), 73, 78,
    89, 91n3
Boindin, Nicolas, 107, 109
Boissy, Louis de, 162–63
Bonin, Louis, 130–31
Booth, Barton, 187, 190
Bourguignon, Erika, 219
Boutade (Rebel), 130–31
Bouteville, S., 127
Bracegirdle, Anne, 192
Brooks, Lynn Matluck: contributor's
    note, 257; introduction by, 3–14
Brunel, Mlle., 109
Buckingham, Duke of (George Villiers),
    74, 75, 76, 77, 78, 79, 185
Burke, Peter, 233
Bussy-Rabutin (Roger de Rabutin,
    Comte de Bussy), 233, 237
Bynum, Carolyn Walker, 209–10, 225

Caciola, Nancy, 220
Caetana, Agnesina Colonna, 50, 51–52,
    55, 57, 60–61
Caetana, Bonifacio, I, 55, 57
Caetana, Caterina Pio, 55
Caetana, Felice Maria Orsini, 50, 61, 63
Caetani family genealogy, *56*
Cahusac, Louis de, 172
Calzabigi, Ranieri, 173
Camargo, Marie Anne Cupis de, Prévost
    and, 123
Cammasse, Lolotte (Charlotte), 170
Campanini, Barbarina, 171, 174
Campra, André, 167, 172, 189, 232
Camus, Jeanne Edmée (Mme. Delastre),
    107
Caprice (Rebel), 130–31, 156n28
Les Caractères de la danse (Rebel), 130, 132–
    33, 137, 138, 156n28, 156–57n32, 188
The Careless Husband (Cibber), 186

Caroso, Fabritio, 39; books on dancing
    by, 50; as choreographer, 51–52;
    patronesses of, 5, 49–67; "perfect
    theory" of dance, 58, 59–60, 61;
    Spanish connections of, 57, 60
Carte de Tendre (Scudéry), 230, 237
*Les Cérémonies et coutomes religieuses de tous
    les peuples du monde* (Picart), 233–34,
    243
"Cesarina" (Caroso), 60
Cesi, Beatrice Caetana, 50, 51–52, 54,
    55, 57–58, 68n14
Cesi, Federico (elder), 63, 66–67
Cesi, Federico (younger), 64–67
Cesi, Olimpia Orsina, 50, 51–52; as
    Caroso's patroness, 50, 51–52, 64,
    67; children of, 64–67; cousins of,
    61–63; family of, 52–57, 59; grand-
    parents of, 52; in-laws of, 55–61;
    marriage to Federico Cesi, 55, 63–
    67; parents of, 52–54; as patroness
    of architecture and arts, 64
Cesi, Onorato, 55, 57, 60–61, 67
Cesi, Paolo Emilio, 54, 55
Chaillou, Mlle., 110, 113
Charles I, King of England, 71, 72, 76,
    78, 93n27; marriage to Henrietta
    Maria, 74, 76, 79, 84, 88; as masque
    performer, 75, 79, 84
Charles II, King of England, 88
Chateauneuf, Marie, 169
Chateauvieux, Mlle., 109
Chesnée, Quesnot de la, 105–6
"Chiaranzana," 32, 39, 60
children: dancers' illegitimate, 107; as
    performers at Paris Opera, 103,
    119–20n11, 126–27, 161; as per-
    formers in English masques, 75,
    89–90; as protégés of Sallé, 168–70
Chloridia: Rites to Chloris and Her Nymphs
    (English court masque), 80–86,
    88, 91
choreography: English court musicians
    as responsible for, 72; extant de-
    scriptions or notations, 12, 21, 110,
    113, 186; "how to dance" books as

record of, 49; principal dancers as choreographers, 131; women and Spanish, 72. *See also specific choreographers; specific works*
Christout, Marie-Françoise, 174
Cibber, Colley, 184
classical and mythological subjects, 81, 83–84, 94, 117
Cochois, Marianne, 170
Cohen, Sarah R., 229
Comédie Française, 105
comedy: comic and grotesque elements in English masques, 77, 88–89; in English theater, 167, 184, 185, 187, 188, 190, 192, 194–95, 196–97, *198;* Sallé as comic dancer, 167
commedia dell'arte, 194, 195, 199
concert dance traditions, twentieth-century, 222
Confesse, Nicholas, 78
Congreve, William, 185–86, 187
The Constant Couple (Farquhar), 192, *193*
"Contezza d'Amore" (Caroso), 53–54
"Contrapasso Nuovo" (Caroso), 59–60
Cooke, Philip (the younger), 169–70, 180n47
Corail, Mlle., 109, 110, 113
Corbière, Mlle., 107, 109
Cordier, Jacques (Bocan), 73, 78, 89
Cornazano, Antonio, 21
Corneille, Pierre, 134
costumes: as conspicuous display of power, 24, 35, 48n93; as depicted in art, 124–25; of Elisabeth of Spalbeek, 215; for English masques, 76, 84–86, *85,* 86, 87, 88; for *Les Indes galantes, 231,* 242–43; for Italian wedding spectacles, 27, 29, 31–32, 40, 46n75; for Paris Opera productions, 107, 124; Sallé and reforms in, 165–66
The Country Wife (Wycherley), 185, 186, 188, 197
Couperin, Louise, 158n57
creativity as gendered, 162, 165
cultural relativity, 245, 252n48

da Bagno, Guido, 21
Dacier, Emile, 161
Dahms, Sibylle, 181n63
dance, difficulty in defining, 218–19
dancer-actresses, 8–9, 183–200
dancing masters. *See* training and instruction
Dangeville, Antoine François *(l'aîné),* 102
Dangeville, Jean-Baptiste *(le cadet),* 102
Dangeville, Michelle, 7, 102, 110, 118, 127
danse d'action, 134
Darnton, Robert, 233
Davenant, William, 71
Davies, Thomas, 188
Davis, Natalie Zemon, 3–4, 10–11
Daye, Anne, 5–6; article by, 71–91; contributor's note, 257
Dazincourt, Mlle., 142
DeJean, Joan, 230, 236–37, 246, 250–51n35, 255n75
Delastre, Jeanne Michelle, 107
Delisle, Mlle., 107, 110
del Soto, Francesco, 64
Denoyer, Mlle., 189
Desaive, Jean-Paul, 11–12
Desmâtins, Marie Louise, 104
Desplaces, Mlle., 110
d'Este, Alfonso, 24
d'Este, Beatrice, 21, 24
d'Este, Isabella: birth of, 24; dancing masters and instruction of, 21, 23–24; genealogy of, *22;* instruction in dance, 21–22; as patroness of arts, 19; as performer, 21, 23; as politician, 19
Destouches, André-Cardinal, 110
Dictionnaire des danseurs de Bruxelles de 1600 à 1830, 105
Dimanche, Louise, 105–6
Domenico of Piacenza, 21
Dryden, John, 192, 194
duets, 111
Du Fort, Elisabeth, 7, 102, 110, 116, 118
The Dumb Farce (Thurmond), 185, 195
Dumirail, S., 127
Dumoulin, David, 113, 171

Dumoulin, François, 113, 116
Duplessis, Louise, 106
Dupré, Emilie, 106
Duval, Mlle., 103

"early dance," use of term, 4, 7
Ebreo, Guglielmo, 21
Eleonora of Aragon, 23–26
Elisabeth of Spalbeek, 9–10, 14, 207–
    22; as Beguin mystic, 209, 210, 211;
    as controversial figure, 226–27n52;
    costume and setting for dances, 215;
    dance as bodily communication
    and, 218–20; description of dances
    of, 211–15, 225n30, 226n40, 226n49;
    stigmata of, 207, 211, 215, 217
embodiment: ballet and the "artful body,"
    229; dance and gender equity, 11–12;
    religion and, 218–20, 225n21
Emperor of the Moon (Behn), 194
The Escapes of Harlequin (Thurmond), 185,
    186, 195
An Essay Towards an History of Dancing
    (Weaver), 191
Essex, John, 190
Etherege, George, 185
l'Europe galante (Campra and La Motte),
    167, 172, 189, 232
exotic subjects and roles, 117; in Italian
    wedding spectacles, 29. See also *Les
    Indes galantes* (Rameau)

The Fair Quaker of Deal (Shadwell), 187
Famiglie celebri italiane (Litta), 51
familial relationships among dancers,
    129–30, 161
Farge, Arlette, 3–4, 10–11
Farnese, Odoardo, 81
Farquhar, George, 185, 192
Fasti (Ovid), 81
Ferrara (Italian city-state), 19–21
Les Fetes d'Hebé (Rameau), 167
Les Fêtes grecques et romains (Blamont),
    170, 176
Feves, Angene, 5; article by, 49–67;
    contributor's note, 257–58

Fleury, René-Julie, 116
La Flora (Salvadori), 81–82, 84
flower roles, 175
Fokine, Michel, 175
Fonte, Moderata, 6
Fontenelle, Bernard le Bouvier de, 167
Foster, Susan Leigh, 173
La France Galante (Bussy-Rabutin), 233;
    illustration from, *234*
Freville, Mlle., 105
Friedler, Sharon, 13
Furetière, Antoine, 230, 235
Fuselier, Louis, 239, 242, 244, 245, 251n45

galanterie, 228, 230, 232, 235–36, 246; sa-
    tirical qualities of, 233–35; sexual
    mores and, 233–35; as subversive,
    233–35
Gallet, Sébastien, 175
Gallonio, Antonio, 64
Gand, Alexander Maximilien Baltha-
    zar, de (Count of Middelbourg,
    "Médor,"), 107, 136, 138–41
Gaultier, Jacques, 89
gender: of audience for *Les Indes galantes*,
    235–36; creativity as gendered, 162,
    165; dance and gender equality,
    11–12; dancing as profession and,
    72; French novel form and, 236–
    37; male dancers in female roles,
    26, 230; masque performance and,
    72; religious expression or demon-
    stration and, 10–11, 217; roles and,
    117; salaries of dancers and, 115–
    16; salon culture and, 229–30,
    232, 236–37, 247n6; semiotics of
    Les Indes galantes and, 10–11, 228–
    46; sixteenth-century power dy-
    namics and, 6; size of male and fe-
    male Paris Opera troupes, 113–15;
    women in recent dance history, 13
Gilbert of Tournai, 217
Gildon, Charles, 191
Giovanni Ambrosio (dancing master),
    23–24
Glazer, Susan, 13

gloire, 228, 230, 232, 235, 248n14
Gluck, Christoph Willibald, 173
Goff, Moira, 8–9; article by, 183–200;
    contributor's note, 258
Goring, Sir George, 75, 77, 78
Graffigny, Mme. de, 244
"Gratie d'amore" (Caroso), 60
Le gratie d'amore (Negri), 50
Greenblatt, Steven, 251n39
Grimaldi, Antoine de, 110, 121n42
Grognet, Manon (Marie), 164–65, 170
Guynemet, Pierre, 131
Guyot, Jean-Baptiste, 100
Guyot, Marie-Catherine, 7, 100, 103,
    110, 118, 137

Handel, George Friedrich, 161, 166–67,
    170, 174, 182n72
Haran, Anne Julienne, 106, 115, 116, 118
Harlequin Doctor Faustus (Thurmond),
    185, 186, 187
Henrietta Anne, Duchess of Orleans, 89
Henrietta Maria, Queen of England:
    childhood of, 73–74; court masque
    production and, 4–5, 80–89, 91;
    dance training of, 72–73, 91n4;
    marriage to Charles I, 72, 74, 76,
    79, 84, 88; masques as political
    acts, 71–72, 91n2; as patroness of
    arts, 4, 14, 89, 92n10; as performer,
    74, 76, 91–92n6
Hesse, Jean-Baptiste de, 174
Hilverding, Franz, 173, 175
Historia deli sante vergini romane (Gallonio),
    64
Holland, Earl of, Lord Kensington
    (Henry Rich), 74–75, 77, 78, 84
Hopper, Simon, 89
Horace (Corneille), 134
Hudson, Jeffrey, 77, 86

Les Incas du Pérou (Rameau), 229, 238–46
Les Indes galantes (Rameau): as cosmo-
    politan and "modern" work, 242;
    discourse analysis of, 228–46; par-
    odies of, 169, 175, 254n65; Sallé's

performance in, 163–64, 167, 169,
    175, 182n72; salon culture reflected
    in, 242; score for, *240*
The Indian Emperor (Dryden), 192, 194
instruction. *See* training and instruction
Isaac, Mr., 186, 187
Isec, Marie-Louise, 115, 116, 118
Isherwood, Robert M., 232
Italy: dance spectacles in, 19–40; map of
    political boundaries (1473–1514), *20*

Les Jalousies de sérail (Noverre), 175–76
James, Duke of York, 89
Javillier, Claude, 107
Jones, Inigo, 5, 71, 76, 77–78, 79, 80, 82, 87
Jonson, Ben, 71, 79, 80, 81, 82, 86, 87
The Judgment of Paris (Weaver), 187

King Lear (Tate), 186, 187
Kirstein, Lincoln, 173
Kleinberg, S. Jay, 3
Kunzmann, Vladia, 130

l'Abbé, Anthony, 186, 187, 189, 190–91
La Camargo, Anne Cupis de, 105, 118,
    132, 170, 178n14; Prévost as teacher
    and mentor of, 123, 132, 137–38,
    141–42
La Ferriere, Mlle., 100, 101, 103, 106, 108,
    109, 111, 113, 116, 118
La Garde, Simon de, 89
La Gorce, Jérôme de, 230, 232
La Mare, Pierre de, 78
La Motte, Antoine Houdar de, 232
Lancret, Nicolas, painting of Sallé by,
    163, 163–64
Lany, Charlotte, 169
Lany, Jean-Barthélemy, 174, 175
La Pierre, Sebastian and Guillaume,
    89, 91
Laudi Spirituali (del Soto), 64
Lavagnolo, Lorenzo, 39
Laval, Antoine, 113
Laval, Antoine Bandieri de, and son,
    243–44
Le Brun, Charles, 191

Lecomte, Nathalie, 6, 7, 8; article by, 99–119; contributor's note, 258
Le Fevre, Mlle., 110, 168
Lemarie, Anne, 103, 116, 118
Le Roy, Anne, 116
Lestang, S., 127
Lettres d'une péruvienne (Graffigny), 244
Levin, Carole, 6
libretti as research documents, 119nn1–2
The Life of Mr. Thomas Betterton (Gildon), 191
Litta, Pompeo, 51, 52, 53, 61, 63, 64–65
Lougee, Carolyn C., 229
Louis XIV, King of France, 89, 91; allusions to, in *Les Indes galantes*, 239, 243; as performer, 88, 230, 232; politics of dance and, 229; reign as context, 91, 133, 232–35; 248n13, religious fanaticism of, 239; theater bylaws of, 107, 142
Love for Love (Congreve), 185–86
The Loves of Mars and Venus (Motteux), 192
The Loves of Mars and Venus (Weaver), 185, 186, 187, 191, 194, 196, 197
Love's Triumph though Callipolis (English court masque), 79–80, 84
"Lucretia Favorita" (Caroso), 54
Lully's privileges, 106
Luminalia (Davenant), 82

Maine, Duchess of (Louise de Bourbon Condé), 134
Le Maître à danser (Rameau), 190, 241–42
Malter, Mons (*l'Anglais*), 171, 179, 181
Mangot, Françoise, 103, 116
The Man of Mode (Etherege), 185, 192
Marcel, François, 113
Marinella, Lucrezia, 6
masques, English, 5; antimasques in, 72, 73, 80, 81, 87–89; choreography of, 72, 78, 88, 89; vs. French masques, 72–73; Jones and development of, 71, 76, 77–78, 79, 80, 82, 87; Jonson and development of, 71; moral masques as genre, 89; as political acts, 71–72,

87–88; royal performers in, 76, 78, 88
McClary, Susan, 229
McCleave, Sarah, 8; article by, 160–77; contributor's note, 258
Medici, Bianca Cappello de, 51
Medici, Margherita de', 81
Medici, Marie de, 82
Meglin, Joellen A., 10–11, 12; article by, 228–46; contributor's note, 258
Menés, Madeleine, 7, 103, 109, 110, 112, 113, 116, 118
Mesmes, Jean-Jacques de, relationship with Prévost, 126, 127–30, 133–37, 138–41
methodologies: analysis of Paris Opera documents, 99–100, 107–9, 110–11; archival sources, 125–26; discourse analysis, 247n1; Italian genealogical records as sources, 50–52; libretti as research documents, 119nn1–2
Michel, François, 169
mime (pantomime), 29, 30, 32; classical antiquity and, 35, 40
Molière, Jean-Baptiste, 91
Montagut, Bartholomew de, 78, 89
Montesquieu, Charles de, 167
Mooser, Aloys, 173
morality: dancers as courtesans, 141–42; *galanterie* and sexual mores, 233–35; performance by nobility as defiance of English decorum, 76, 78; Prévost's sexual freedom and love affairs, 127–30, 133–36; of public performances by Henrietta Maria, 76; reputation of professional dancers, 7, 106–7, 110, 178n14; Sallé's costumes and, 165–66; stereotypes of dancers, 142, 162–65, 167
moresche, 28, 29, 31–32, 34–36, 40, 44n41, 46n63, 47n86; as political exhibitions, 35; as specific dance type, 35, 47n79
Mouret, Jean-Joseph, 134
Moylin, François, and Moylin Dance Troupe, 169, 170, 174, 180

Moylin, Simon, 169
Munro, James, 241

Nadal, Mlle., 116
Najinsky, Vaslav, 175
narrative dance: Elisabeth of Spalbeek's
    liturgical performance as, 212–13,
    221; pantomime and *danse d'action*,
    134; in the fifteenth century, 32,
    35, 40
The Necromancer (Rich), 186, 196
Negri, Cesare, 39, 48n93, 49, 50, 58
Nicholson, Eric A., 7
*The Nobility and Excellence of Women, and the
    Defects and Vices of Men* (Marinella), 6
Nobiltà di dame (Caroso), 50, 54, 57, 58,
    59–60, 61, 64
novels, French, 236–37, 244, 255n75
Noverre, Jean-Georges, 134, 168–69, 171,
    175–76; Sallé as influence, 182n71

Opéra-Comique, 161, 170, 174
Opera Statutes (1713), 142
Orchesographie (Arbeau), 49
Orgel, Stephen, 82
Orpheus and Eurydice (Weaver), 185, 187
Orsina, Giovanna Caetana, 50, 51–52,
    55, 57, 58, 59–60, 64
Orsini, Camillo, 52
Orsini, Elisabetta Baglione, 52
Orsini, Giovanni, 52–53
Orsini, Portia dell'Anguillara (Duchess
    of Cere), 52–54, 55, 57
Orsini family genealogy, 65

pantomime, 173; *danse d'action* and, 134;
    Elisabeth of Spalbeek's perform-
    ances and, 220; Weaver on, 191,
    199–200
Parfaict brothers, 102–3, 171
Paris Opera, 6–7; English theater influ-
    enced by, 199; female dancers listed
    in index of, 100–103; hierarchy of,
    110–12, 131, 142–43; itinerant danc-
    ers and, 105, 107; legal freedoms ac-
    corded dancers, 106, 142; *pantomimes

heroique in productions, 134; partner-
    ships among dancers, 113; as patri-
    archal institution, 142–44; Pécour as
    director of, 99; pensions for retired
    dancers, 141, 167; principal dancers
    of, 110–12 *(see also specific individuals)*;
    role specialization by dancers of,
    116–18; salaries of dancers, 115–16,
    131, 143; singing careers of dancers,
    104–5; size of troupes, 113–15
parodies, 6, 169, 175, 196, 233, 237,
    254n65
"Passagalia of Venus and Adonis"
    (l'Abbe), 187, 190–91
"Passo e mezo" (Caroso), 61
pastoral subjects, 117
patronage: admission to Paris Opera
    company contingent upon, 142; Fa-
    britio Caroso's patronesses, 49–67;
    Henrietta Maria as patroness, 4, 14,
    89, 92n10; Sallé and, 167; women as
    dance patrons, 4–6, 49–67; women
    as patronesses of arts and architec-
    ture, 51, 64
Pécour, Guillaume Louis, 99, 113, 116,
    144, 253n59
Perseus and Andromeda (Rich), 186, 187,
    196, 197
Petit, Mlle., 110, 118
Philip of Clairvaux, description of Eli-
    sabeth of Spalbeek's dances by, 10,
    12, 211–15
Pigmalion (Hilverding), 174
Pigmalion (Riccoboni), 173–74
Pigmalion (Sallé), 161, 166, 167, 170, 171,
    172, 173–74
Pignatelli, Girolama Colonna, 61
politics: absolutism, 229, 233, 235, 246,
    248n13; allusions to, in *Les Indes
    galantes*, 239; dance as political act,
    35, 73–74, 77, 87–88, 91n2, 93n17,
    229; dance as propaganda, 230,
    232; French novel as political sub-
    version, 236–37; geopolitics and
    Les Indes galantes, 228–46
Potts, Shona, 178

power: dance as expression of, 4–5; public performance as display of, 24. *See also* patronage; politics

préciosité, 236–37, 246, 250–51n35

Prévost, Abbe, 166

Prevost, Camille, 78

Prévost, Françoise: childhood of, 103, 126–29; children of, 107, 136–37, 139–41; as choreographer, 131, 132; dance training of, 126–27; death of, 141; innovative style of, 131–32, 134–35, 199; list of dances for, *127;* professional career of, 7–8, 14, 110, 123, 126–27, 130–33, 137–38, 188; professional reputation of, 125, 134, 190; Raoux portrait of, 123–25, *124;* relationship with de Mesmes, 126, 127–30, 133–37, 138–40; reputation of, 125; roles danced by, 118, 125, *127,* 144–54; sexual freedom and love affairs of, 127–30, 133–36; signature of, *139;* as teacher or mentor, 104, 123, 132

professional dancers: dual singing careers of, 104–5; English dancer-actresses, 8–9, 183–200; familial relationships among, 100, 102–3, 104, 169–70, 171, 179n34; gender and, 72; impact of English regulations on, 185; institutional hierarchy and, 142–43; legal freedom of, 142; length of careers of, 101–2, 103; names and identification of, 100, 105–6; partnerships among Paris Opera dancers, 113; pensions for retired dancers, 141, 167; salaries of dancers, 131. *See also* Paris Opera

prostitution, 107

The Provoked Wife (Vanbrugh), 187

Pure, Michel de, 131–32

Puvignée, Mlle., 169, 174, 175

Rabutin, Roger de, 233, 237

Rameau, Jean-Phillip, 161, 182n72, 245; Sallé as collaborator with, 174; score for *Les Indes galantes* written by, *240*

Rameau, Mlle., 107, 109

Rameau, Pierre, 102, 110, 113, 118, 125, 190, 241–42, 253–54nn63–64

Raoux, Jean, portrait of Prévost by, 123–25, *124*

The Rape of Proserpine (Theobald), 177n6, 186

Rebel, François, 140

Rebel, Jean-Féry, 130–33, 137–38, 140; signature of, *139*

The Recruiting Officer (Farquhar), 185–86

The Rehearsal (Buckingham), 185

The Relapse (Vanbrugh), 186

religion: Beguines and other lay orders, 208–10, 215, 217; churches as sites of dancing, 215; as context for works, 11; dance as religious expression and communication, 9–10, 207–22; dramatic performance as imitation of Christ, 209–10; gender and, 10–11; as subject in English masque, 93n17; as subject in *Les Inca du Pérou*, 242; trance states and dance as, 210, 211, 221; women as architectural patronesses, 58

Retrieving Women's History (Kleinberg), 3

Riccoboni, Lélio, 173–74

Rich, John, 167, 178, 184, 196–97

Richalet, Mlle., 104, 132

Richard, Louis, 78

Rochefoucauld, François de La, 229

Roger, M., 187

Rogers, Elizabeth, 168

Roland, Catherine, 104, 156n32, 170, 173–74

roles: amazons or *fortes femmes*, 230–31; "Colombine" in English productions, 185, 186, 194–99; exotic, 29, 117 (see also *Les Indes galantes* [Rameau]); flower roles, 175; gender, 26, 117, 230; Harlequin, 184, 185, 187, 190, 194–95, 196–97, *198;* "lines" of English dancer-actresses, 191–92, 195; multiple roles danced by single artist in production, 115; religious devotion and *imitatio Christ*,

9–10, 207–22; specializations at the Paris Opera, 116–18

"Rosa Felice" (Caroso), 61, 63

Rousseau, Jean-Jacques, 130, 131

The Rover (Behn), 186, 187

Rowe, Nicholas, 186, 192

Saint-Simon, Claude Henri de Rouvroy, 133

Sallé, Francis, 171

Sallé, Marie, 8, 14, 132; childhood and family of, 161; as choreographer, 160, 161, 167, 173–76; as comic dancer, 167; as creative, 167, 172; dance training of, 161; death of, 167–68; English career of, 161, 167, 169–71; Handel's collaboration with, 161, 167, 170, 182n72; innovations linked to, 175–76; Lancret's painting of, *163*, 163–64; Opéra-Comique and, 168; patrons of, 167; Prévost as teacher and mentor of, 123, 125, 134, 138, 161; professional career of, 118, 160, 166–68, 171–73, 176–77; relationship with Grognet, 164–65; retirement of, 171; sensual dancing style of, 163–64; sexual morality of, 163–65; social reputation of, 160, 162–65; as teacher and mentor, 160, 168–71, 175–76; as virginal and virtuous, 162–63, 164, 167

Salmacida Spolia (Davenant), 88, 89, 92n12

salon culture, 229–30, 232, 236–37, 242, 247n6

Salvadori, Andrea, 81

Salvetti, Amerigo, 75, 77, 93

Salviati, Lucretia, 54, 57

Santlow, Hester (Mrs. Booth), 9, 186–87, 189–91, 192, 194, 199–200

Santucci, Ercole, 58

Sceaux, dance performances at, 134

La Sceptre de la Rose (Fokine), 175

scope, chronological, 4

Scudéry, Madeleine de, 230, 236–37, 241

sensibilité, 241, 242, 246

sexuality: dancers as courtesans, 141–42; *galanterie* and sexual mores, 233–35; military language and sexual conquest, 232–33, 238–42; Prévost and, 135–36; Sallé and, 163–65

Sforza, Tristano, 21

Shadwell, Charles, 187

The Shipwreck (Weaver), 185, 194, 195

Silen, Karen, 9–10, 12; article by, 207–22; contributor's note, 258–59

Simons, Walter, 209, 215

singing, 104–5

sociabilité, 236, 238, 246

social dancing, 25, 43n28, 72–73, 78

solos, 111

Sorin, Joseph, 195

Sparti, Barbara, 4–5, 12; article by, 19–40; contributor's note, 258–59

Steele, Richard, 187–88, 194, 195

stigmata, 207, 210, 211, 215, 217

Strong, Roy, 82

Subligny, Marie Thérèse de, 105, 110, 113, 116, 118, 142

Sullam, Sara Copio, 6

Sullivan, Patricia A., 6

Tamerlane (Rowe), 186, 192, 194

Tancrède (French court ballet), 86

Tarabotti, Arcangela, 6

Tate, Nahum, 186, 187

tendresse, 230, 237, 241, 244–45, 246

Terpsichore (Rebel), 130–31, 133

Tethys' Festival (English court masque), 84

Thibaud (Parisian dance master), 126–27

Thierot, Nicolas-Clause, 165

Thurmond, John, Jr., 185, 186, 187, 195

training and instruction: distinction between dance masters and dancing masters, 67n1; "how to dance" books as means of, 49; in noble and royal households, 21, 23–24, 32, 36, 43n27, 49, 51–52, 57, 89, 91n3, 167, 181n63; at Paris Opera, 103–4, 116; women as dance instructors, 120n15

The Tricks of Harlequin (Rich), 197

trios, 111

Le Turc généreux (Rameau), 244–45
Turgis, George, 89
"Turkish Dance" (l'Abbe), 189

"The Union" (Isaac), 186, 187
universality, dance as universal language,
    251n39

Valjoly, Anne-Auguste de, 107
Valone, Carolyn, 51, 53, 64, 68n5
Vanbrugh, John, 184, 187
Verbruggen, Susanna, 188
Viala, Alain, 236, 250nn30–31
Victoire, Mlle., 110, 116, 118
Victor, Benjamin, 166
Voltaire, 163, 165

Weaver, John, 9, 184, 185, 186, 187, 191–
    94, 195, 199–200
weddings: dance in noble Italian, 19–40;
    French ballet or opera performances
    at, 82, 86; masques at, 72, 92n12; as
    political alliances, 74; social dancing
    at, 60
Wick, Rebecca, 168
Winter, Marian Hannah, 170
Wycherley, William, 185

Younger, Elizabeth, 9, 185–86, 188–89,
    192, 194, 196–97, 199–200

Zéphire et Flore (Angiolini), 175
Ziegler, Joanna, 215